GREAT AMERICAN WAR STORIES

GREAT AMERICAN WAR STORIES

WAR

STORIES

EDITED BY
TOM McCARTHY

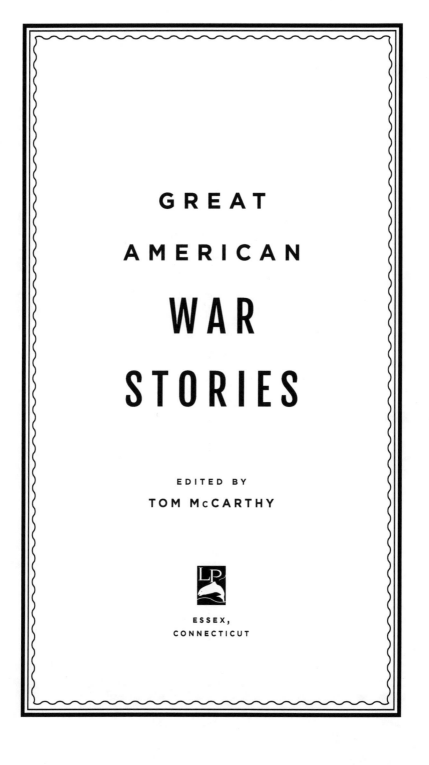

ESSEX,
CONNECTICUT

An imprint of Globe Pequot, the trade division of The Rowman &
Littlefield Publishing Group, Inc.
4501 Forbes Blvd., Ste. 200
Lanham, MD 20706
www.rowman.com

Distributed by NATIONAL BOOK NETWORK

British Library Cataloguing in Publication Information available

Library of Congress Cataloging-in-Publication Data

Names: McCarthy, Tom, 1952- editor of compilation.
Title: Great American war stories / Tom McCarthy.
Description: Essex, Connecticut : Lyons Press, [2023] | Includes
bibliographical references. | Summary: "A magnificent collection of
gripping accounts of battles great and small throughout history"—
Provided by publisher.
Identifiers: LCCN 2023015408 (print) | LCCN 2023015409 (ebook) | ISBN
9781493072194 (trade paperback) | ISBN 9781493072200 (epub)
Subjects: LCSH: United States—History, Military—Antecdotes. | United
States—Armed Forces—History—Antecdotes.
Classification: LCC E181 .G735 2023 (print) | LCC E181 (ebook) | DDC
355.00973—dc23/eng/20230418
LC record available at https://lccn.loc.gov/2023015408
LC ebook record available at https://lccn.loc.gov/2023015409

♾™ The paper used in this publication meets the minimum requirements
of American National Standard for Information Sciences—Permanence of
Paper for Printed Library Materials, ANSI/NISO Z39.48-1992.

CONTENTS

INTRODUCTION

It is impossible to write of war without recounting death. It is equally impossible to write of war without mentioning honor and bravery and courage.

No one wants war, but if wars must be fought, they require men and women who are selfless and willing to take part in an effort that might lead to their deaths. *Great American War Stories* celebrates the warriors, if not the wars themselves, for without soldiers willing to go to war and face the inevitable, we would have no hope that perhaps our latest war will be our last.

General William Tecumseh Sherman, for whom the practice of war was an art form, once wrote, "War is cruelty. There is no use trying to reform it. The crueler it is, the sooner it will be over." Sherman certainly practiced what he preached, and his 1864 March to the Sea after setting Atlanta ablaze was remarkable for its cruelty. But it hastened the war's end and, despite its harshness, perhaps saved lives.

These stories are a tribute to the solders, sailors, and Marines who fought and died for a higher cause, who found themselves in battle, whether voluntarily or not, because they felt the inexorable pull of a higher calling.

Great American War Stories is a celebration of hidden gems lost to generations of readers. They are startling for their rawness and reportage, for their emotion and insights.

Here are Paul Revere, the Battle of Bunker Hill, and Benedict Arnold during the American Revolution. And Ulysses S. Grant's own perspective on the Mexican War and American presidential politics long before he rose to fame.

Here also is West Point graduate and Union officer Milo Hascall's report on the Union's failure at the Battle of Stone River. It is an eviscerating indictment of ego and ambition.

No collection of the best American writing should be without Mark Twain. Here you will find his practiced eye focused on Vicksburg and its inhabitants during tumultuous times. William Pittenger, a participant, recounts the cinematic and ultimately unsuccessful attempt to hijack a Confederate train, an effort that led to the first Congressional Medals of Honor.

You will read of George Armstrong Custer's final moments at the Battle of Little Bighorn during the Sioux Wars, a battle Custer and his men had no chance of winning. Theodore Roosevelt himself recounts the bloody struggle and his own involvement in the fighting at Las Guasimas with the Rough Riders, a battle during the Spanish-American War long forgotten and often viewed as a walk in the park. It was not.

Raymond B. Lech's "The Loss of the *Indianapolis*" will immerse you in the terrifying shark-filled waters of the South Pacific during World War Two, where sailors drifted for days before anyone knew they were missing. And you will read of the courage of Marines at Mount Suribachi, and decades later at Khe Sanh.

This collection focuses not on the results—not who won or lost—but on the sacrifice. Here, startling and perhaps uncomfortable, is what is was really like to feel the pain and the loss and the tension. Here is the viscera and the horror and the heroism.

Great American War Stories focuses on the humanity of war, of the extreme efforts and discomfort of soldiers under the worst possible pressure a human can endure. Here are the unsung heroes we celebrate each July Fourth, the people we mourn and admire on Veterans Day.

Nations go to war for a variety of reasons. Soldiers go to war for something quite different. Before their wars, the soldiers in these pages—from the Revolutionary War through Viet Nam—had been ordinary men, normal citizens going about their normal routines. They found themselves in the military for a variety of reasons—the draft, an urge to volunteer to help a larger purpose, maybe a desire to do something for the common good. They were not, before these wars, extraordinary soldiers.

Those who survived the infernos they were thrust into became something quite different afterward, and that is what we celebrate here.

1

PAUL REVERE

WALTER A. DYER

Paul Revere was keenly alive to the importance of the trust thus placed in him, and he watched the course of events like a cat. No slightest detail escaped him. It was not wholly easy to get news in and out of Boston promptly, but Revere managed it. Newton had all the members of the watch under surveillance, but Peter Brackett was still a free lance, so far as the organization was concerned. And if anybody could slip through the lines, the wily Peter could. Arrangements were made whereby he could leave town quietly on foot and then ride to Concord, and the result was that Paul Revere received daily bulletins from the seat of the Provincial Government.

On Saturday, April 15th, Congress adjourned, to reconvene in one month, but Hancock and Adams, made fully aware of their peril by messages delivered by Peter, did not return to Boston. Instead they went to Lexington and accepted the hospitality of Hancock's cousin and her husband, the Rev. Jonas Clark. Hither, in a panic after another raid on Hancock's house, came Madam Lydia Hancock, the aunt who acted as hostess in his establishment, and with her came her young and pretty friend Dorothy Quincy, a relative of Mr. Clark's. In spite of her panic, Madam Hancock had a method in this, for she was a shrewd and confirmed old matchmaker, and she had long ago selected Dorothy to be Hancock's bride. He had remained a bachelor altogether too long, according to her way of thinking, and Mr. Clark's quiet house seemed to her an ideal place for courting. That her plot was successful is evidenced by the fact that Hancock and Dorothy were married the following August. Meanwhile, however, the Clark house proved to be anything but the quiet rendezvous that Madam Hancock had pictured it.

In Boston, Revere felt now somewhat less alarmed for Hancock and Adams, since Peter reported them prepared to leave on short notice, but he felt a growing concern for the supplies that the Committee of Safety had been collecting at Concord. They seemed dangerously near Boston. Gage had learned through his secret informant that these stores were of considerable importance, and Revere knew that Gage knew. Any move in that direction must be thwarted or the Committee of Safety might lose what it had taken them months to collect. Revere ordered the Committee of Six and the Watch of Thirty to redouble their vigilance. They must not let the smallest trifle escape them.

The legends that attribute the leaking out of Gage's plans to the fact that his wife was an American woman of Whig sympathies have been the cause of considerable debate, but they are not needed to explain the situation. Indiscreet soldiers talked too much, and wherever there were ears, those ears were used to serve Paul Revere.

Indeed, it was very evident that some sort of expedition was being planned. The small boats of the transport fleet had been drawn up and repaired. That looked like some sort of expedition by water. On the other hand, there were military preparations reported that suggested a march by land. In any case Revere felt certain that Concord would be the objective and he laid his plans accordingly.

On Saturday evening, April 15th, Revere's patrols brought him reports that something was in the wind. Details began to reach him, and at midnight he went to Warren.

"Something is up," said he. "All the grenadiers and light infantry have been taken off sentry duty and are held in barracks. All the small boats of the transports have been launched and are lying hidden under the sterns of the men-o'-war. What do you make of it?"

"An expedition, undoubtedly," said Warren. "Perhaps they mean to cross to Charlestown in force. At any rate, you had better prepare for that contingency. They may be after Hancock and Adams at Lexington or the stores at Concord—perhaps both. There must be no sleep for us this night."

There was no sleep for Paul Revere. Indeed, the Sons of Liberty were so active about the town that Gage must have decided to postpone action until his plans were more fully matured. At all events, morning found the soldiers still in their barracks.

Warren, however, was not to be lulled into a false sense of security. He knew that Peter Brackett had warned the patriots at Lexington and Concord, but he could not feel quite content until he knew that Paul Revere himself had been to see them. Accordingly, on Sunday morning, April 16th, he summoned Revere and requested him to take the dangerous ride himself to Lexington and Concord in order to see to it that the facts were fully set before Hancock and Adams and the Committee of Safety.

This proved to be one of the most important if one of the least spectacular of all Paul Revere's rides. He managed to slip quietly out of town by way of the Neck and found the horse that was held for Peter's use. Then, jogging slowly along the back roads, attracting as little attention as possible, and making sure that Newton's men were thrown off the scent, he made his way to Lexington.

Revere did not mince matters, and Hancock, now thoroughly aroused to the seriousness of the situation, began to take immediate action. He sent out a call to the members of the Provincial Congress to meet in Watertown on April 22nd instead of May 15th. Then he sent Revere on to Concord with messages for the Committee of Safety and Supplies which was still in session there.

As a result of this timely warning, the stores were removed to places of greater security. On the following day, the 17th, they were quietly disposed of. Two four-pounders were hidden in Concord in charge of the artillery company there. Four six-pounders were sent to Groton under Colonel Prescott. Two seven-inch mortars were taken to Acton. The ammunition in the hands of Colonel Barrett, and also the intrenching implements, medical supplies, etc., were distributed in like manner among the towns of Worcester, Lancaster, Groton, Mendor, Leicester, and Sudbury. Revere, with a less anxious heart, rode home by way of Charlestown.

It proved easier to get into Boston than to get out again. On Tuesday soldiers were guarding every exit and the challenges of the sentries were more peremptory. The ferries ceased running. The *Somerset* moved from the bay into the Charles River and her guns covered the ferry ways. At 9 o'clock in the evening, orders were issued forbidding all exit from the town; Boston was closed up tight.

But if the soldiers were watchful, so were the Sons of Liberty, especially the vigilant Thirty. During the evening, reports reached Revere that the troops were being mustered. The movement appeared to be not toward the Neck, but toward the bottom of the Common.

At 10 o'clock Warren sent for him in great haste.

"What have you learned?" asked Warren.

"Enough to convince me," replied Revere, "that the troops will move to-night and that they will go by water rather than by land. They are not moving toward the Neck."

"I agree with you," said Warren. "Gage's promised expedition is on foot. I am told that 1,500 men have been mobilized. Hancock and Adams must be warned at once and persuaded to leave Lexington for a place of greater safety. The remaining stores are also in danger. We must guard against every chance of failure. To that end I have already dispatched William Dawes, who said that he was confident of being able to slip through the lines and across the Neck. But we must not depend on one man. You we have learned to trust. Do you cross the river and proceed through Charlestown, Revere?"

"I will undertake to win through," said Revere. "But to make assurance doubly sure, I have already arranged a signal to acquaint our friends in Charlestown with what is going forward. They will take the message in case I am intercepted."

"Good," said Warren.

No further time was wasted in words. Revere started at once.

His first move was to find Peter Brackett.

"Peter," said he, "there are important tasks ahead of us all this night. I ride secretly to Lexington. Captain Pulling will also have a difficult duty to perform and he will remain here in Boston, in great danger. If he is discovered and caught, you know that Newton will see to it that short work is made of him. Newton hates Pulling almost as well as he hates me. You have two sharp eyes, Peter. Let one of them watch Newton's men, whom you know well. Keep the other on Captain Pulling and see that he is warned if danger threatens."

Peter nodded and slipped silently away.

Revere found Pulling at his home in Salem Street and quietly entered the house by a back door.

"The hour has struck," said Pulling.

"It has, John," said Revere. "And I have a hazardous task for you. If I can get cross the river, I ride express to Lexington to warn Hancock and Adams. God grant that I may be in time."

"But the river is guarded," said Pulling.

"True," replied Revere. "I may fail at the outset. But I have taken steps to get a message through in case I fail. On my return from Lexington yesterday I passed through Charlestown. There I put the case before our friend Colonel Conant. He will have a horseman ready and as soon as he sees our signals he will know what the message will be. Then he will wait a reasonable time, and if I do not appear, he will dispatch his messenger. I must hurry. With you I leave the responsibility of the signals. I depend upon your resourcefulness."

"What were the signals agreed upon?" asked Pulling.

"Lanterns in the belfry of the North Church," replied Revere. "Conant will see them. I promised to show two lanterns if the troops should embark in the boats; one if they start off by land. They are moving now, and it looks as though they would proceed by water. Make sure, John, and then show the signals."

The two friends gripped hands and Revere departed as quietly as he had come.

John Pulling lost no time. He was a vestryman in the Old North Church and he knew where to get the keys. He started at once for the home of Robert Newman, the sexton, who lived in the same street.

Reaching the house he took the precaution of peering in at the window. In the living room sat the sexton with four soldiers who were quartered on him. Pulling was perplexed. As he stood there cogitating, he heard a slight noise by his side which startled him, and then a cautious whisper.

"It's Peter Brackett. Mr. Revere told me to help you. Do you want to speak to Mr. Newman?"

"Very much I do," whispered Pulling.

"Leave that to me," said Peter.

"Be careful," said Pulling.

"I will," said Peter.

He hurried up the steps and banged at the knocker. Newman opened the door. Behind him loomed the figure of one of the soldiers.

"I am sorry to trouble you, Mr. Newman," said Peter, "but Mistress Hunter is much disturbed because no arrangements have been made for her son's funeral."

"Mistress Hunter?" echoed Newman, to whom the name meant nothing.

"If you will step out here just a minute, Mr. Newman, perhaps she can explain to you. She is much perturbed."

The weary soldier grunted and stepped back into the room while the puzzled sexton followed Peter into the shadow of a big maple.

"That was just a trick," whispered Peter in hurried explanation. "It's Captain Pulling that wants to speak with you."

Robert Newman, though not an active Son of Liberty, was known to Pulling as a faithful friend of the cause. At any rate, he had no choice but to trust him. In as few words as possible he acquainted him with the situation. Newman hesitated for a moment, and then answered, "All right; I'll chance it."

"Have you lanterns at the church?" asked Pulling.

"I have one," said the sexton. "I will fetch another and the keys."

He reentered his house, grumbling audibly, and closed the door behind him. In a short time he emerged through a kitchen window with an unlighted lantern in his hand and rejoined Pulling. Together the two made their way by a roundabout route to the church, while Peter vanished in the shadows.

The sound of marching feet was heard, and as they neared the water front they observed torches.

"The soldiers are taking to the boats," remarked Pulling. "It is by water, then, and two lanterns will be the signal."

They entered the empty church, but Pulling advised against lighting the lanterns until the last moment.

"Can you do it, Newman?" he asked. "You alone know those belfry stairs in the dark."

The sexton held back at first, but was at last persuaded.

"Light both lanterns and place them where they can be seen from the Charlestown shore," directed Pulling. "I'll remain here to keep watch."

Christ Church, or Old North, had been erected in 1723, and its graceful spire had long been a landmark for home-coming mariners. Never, however, had eyes sought it more eagerly than on that night, when Conant and his friends waited on the other side of the river for the promised signals. Slowly and somewhat fearfully the sexton mounted the creaking old stairs, while Pulling waited anxiously below.

At last Newman gained the belfry, and the watchful Conant saw first one point of light and then another.

"They come by water," said he. "It is well. Whatever may happen to Paul Revere, the warning will be sent before a British foot is set on Charlestown or Cambridge soil."

The sexton presently rejoined Pulling and they locked the door of the church behind them. Pulling slipped off toward the water front to observe the embarkation of the troops and to make sure that the lanterns were properly set, while Newman hurried home and reëntered his kitchen window.

Every available man that James Newton could command was on duty that night to guard against any leaking out of Gage's plan. And Newton had given special orders to watch Revere and Pulling, hoping that this time he might be able to catch them red-handed. Sharp eyes, therefore, spied those lanterns as soon as they flashed forth. Newton's men rushed to the church, but the door was already locked. Suspicion at once turned toward the sexton, who kept the keys.

Newton's men hurried to Newman's house, which was near by, and aroused the soldiers there. Their story was quickly told. The house was searched, and Robert Newman was found in bed. At first he appeared to have awakened from a sound sleep, and was extraordinarily stupid. The soldiers placed him under arrest and an officer, summoned to the house, began to question him.

No evidence against himself could be wormed out of the man, and at last he was released. But the officer was clever and persistent, and the sexton began to weaken under the rapid cross questioning. Finally they forced him to state that he had lent his keys to John Pulling.

That was enough for Newton's men. Here was the longed-for chance to win the reward their chief had offered. Out of the house they hurried with the soldiers, leaving the remorseful sexton to pray for the safety of his accomplice.

But there was one who had left ahead of the soldiers. Peter Brackett had been listening to the inquisition from the limb of a tree that reached close to Newman's window. As soon as he heard Pulling's name mentioned he dropped to the ground and was off like a deer.

By a happy chance he came upon Pulling, who was just returning home from the water front.

"They are after you," panted Peter. "There's not a moment to be lost. No, you must not go home. I'll explain to your family. You must hide at once. Newton has sworn to have his revenge on you and he will show no mercy. You must not be taken. The old tobacco shed by the Mill Pond. Hide there and I will come to you before morning with something to eat. Meanwhile I'll try to throw them off the track."

John Pulling hated to flee, but there was no alternative. He hid himself securely and the soldiers and Newton's men never found him. The next day, with Peter Brackett's help, he disguised himself as a laborer and escaped to Nantasket with his family in a small boat, leaving all his worldly goods behind him.

To return to Paul Revere. Longfellow has made famous the ride he took that night in a poem that is spirited and unforgettable if not entirely accurate. Neither the episode of the lanterns nor the details of the ride are quite correct in that version, though it has served a noble end. Some years later Paul Revere wrote out two versions of his own which the historian may more safely follow.

Leaving his friend Pulling, assured that the signals would be shown, he hastened home for his boots and surtout and kissed his wife a hurried good-by. Then, avoiding the marching columns of red-coats, he hastened to the water front. To get across the Charles River was no easy task. All egress had been stopped at 9 o'clock. The ferry boats had been tied up and the guns of the *Somerset* covered the river.

But Revere was prepared for that. He had kept in constant readiness for such emergency a small boat, hidden beneath a cob-wharf on the Mill Pond side, in the custody of two loyal Sons of Liberty, John Richardson and Joshua Bentley, both of whom afterward fought gallantly in the Revolution. They lived near at hand and Revere quickly found them. They brought out the boat and prepared to put off, when Revere halted them.

"The oars must be muffled," said he. "They will hear us else on the *Somerset*."

"A plague on it!" exclaimed Bentley. "We have no cloth."

"That is easily remedied, I think," said Richardson, and hurried to a house close by.

Under a window the young man gave a low whistle. The sash was stealthily raised and a hurried colloquy followed in guarded whispers. Revere heard a low feminine laugh and something white fluttered down to the ground. In triumph Richardson bore it back to the boat. It was a woman's skirt, suspiciously warm.

The thole pins were carefully wrapped in the cloth and the boat pushed out upon the water. Richardson and Bentley took the oars and Revere sat in the stern. With the utmost caution the men guided the precious craft across the river, under the very guns of the frowning man-of-war. An unwary splash or a cough would have betrayed them. It was a tense moment for Paul Revere as they crossed the *Somerset*'s bows and made for the Charlestown shore. The rising moon broke through the low clouds as the men bent to their oars for the final pull. They were just in time.

They landed near the old battery in Charlestown, and there found Colonel Conant, Richard Devens, a member of the Committee of Safety, and two or three others.

"Well met, Revere," cried Conant. "We saw your signals and have a post rider all ready to start for Lexington. Shall we send him?"

"No," said Revere, "though I do thank you. I have got thus far; I will press on. The soldiers are already embarking; there is no time to lose. Can you get me a good horse?"

"At once," said Conant, and dispatched a man.

"Be cautious, Revere," warned Devens. "There are scouts upon the road. I myself came from Lexington to-day, and just after sunset I met with nine or ten British officers, armed and well mounted, going toward Concord."

"I'll be on my guard," said Revere.

The man appeared with a horse, saddled and bridled.

"It is Deacon Larkin's horse, and a good one," said the man. "I promised that no harm should befall it."

Revere laughed. "It were easy to promise," said he.

With all that had taken place, only an hour had elapsed since Revere had called on Dr. Warren. It was now about 11 o'clock, a full moon had risen, and the night was, as Revere puts it, "very pleasant." Pleased with the success of his crossing and enjoying the prospect of further adventure, he set off, riding cautiously at first.

He passed Charlestown Neck and took the open road. He had ridden a little way in the moonlight when his sharp eyes detected two horsemen waiting in the shade of a tree. The road was narrow here, and Revere saw that he would have to pass close to them. As he approached he discerned holsters and cockades; they were British officers.

He was about to make a dash for it when one of them rode directly toward him and the other took his place in the road ahead.

Revere suppressed the temptation to risk an encounter. Turning his horse short about, he made off at full speed as though to return to Charlestown. One of the officers was close at his heels, the other farther behind.

Selecting a dark spot in the road, he turned at right angles, struck off cross country, and made for the Medford Road. It was not easy going, for the spring mud had not dried up, but Revere knew the lay of the land like a book. His pursuer, less familiar with it, presently came to grief in a clay bank. Revere flung him back a taunting laugh. The other followed for a quarter of a mile and then gave it up.

Reaching the road, Revere let out his horse and proceeded at a rapid pace along the Mystic River to Medford. There he awoke the Captain of the minute-men.

"The British are on the way to Lexington and Concord," he cried. "They must be delayed as much as possible."

Then he dashed across the bridge and on toward Menotomy, now Arlington. Behind him the ringing church bells told him that the minute-men were gathering.

"They will fight!" he cried exultantly, urging his horse to greater speed. "The farmers will fight!"

The spirit of the situation was getting into his blood, and as he rode he shouted aloud to every farmhouse, "To arms, patriots! The red-coats are coming!"

> A hurry of hoofs in a village street,
> A shape in the moonlight, a bulk in the dark,
> And beneath, from the pebbles, in passing, a spark
> Struck out by the steed flying fearless and fleet:
> That was all! And yet, through the gloom and the light,
> The fate of a nation was riding that night.

Back in Boston the soldiers were rapidly embarking. Warren knew that this was to be Gage's supreme effort. There was no sleep for him that night. The lives of Adams and Hancock were in dire peril; the fate of a nation hung in the balance. Would Revere be in time?

In Lexington the militia, warned by Revere the previous Sunday, were ready for whatever might happen. British officers had been seen on the road and the Clark house, with its precious occupants, was guarded by eight men under Sergeant William Monroe.

Meanwhile Deacon Larkin's horse was eating up the miles and Paul Revere was everywhere spreading the alarm. Farmers and townsmen tumbled out of bed and sought their weapons.

> *So through the night rode Paul Revere!*
> *And so through the night went his cry of alarm*
> *To every Middlesex village and farm,—*
> *A cry of defiance and not of fear,*
> *A voice in the darkness, a knock at the door,*
> *And a word that shall echo forevermore!*
> *For, borne on the night-wind of the Past*
> *Through all our history to the last,*
> *In the hour of darkness and peril and need*
> *The people will waken and listen to hear*
> *The hurrying hoof-beats of that steed,*
> *And the midnight message of Paul Revere.*

On the stroke of twelve, Revere came galloping up to Mr. Clark's door.

"Halt!" challenged Monroe. "Who goes there?"

"A friend," answered Revere, "and in a precious hurry."

"Hush!" cautioned Monroe. "Don't make so much noise. Everybody's asleep inside."

"Noise?" cried Revere. "There'll be noise soon enough. Why, man, the regulars are coming!"

The clattering hoofs and Revere's shouts had awakened Hancock, and he thrust his head out of an open window.

"Come on in, Revere," he called. "We're not afraid of you."

Revere dismounted and went inside. Mr. Clark brought candles and they were soon joined by Adams and Hancock.

"What's up, Revere?" asked Adams sleepily.

"No false alarm this time, Mr. Adams," replied Revere. "There are some 1,500 red-coats on the way from Boston. They will be here by daybreak."

"Are you sure?" demanded Adams, his face betraying his consternation.

"I saw them embarking myself," said Revere. "Dr. Warren sent me post haste to warn you, and I have alarmed everybody on the way. Hasn't William Dawes told you?"

"No," said Hancock, "no one has told us."

"That is strange," said Revere. "Dr. Warren sent Dawes first and he did not have to get across the water. He must have been intercepted. At all events, there is no time to waste. Dr. Warren said to urge you to leave on the instant. The British mean to make a thorough job of it this time. You should leave at once, Dr. Warren says, and not stop until you are safe in New York or Philadelphia."

"But," demurred Hancock, "we cannot leave the Provincial Congress in the lurch. I have called them to meet on the 22nd."

"They would be left more in the lurch if you were to be captured, Mr. Hancock. I tell you the whole British army is after you. Gage has vowed that you shall not escape."

John Hancock, for all his elegance, did not lack heroic qualities in an emergency. Though aroused to a sense of his personal peril, his first thought was for his followers and for the remaining stores. He sent word at once to Buckman's Tavern, the militia headquarters. Soon a bell raised its clamor, and militia and citizens gathered to the number of about 150.

While Hancock and Adams were taking counsel together, William Dawes arrived on a spent horse, after a difficult journey. He did not wait to tell his story but sought at once a fresh mount and proposed that he and Revere should carry the news on to Concord where there were still some valuable stores to be secreted.

After a bare half hour's rest they set off again along the Concord road. They had not proceeded far when they heard hoof-beats on the road behind them.

"There is but one of them," said Revere. "We need not fear."

Presently they were overtaken by a horseman who was evidently not a British officer.

"Good evening to you, gentlemen," said he. "It is good to have company on the road in these times."

"It is indeed," replied Revere, "so be it the company be friendly."

"I will be bold," laughed the stranger. "If you be friends of King George, we may as well part company."

"Not so," said Dawes. "We be friends of freedom, and we ride, Revere and I, to tell the militia at Concord that the British are coming."

"Then that rumor is true?" said the stranger. "And you are Paul Revere? Well met, Revere. My name is Prescott, Dr. Prescott of Concord."

"Well met, indeed," said Revere, "for I know your name as that of a loyal Son of Liberty. But have you no errand this time of night?"

"No errand but to get home," said Prescott. "I fear I lingered over-long with a certain lady in Lexington."

"So that's the quarter in which the wind sets," laughed Revere. "Well, you had best put from your mind thoughts of courting now. We must keep a sharp lookout, for scouts have been seen on the road by both Dawes and myself, and by Richard Devens earlier in the day. We may be stopped if we don't look out."

"We'd better spread the alarm as we go, in any case," said Dawes.

"I know every farmer between here and Concord. I'll attend to that," said Prescott.

So they began spreading the alarm as they rode. While Prescott and Dawes were engaged in trying to get the facts into the head of a sleepy farmer, Revere went on ahead. He had gone about 200 yards when he became aware of two horsemen in the road ahead of him. He turned and shouted back to Dawes and Prescott:

"Look out! Scouts ahead!"

The two horsemen bore down upon him at that and two more suddenly appeared from the shadow of a tree in the pasture close by. Revere was immediately surrounded and one of the horsemen clapped a pistol to his breast.

"Move an inch farther and you're a dead man," cried the officer.

Revere was unable to give a second warning and Dawes and Prescott came riding up to be stopped in like manner. Then all three were forced through a bar-way into the pasture.

Each one of the three fully intended to make a dash for liberty, and as soon as they reached the shadow of the tree Revere gave a yell and struck spurs to his horse. A hand clutched Dawes's bridle and held him, but Revere and Prescott started off full tilt.

Prescott was the lucky one. He turned his horse sharply to the right, jumped the stone wall, gained the road, and escaped to carry the alarm to Concord. Revere, who knew nothing of the jumping abilities of Deacon Larkin's horse, turned to the left and made for the wood at the foot of the pasture. He might have shaken his pursuers there, but as luck would have it six more horsemen emerged from the wood and blocked his way. Again a pistol was presented to Revere's breast and he was ordered to dismount. There was nothing for it but to comply. Then the leader of the six, who appeared to be a gentlemanly fellow, came forward.

"What is your name?" he demanded.

"Revere."

"Paul Revere?" asked the officer, not without a sort of respect in his tone.

"Yes."

"You ride express from Boston?"

"Yes."

The others crowded about and seemed desirous of abusing Revere, but the leader restrained them.

"He's the man we want," they said.

"He will serve us better alive than dead," said the officer.

"Gentlemen," said Revere, "I know what you are after, but you have missed your aim. You are after bigger game than me but you will not find it. I left Boston after your troops had landed at Lechmere Point and if I were not certain that the people to the distance of fifty miles into the country had been notified of your movements, I would have risked one shot before you should have taken me. We shall have 500 men here forthwith."

"But we have 1,500 coming," indiscreetly answered the officer.

"I know that well enough," said Revere, "but they will not be enough and they will not come soon enough. The whole countryside is aroused, I tell you. It is you who are in danger, not I."

Now the other four came on the scene, with the captured Dawes. One of them was Major Mitchell of the Fifth Regiment. He pointed his pistol at Revere and frowned menacingly.

"Tell me the truth or I will blow your brains out," said he.

He asked several questions and got much the same answers that Revere had given before. The soldiers were evidently disturbed by his replies and his fearless bearing. Then they took away his pistols and ordered him to remount. An officer grasped his bridle. Four other prisoners were now brought from the woods and all returned to the road. It was a Sergeant who guided Revere's horse, and he held his pistol in readiness.

"Remember," said he, "I will shoot if you attempt to escape or if any attempt at rescue appears."

On the road the soldiers arranged themselves in a circle with their prisoners in the center. Revere was too well guarded by the Sergeant to attempt escape, but the soldiers had become alarmed, some of them relaxed their vigilance, and suddenly William Dawes tore his bridle from the hand of his captor and made a dash for it.

Three of the horsemen started pell mell on his heels. He kept well ahead at first, but his horse was not a fast one, and they began to gain on him. As he approached a darkened farmhouse he raised his voice in an exultant shout.

"Hello, boys," he yelled, "I've got three of 'em!"

The ruse succeeded, the soldiers turned and fled without more ado, and Dawes escaped.

The others pressed on toward Lexington. Suddenly the report of a musket was heard.

"What was that?" cried Major Mitchell.

"An alarm gun," replied Revere quite truthfully. "The countryside is gathering. You will soon find yourselves in hot water."

"We can't be bothered with these fellows," said the Major. He caused all the prisoners to dismount except Revere, removed their saddles and bridles, turned the horses loose, and sent the men about their business. Then they rode cautiously on again.

More guns were heard. The Major ordered a halt and commanded the Sergeant to take Revere's horse, his own being [fatigued]. The saddle and bridle were cut from the Sergeant's mount and he was turned loose. Revere was compelled to proceed on foot.

As they approached Lexington they could see the minute-men gathering. The soldiers began to look to their arms and their horses, and in the midst of the confusion Revere slipped quietly away. What eventually happened to Deacon Larkin's beloved horse, history, unfortunately, does not tell.

Meanwhile the British troops—though not the full 1,500 of them—had indeed crossed the Charles River and had landed about midnight near Phipps's Farm, Lechmere Point, Cambridge. They heard the church bells and saw the minute-men gathering as they started on the road toward Lexington. Lieutenant-Colonel Smith, who was in command of the force, alarmed at these evidences of preparedness against them, ordered a rapid march, sent back to Boston for reinforcements, and bade Major Pitcairn of the Marines, with one company, to push on ahead with all speed.

Revere, finding himself free at last, though without a horse, and knowing the roads to be filled with peril for the fugitives, hurried across the burying-ground to the Clark house. Much to his dismay he found Hancock and Adams still there. Hancock, indeed, had announced his firm intention of remaining to fight.

Revere, who understood the danger better than they, was beside himself with anxiety. He did not mince matters. Forgetting for a moment their relative positions, he all but ordered them out of the house.

"The time has come to strike a blow for Liberty," said Hancock. "Shall it be said that John Hancock fled in that hour of need?"

But Adams had the wiser head of the two.

"Revere is right," said he. "This is not our business, this fighting. Remember, Hancock, we belong to the Cabinet."

Very tactfully he argued with the headstrong leader and at last, about daybreak, persuaded him to go. Hancock's secretary, Lowell, had been making the arrangements, and said that they should go at once to Woburn, and on from there the next night.

At last, when it seemed as though the British must be nearly upon them, Adams and Hancock started. Lowell and Revere accompanied them for about two miles to guard against an encounter with the scouts, and Revere at least was prepared to fight to death for them if need arose. But they were not molested, and finally Revere and Lowell, assured of their safety, turned back.

Hancock and Adams proceeded to the home of the Rev. Samuel Sewell in Woburn where they were carefully protected against capture. Dorothy Quincy and Mrs. Hancock joined them later and they were escorted by easy stages out of the dangerous country. Hancock and Dorothy were married in Fairfield, Conn., on August 28th, and thence they went on to New York and Philadelphia.

As Revere and Lowell turned back toward Lexington, the latter bethought him of a trunk filled with valuable papers belonging to Hancock.

"Those must certainly be rescued," said Lowell, "or I shall sweat for it. They must be sent on to Philadelphia."

"Where are they?" asked Revere.

"In the tavern," said Lowell.

"Well, then let us get them," said Revere. "That is certainly no safe place for them."

As they hurried on they met a man on horseback.

"What news?" cried Revere.

"The troops are less than two miles away," shouted the man as he dashed past on his errand.

Lowell's face turned a sickly hue, but Revere urged him to hurry on.

"Thank God, Hancock and Adams are safe," said he. "They started none too soon."

Revere stopped for a moment at the Clark house to give the ladies tidings of Hancock and then hastened with Lowell to the tavern. From a chamber window they could see the troops approaching up the road in the distance.

"We have no time to get this away now," said Revere, as they bore the trunk down stairs. "We must hide it in Mr. Clark's garret. It will look like any other trunk up there, if a search should be made. Judging by what is acting here they may have small chance to search for anything but the way back to Boston."

As he spoke they were passing through a body of fifty or sixty militia standing with weapons ready. Lowell, taking the small trunk in his arms, started on a run for the Clark house. Revere tarried.

He beheld about 800 British soldiers, with a mounted officer at their head, appear around both sides of the meeting-house. Facing them, across the green, was the handful of minute-men.

As Revere started on toward the Clark house he heard a pistol shot, followed by two musket shots. Then he turned just in time to see the troops fire a volley.

2

BUNKER HILL

BENSON J. LOSSING

In May 1775, the British force in Boston had increased by fresh arrivals from England and Ireland to ten thousand men. The man-of-war *Cerberus* arrived on the 25th with Generals Howe, Clinton, and Burgoyne—three officers experienced in the military tactics of Europe, but little prepared for service here.

They were surprised at the aspect of affairs, and Gage was reproached for his apparent supineness. However, unity of action was necessary, and the new-comers heartily co-operated with Gage in his plans, such as they were, for dispersing the rebel host that hemmed him in.

He issued a proclamation on June 12, insulting in words and menacing in tone. It declared martial law; pronounced those in arms and their abettors "rebels, parricides of the Constitution," and offered a free pardon to all who would forthwith return to their allegiance, except John Hancock and Samuel Adams, who were outlawed, and for whose apprehension as traitors a reward was offered. This proclamation, so arrogant and insulting, served only to exasperate the people. In the meanwhile, several skirmishes had occurred between parties of the British regulars and the provincials, upon some of the cultivated islands that dot the harbor of Boston.

At this time (May 1775), little progress had been made by the Americans in erecting fortifications. Some breastworks had been thrown up at Cambridge, near the foot of Prospect Hill, and a small redoubt had been formed at Roxbury. The right wing of the besieging army, under General Thomas, was at Roxbury, consisting of four thousand Massachusetts troops, including four artillery companies, with field-pieces and a few heavy cannon. The Rhode Island forces, under Greene, were at Jamaica Plains, and near there was a greater part of General Spencer's Connecticut regiment. General Ward commanded the left wing at Cambridge, which consisted of fifteen Massachusetts regiments, the battalion of artillery under Gridley, and Putnam's regiment, with other Connecticut troops.

Most of the Connecticut forces were at Inman's farm. Paterson's regiment was at the breastwork on Prospect Hill, and a large guard was stationed at Lechmere's Point. Three companies of Gerrish's regiment were at Chelsea; Stark's regiment was at Medford, and Reid's at Charlestown Neck, with sentinels reaching to Penny Ferry and Bunker Hill.

It was made known to the Committee of Safety that General Gage had fixed upon the night of June 18 to take possession of and fortify Bunker Hill and Dorchester Heights. This brought matters to a crisis, and measures were taken to perfect the blockade of Boston. The Committee of Safety ordered Colonel Prescott, with a detachment of one thousand men, including a company of artillery, with two field-pieces, to march at night and throw up intrenchments upon Bunker Hill, an eminence just within the peninsula of Charlestown, and commanding the great northern road from Boston, as well as a considerable portion of the town.

Bunker Hill begins at the isthmus, and rises gradually for about three hundred yards, forming a round, smooth hill, sloping on two sides toward the water, and connected by a ridge of ground on the south with the heights now known as Breed's Hill. This was a well-known public place, the name, "Bunker Hill," being found in the town records and in deeds from an early period.

Bunker Hill was one hundred and ten feet high, Breed's Hill sixty-two feet, and Moulton's Hill thirty-five feet. The principal street of the peninsula was Main Street, which extended from the Neck to the ferry. A road ran over Bunker Hill, around Breed's Hill, to Moulton's Point. The westerly portions of these eminences contained fine orchards.

A portion of the regiments of Prescott, Frye, and Bridge, and a fatigue party of two hundred Connecticut troops with intrenching tools, paraded in the Cambridge camp at six o'clock in the evening. They were furnished with packs and blankets, and ordered to take provisions for twenty-four hours. Samuel Gridley's company of artillery joined them, and the Connecticut troops were placed under the command of Thomas Knowlton, a captain in Putnam's regiment, who was afterward killed in the battle on Harlem Heights.

After an impressive prayer from the lips of President Langdon, of Harvard College, Colonel Prescott and Richard Gridley, preceded by two servants with dark lanterns, commenced their march, at the head of the troops, for Charlestown. It was about nine o'clock at night, the sky clear and starry, and the weather very warm. Strict silence was enjoined, and the object of the expedition was not known to the troops until they arrived at Charlestown Neck, where they were joined by Major Brooks, of Bridge's regiment, and General Putnam. A guard of ten men was placed in Charlestown, and the main body marched over Bunker Hill.

A council was held, to select the best place for the proposed fortification. The order was explicit, to fortify Bunker Hill; but Breed's Hill being nearer Boston, and appearing to be a more eligible place, it was concluded to proceed to fortify it, and to throw up works, also, on Bunker Hill, to cover a retreat, if necessary, across Charlestown Neck. Colonel Gridley marked out the lines of the proposed fortifications, and, at about midnight, the men, having thrown off their packs and stacked their arms, began their perilous work—perilous, because British sentinels and British ships-of-war were almost within sound of their picks.

Officers and men labored together with all their might, with pickaxes and spades, and were cheered on in their work by the distant signals of safety—"All's well!"—that came from the shipping and the sentinels at the foot of Copp's Hill. It proclaimed that they were still undiscovered; and at every cry of "All's well!" they plied their tools with increased vigor.

When the day dawned, at about four o'clock, they had thrown up intrenchments six feet high; and a strong redoubt, which was afterward the admiration of the enemy, loomed up on the green height before the wondering eyes of the astonished Britons like a work of magic. The British officers could hardly be convinced that it was the result of a few hours' labor only, but deemed it the work of days. Gage saw at once how foolish he had been in not taking possession of this strong point, as advised, while it was in his power to do so.

The fortification was first discovered at dawn, by the watchmen on board the British man-of-war *Lively*. Without waiting for orders, the captain put springs upon his cables, and opened a fire on the American works. The noise of the cannon aroused the sleepers in Boston, and when the sun arose on that bright morning, every eminence and roof in the city swarmed with people, astonished at the strange apparition upon Breed's Hill. The shots from the *Lively* did no harm, and, defended by their intrenchments, the Americans plied their tools in strengthening their works within, until called to lay aside the pick and shovel for gun and knapsack.

On June 17, Admiral Graves, the naval commander at Boston, ordered the firing to cease; but it was soon renewed, not only by the shipping, but from a battery of six guns upon Copp's Hill in the city. Gage summoned a council of war early in the morning. As it was evident that the Americans were rapidly gaining strength, and that the safety of the town was endangered, it was unanimously resolved to send out a force to drive them from the peninsula of Charlestown and destroy their works on the heights.

It was decided, also, to make the attack in front, and preparations were made accordingly. The drums beat to arms, and Boston was soon in a tumult. Dragoons galloping, artillery trains rumbling, and the marching and countermarching of the regulars and loyalists, together with the clangor of the church bells, struck dismay into many a heart before stout in the presence of British protectors. It is said that the danger which surrounded the city converted many Tories into patriots; and the selectmen, in the midst of that fearful commotion, received large accessions to their list of professed friends from the ranks of the timid loyalists.

Toward noon between two and three thousand picked men from the British army, under the command of General Sir William Howe and General Pigot, embarked in twenty-eight barges, part from the Long Wharf and some from the North Battery, in Boston, and landed at Morton's, or Moulton's Point, beyond the eastern foot of Breed's Hill, covered by the guns of the *Falcon* and other vessels.

The Americans had worked faithfully on their intrenchments all the morning, and were greatly encouraged by the voice and example of Prescott, who exposed himself, without care, to the random shots of the battery on Copp's Hill. He supposed, at first, that the enemy would not attack him, but, seeing the movements in the city, he was convinced to the contrary, and comforted his toiling troops with assurances of certain victory.

Confident of such a result himself, he would not at first send to General Ward for a reinforcement; but between nine and ten o'clock, by advice of his officers, Major Brooks was dispatched to headquarters for that purpose. General Putnam had urged Ward early in the morning to send fresh troops to relieve those on duty; but only a portion of Stark's regiment was allowed to go, as the general apprehended that Cambridge would be the principal point of attack.

Convinced otherwise, by certain intelligence, the remainder of Stark's regiment, and the whole of Reed's corps, on the Neck, were ordered to reinforce Prescott. At twelve o'clock the men in the redoubt ceased work, sent off their intrenching tools, took some refreshments, hoisted the New England flag, and prepared to fight.

The intrenching tools were sent to Bunker Hill, where, under the directions of General Putnam, the men began to throw up a breastwork. Some of the more timid soldiers made the removal of the tools a pretext for leaving the redoubt, and never returned.

It was between twelve and one o'clock when the British troops, consisting of the fifth, thirty-eighth, forty-third, and fifty-second battalions of infantry, two companies of grenadiers, and two of light infantry, landed, their rich uniforms and arms flashing and glittering in the noonday sun, making an imposing and formidable display.

General Howe reconnoitred the American works, and, while waiting for reinforcements, which he had solicited from Gage, allowed his troops to dine. When the intelligence of the landing of the enemy reached Cambridge, two miles distant, there was great excitement in the camp and throughout the town. The drums beat to arms, the bells were rung, and the people and military were speedily hurrying in every direction.

General Ward used his own regiment, and those of Paterson and Gardner and a part of Bridge's, for the defence of Cambridge. The remainder of the Massachusetts troops were ordered to Charlestown, and thither General Putnam conducted those of Connecticut.

At about two o'clock the reinforcement for Howe arrived, and landed at the present navy-yard. It consisted of the forty-seventh battalion of infantry, a battalion of marines, and some grenadiers and light infantry. The whole force (about four thousand men) was commanded and directed by the most skilful British officers then in Boston; and every man preparing to attack the undisciplined provincials was a drilled soldier, and quite perfect in the art of war.

It was an hour of the deepest anxiety among the patriots on Breed's Hill. They had observed the whole martial display, from the time of the embarkation until the forming of the enemy's line for battle. For the Americans, as yet, very little succor had arrived. Hunger and thirst annoyed them, while the labors of the night and morning weighed them down with excessive fatigue.

Added to this was the dreadful suspicion that took possession of their minds, when only feeble reinforcements arrived, that treachery had placed them there for the purpose of sacrifice. Yet they could not doubt the patriotism of their principal officers, and before the action commenced their suspicions were scattered to the winds by the arrival of their beloved Doctor Warren and General Pomeroy.

Warren, who was president of the Provincial Congress, then sitting at Watertown, seven miles distant, informed of the landing of the enemy, hastened toward Charlestown, though suffering from sickness and exhaustion. He had been commissioned a major-general four days before. Putnam, who was at Cambridge, forwarding provisions and reinforcements to Charlestown, tried to dissuade him from going into the battle. Warren was not to be diverted from his purpose, and, mounting a horse, he sped across the Neck and entered the redoubt, amid the loud cheers of the provincials, just as Howe gave orders to advance.

Colonel Prescott offered the command to Warren, as his superior, when the latter replied, "I am come to fight as a volunteer, and feel honored in being allowed to serve under so brave an officer."

While the British troops were forming, and preparing to march along the Mystic River for the purpose of flanking the Americans and gaining their rear, the artillery, with two field-pieces, and Captain Knowlton, with the Connecticut troops, left the redoubt, took a position near Bunker Hill, and formed a breastwork seven hundred feet in length, which served an excellent purpose.

A little in front of a strong stone and rail fence, Knowlton built another, and between the two was placed a quantity of new-mown grass. This apparently slight breastwork formed a valuable defence to the provincials.

It was now three in the afternoon. The provincial troops were placed in an attitude of defence as the British column moved slowly forward to the attack. Colonel Prescott and the original constructors of the redoubt, except the Connecticut troops, were within the works. General Warren also took post in the redoubt.

Gridley and Callender's artillery companies were between the breastworks and rail fence on the eastern side. A few troops, recalled from Charlestown after the British landed, and a part of Warner's company, lined the cart-way on the right of the redoubt. The Connecticut and New Hampshire forces were at the rail fence on the west of the redoubt, and three companies were stationed in the main street at the foot of Breed's Hill.

Before General Howe moved from his first position he sent out strong flank guards, and directed his heavy artillery to play upon the American line. At the same time a blue flag was displayed as a signal, and the guns upon Copp's Hill and the ships and floating batteries in the river poured a storm of round-shot upon the redoubt.

A furious cannonade was opened at the same moment upon the right wing of the provincial army at Roxbury, to prevent reinforcements being sent by General Thomas to Charlestown. Gridley and Callender, with their field-pieces, returned a feeble response to the heavy guns of the enemy.

Gridley's guns were soon disabled; while Callender, who alleged that his cartridges were too large, withdrew to Bunker Hill. Putnam was there, and ordered him back to his first position. He disobeyed, and nearly all his men, more courageous than he, deserted him.

In the meanwhile, Captain Walker, of Chelmsford, with fifty resolute men, marched down the hill near Charlestown and greatly annoyed the enemy's left flank. Finding their position very perilous, they marched over to the Mystic, and did great execution upon the right flank. Walker was there wounded and made prisoner, but the greater part of his men succeeded in gaining the redoubt.

Under cover of the discharges of artillery the British army moved up the slope of Breed's Hill toward the American works in two divisions, General Howe with the right wing, and General Pigot with the left. The former was to penetrate the American lines at the rail fence; the latter to storm the redoubt.

They had not proceeded far before the firing of their artillery ceased, in consequence of discovering that balls too large for the field-pieces had been sent over from Boston. Howe ordered the pieces to be loaded with grape; but they soon became useless, on account of the miry ground at the base of the hill. Small arms and bayonets now became their reliance.

Silently the British troops, burdened with heavy knapsacks, toiled up the ascent toward the redoubt in the heat of a bright summer's sun. All was silent within the American intrenchments, and very few provincials were to be seen by the approaching battalions; but within those breastworks, and in reserve behind the hills, crouched fifteen hundred determined men, ready, at a prescribed signal, to fall upon the foe.

The provincials had but a scanty supply of ammunition, and, to avoid wasting it by ineffectual shots, Prescott gave orders not to fire until the enemy were so near that the whites of their eyes could be seen.

"Then," he said, "aim at their waistbands; and be sure to pick off the commanders, known by their handsome coats!" The enemy were not so sparing of their powder and ball, but when within gunshot of the apparently deserted works commenced a random firing.

Prescott could hardly restrain his men from responding, and a few did disobey his orders and returned the fire. Putnam hastened to the spot, and threatened to cut down the first man who should again disobey orders, and quiet was restored. At length the enemy reached the prescribed distance, when, waving his sword over his head, Prescott shouted, "Fire!"

Terrible was the effect of the volley that ensued. Whole platoons of the British regulars were laid upon the earth like grass by the mower's scythe. Other deadly volleys succeeded, and the enemy, disconcerted, broke and fled toward the water. The provincials, joyed at seeing the regulars fly, wished to pursue them, and many leaped the rail fence for the purpose; but the prudence of the American officers kept them in check, and in a few minutes they were again within their works, prepared to receive a second attack from the British troops, that were quickly rallied by Howe.

Colonel Prescott praised and encouraged his men, while General Putnam rode to Bunker Hill to urge on reinforcements. Many had arrived at Charlestown Neck, but were deterred from crossing by the enfilading fire of the *Glasgow* and two armed gondolas near the causeway. Portions of regiments were scattered upon Bunker Hill and its vicinity, and these General Putnam, by entreaties and commands, endeavored to rally. Colonel Gerrish, who was very corpulent, became completely exhausted by fatigue; and other officers, wholly unused to warfare, coward-like kept at a respectful distance from danger. Few additional troops could be brought to Breed's Hill before the second attack was made.

The British troops, reinforced by four hundred marines from Boston, under Major Small, accompanied by Doctor Jeffries, the army surgeon, advanced toward the redoubt in the same order as at first, General Howe boldly leading the van, as he had promised.

It was a mournful march over the dead bodies of scores of their fellow soldiers; but with true English courage they pressed onward, their artillery doing more damage to the Americans than at the first assault. It had moved along the narrow road between the tongue of land and Breed's Hill, and when within a hundred yards of the rail fence, and on a line with the breastworks, opened a galling fire, to cover the advance of the other assailants.

In the meanwhile, a carcass and some hot shot were thrown from Copp's Hill into Charlestown, which set the village on fire. The houses were chiefly of wood, and in a short time nearly two hundred buildings were in flames, shrouding in dense smoke the heights in the rear whereon the provincials were posted.

Beneath this veil the British hoped to rush unobserved up to the breastworks, scale them, and drive the Americans out at the point of the bayonet. At that moment a gentle breeze, which appeared to the provincials like the breath of a guardian angel—the first zephyr that had been felt on that sultry day—came from the west and swept the smoke away seaward, exposing to the full view of the Americans the advancing columns of the enemy, who fired as they approached, but with little execution.

Colonels Brener, Nixon, and Buckminster were wounded, and Major Moore was killed. As before, the Americans reserved their fire until the British were within the prescribed distance, when they poured forth their leaden hail with such sure aim and terrible effect that whole ranks of officers and men were slain.

General Howe was at the head, and once he was left entirely alone, his aides and all about him having perished. The British line recoiled, and gave way in several parts, and it required the utmost exertion in all the remaining officers, from the generals down to the subalterns, to repair the disorder which this hot and unexpected fire had produced. All their efforts were at first fruitless, and the troops retreated in great disorder to the shore.

General Clinton, who had beheld the progress of the battle with mortified pride, seeing the regulars repulsed a second time, crossed over in a boat, followed by a small reinforcement, and joined the broken army as a volunteer.

Some of the British officers remonstrated against leading the men a third time to certain destruction; but others, who had ridiculed American valor, and boasted loudly of British invincibility, resolved on victory or death.

The incautious loudness of speech of a provincial, during the second attack, declaring that the ammunition was nearly exhausted, gave the enemy encouraging and important information. Howe immediately rallied his troops and formed them for a third attack, but in a different way. The weakness of the point between the breastwork and the rail fence had been discovered by Howe, and thitherward he determined to lead the left wing with the artillery, while a show of attack should be made at the rail fence on the other side. His men were ordered to stand the fire of the provincials, and then make a furious charge with bayonets.

So long were the enemy making preparations for a third attack that the provincials began to imagine that the second repulse was to be final. They had time to refresh themselves a little and recover from that complete exhaustion which the labor of the day had produced.

It was too true that their ammunition was almost exhausted, and, being obliged to rely upon that for defence, as comparatively few of the muskets were furnished with bayonets, they began to despair. The few remaining cartridges within the redoubt were distributed by Prescott, and those soldiers who were destitute of bayonets resolved to club their arms and use the breeches of their guns when their powder should be gone.

The loose stones in the redoubt were collected for use as missiles if necessary, and all resolved to fight as long as a ray of hope appeared.

During this preparation on Breed's Hill, all was confusion elsewhere. General Ward was at Cambridge, without sufficient staff-officers to convey his orders. Henry (afterward General) Knox was in the reconnoitring service, as a volunteer, during the day, and upon his reports Ward issued his orders.

Late in the afternoon, the commanding general despatched his own, with Paterson and Gardner's regiments, to the field of action; but to the raw recruits the aspect of the narrow Neck was terrible, swept as it was by the British cannon. Colonel Gardner succeeded in leading three hundred men to Bunker Hill, where Putnam set them intrenching, but soon ordered them to the lines.

Gardner was advancing boldly at their head, when a musket-ball entered his groin and wounded him mortally. His men were thrown into confusion, and very few of them engaged in the combat that followed, until the retreat commenced. Other regiments failed to reach the lines.

A part of Gerrish's regiment, led by Adjutant Christian Febiger, a Danish officer, who afterward accompanied Arnold to Quebec and was distinguished at Stony Point, reached the lines just as the action commenced, and effectually galled the British left wing. Putnam, in the meantime, was using his utmost exertions to form the confused troops on Bunker Hill and get fresh corps with bayonets across the Neck.

All was order and firmness at the redoubt on Breed's Hill as the enemy advanced. The artillery of the British swept the interior of the breastwork from end to end, destroying many of the provincials, among whom was Lieutenant Prescott, a nephew of the colonel commanding.

The remainder were driven within the redoubt, and the breastwork was abandoned. Each shot of the provincials was true to its aim, and Colonel Abercrombie and Majors Williams and Speedlove fell. Howe was wounded in the foot, but continued fighting at the head of his men. His boats were at Boston, and retreat he could not. His troops pressed forward to the redoubt, now nearly silent, for the provincials' last grains of powder were in their guns. Only a ridge of earth separated the combatants, and the assailants scaled it.

The first that reached the parapet were repulsed by a shower of stones. Major Pitcairn, who led the troops at Lexington, ascending the parapet, cried out, "Now for the glory of the marines!" and was immediately shot.

Again numbers of the enemy leaped upon the parapet, while others assailed the redoubt on three sides. Hand to hand the belligerents struggled, and the gun-stocks of many of the provincials were shivered to pieces by the heavy blows they were made to give. The enemy poured into the redoubt in such numbers that Prescott, perceiving the folly of longer resistance, ordered a retreat. Through the enemy's ranks the Americans hewed their way, many of them walking backward and dealing deadly blows with their musket-stocks.

Prescott and Warren were the last to leave the redoubt. Colonel Gridley, the engineer, was wounded, and borne off safely. Prescott received several thrusts from bayonets and rapiers in his clothing, but escaped unhurt. Warren was the last man that left the works. He was a short distance from the redoubt, on his way toward Bunker Hill, when a musket-ball passed through his head, killing him instantly. He was left on the field, for all were flying in the greatest confusion, pursued by the victors, who remorselessly bayoneted those who fell in their way.

Major Jackson had rallied Gardner's men upon Bunker Hill, and, pressing forward with three companies of Ward's, and Febiger's party from Gerrish's regiment, poured a destructive fire upon the enemy between Breed's and Bunker Hill, and bravely covered the retreat from the redoubt.

The Americans at the rail fence, under Stark, Reed, and Knowlton, reinforced by Clark, Coit, and Chester's Connecticut companies and a few other troops, maintained their ground, in the meanwhile, with great firmness, and successfully resisted every attempt of the enemy to turn their flank.

This service was very valuable, for it saved the main body, retreating from the redoubt, from being cut off. But when these saw their brethren, with the chief commander, flying before the enemy, they too fled. Putnam used every exertion to keep them firm. He commanded, pleaded, cursed and swore like a madman, and was seen at every point in the van trying to rally the scattered corps, swearing that victory should crown the Americans.

"Make a stand here!" he exclaimed; "we can stop them yet! In God's name, fire and give them one shot more!"

The gallant old Pomeroy, also, with his shattered musket in his hand, implored them to rally, but in vain. The whole body retreated across the Neck, where the fire from the *Glasgow* and gondolas slew many of them.

They left five of their six field-pieces and all their intrenching tools upon Bunker Hill, and they retreated to Winter Hill, Prospect Hill, and to Cambridge. The British, greatly exhausted, and properly cautious, did not follow, but contented themselves with taking possession of the peninsula.

Clinton advised an immediate attack upon Cambridge, but Howe was too cautious or too timid to make the attempt. His troops lay upon their arms all night on Bunker Hill, and the Americans did the same on Prospect Hill, a mile distant.

Two British field-pieces played upon them, but without effect, and, both sides feeling unwilling to renew the action, hostilities ceased. The loss of the Americans in this engagement was one hundred and fifteen killed and missing, three hundred and five wounded, and thirty who were taken prisoners; in all, four hundred and fifty.

The British loss is not positively known. Gage reported two hundred and twenty-six killed, and eight hundred and twenty-eight wounded; in all, ten hundred and fifty-four. In this number are included eighty-nine officers. The Provincial Congress of Massachusetts, from the best information they could obtain, reported the British loss at about fifteen hundred.

The number of buildings consumed in Charlestown, before midnight, was about four hundred; and the estimated loss of property (most of the families, with their effects, having moved out) was nearly six hundred thousand dollars.

The number engaged in this battle was small, yet contemporary writers and eye-witnesses represent it as one of the most determined and severe on record. There was absolutely no victory in the case.

The most indomitable courage was displayed on both sides; and when the provincials had retired but a short distance, so wearied and exhausted were all that neither party desired more fighting, if we except Colonel Prescott, who earnestly petitioned to be allowed to lead a fresh corps that evening and retake Breed's Hill.

It was a terrible day for Boston and its vicinity, for almost every family had a representative in one of the two armies. Fathers, husbands, sons, and brothers were in the affray, and deep was the mental anguish of the women of the city, who, from roofs and steeples and every elevation, gazed with streaming eyes upon the carnage, for the battle raged in full view of thousands of interested spectators in the town and upon the adjoining hills. In contrast with the terrible scene were the cloudless sky and brilliant sun.

3

BENEDICT ARNOLD'S NAVY

ALFRED THAYER MAHAN

At the time when hostilities began between Great Britain and her American Colonies, the fact was realised generally, being evident to reason and taught by experience, that control of the water, both ocean and inland, would have a preponderant effect upon the contest. It was clear to reason, for there was a long seaboard with numerous interior navigable watercourses, and at the same time scanty and indifferent communications by land.

Critical portions of the territory involved were yet an unimproved wilderness. Experience, the rude but efficient schoolmaster of that large portion of mankind which gains knowledge only by hard knocks, had confirmed through the preceding French wars the inferences of the thoughtful. Therefore, conscious of the great superiority of the

British Navy, which, however, had not then attained the unchallenged supremacy of a later day, the American leaders early sought the alliance of the Bourbon kingdoms, France and Spain, the hereditary enemies of Great Britain. There alone could be found the counterpoise to a power which, if unchecked, must ultimately prevail.

Nearly three years elapsed before the Colonists accomplished this object, by giving a demonstration of their strength in the enforced surrender of Burgoyne's army at Saratoga. This event has merited the epithet "decisive," because, and only because, it decided the intervention of France. It may be affirmed, with little hesitation, that this victory of the colonists was directly the result of naval force—that of the colonists themselves.

It was the cause that naval force from abroad, entering into the contest, transformed it from a local to a universal war, and assured the independence of the Colonies. That the Americans were strong enough to impose the capitulation of Saratoga, was due to the invaluable year of delay secured to them by their little navy on Lake Champlain, created by the indomitable energy, and handled with the indomitable courage, of the traitor Benedict Arnold.

That the war spread from America to Europe, from the English Channel to the Baltic, from the Bay of Biscay to the Mediterranean, from the West Indies to the Mississippi, and ultimately involved the waters of the remote peninsula of Hindustan, is traceable, through Saratoga, to the rude flotilla which in 1776 anticipated its enemy in the possession of Lake Champlain. The events which thus culminated merit therefore a clearer understanding, and a fuller treatment, than their intrinsic importance and petty scale would justify otherwise.

In 1775, only fifteen years had elapsed since the expulsion of the French from the North American continent. The concentration of their power, during its continuance, in the valley of the St. Lawrence, had given direction to the local conflict, and had impressed upon men's minds the importance of Lake Champlain, of its tributary Lake George, and of the Hudson River, as forming a consecutive, though not continuous, water line of communications from the St. Lawrence to New York. The strength of Canada against attack by land lay in its remoteness, in the wilderness to be traversed before it was reached, and in the strength of the line of the St. Lawrence, with the fortified posts of Montreal and Quebec on its northern bank.

The wilderness, it is true, interposed its passive resistance to attacks from Canada as well as to attacks upon it; but when it had been traversed, there were to the southward no such strong natural positions confronting the assailant. Attacks from the south fell upon the front, or at best upon the flank, of the line of the St. Lawrence. Attacks from Canada took New York and its dependencies in the rear.

These elements of natural strength, in the military conditions of the North, were impressed upon the minds of the Americans by the prolonged resistance of Canada to the greatly superior numbers of the British Colonists in the previous wars. Regarded, therefore, as a base for attacks, of a kind with which they were painfully familiar, but to be undergone now under disadvantages of numbers and power never before experienced, it was desirable to gain possession of the St. Lawrence and its posts before they were strengthened and garrisoned. At this outset of hostilities, the American insurgents, knowing clearly their own minds, possessed the advantage of the initiative over the British government, which still hesitated to use against those whom it styled rebels the preventive measures it would have taken at once against a recognised enemy.

Under these circumstances, in May 1775, a body of two hundred and seventy Americans, led by Ethan Allen and Benedict Arnold, seized the posts of Ticonderoga and Crown Point, which were inadequately garrisoned. These are on the upper waters of Lake Champlain, where it is less than a third of a mile wide; Ticonderoga being on a peninsula formed by the lake and the inlet from Lake George, Crown Point on a promontory twelve miles lower down. They were positions of recognised importance, and had been advanced posts of the British in previous wars. A schooner being found there, Arnold, who had been a seaman, embarked in her and hurried to the foot of the lake.

The wind failed him when still thirty miles from St. John's, another fortified post on the lower narrows, where the lake gradually tapers down to the Richelieu River, its outlet to the St. Lawrence. Unable to advance otherwise, Arnold took to his boats with thirty men, pulled through the night, and at six o'clock on the following morning surprised the post, in which were only a sergeant and a dozen men. He reaped the rewards of celerity. The prisoners informed him that a considerable body of troops was expected from Canada, on its way to Ticonderoga; and this force in fact reached St. John's on the next day.

When it arrived, Arnold was gone, having carried off a sloop which he found there and destroyed everything else that could float. By such trifling means two active officers had secured the temporary control of the lake itself and of the approaches to it from the south. There being no roads, the British, debarred from the water line, were unable to advance. Sir Guy Carleton, Governor and Commander-in-Chief in Canada, strengthened the works at St. John's, and built a schooner; but his force was inadequate to meet that of the Americans.

The seizure of the two posts, being an act of offensive war, was not at once pleasing to the American Congress, which still clung to the hope of reconciliation; but events were marching rapidly, and ere summer was over the invasion of Canada was ordered. General Montgomery, appointed to that enterprise, embarked at Crown Point with two thousand men on September 4th, and soon afterwards appeared before St. John's, which after prolonged operations capitulated on the 3d of November.

On the 13th, Montgomery entered Montreal, and thence pressed down the St. Lawrence to Pointe aux Trembles, twenty miles above Quebec. There he joined Arnold, who in the month of October had crossed the northern wilderness, between the head waters of the Kennebec River and St. Lawrence. On the way he had endured immense privations, losing five hundred men of the twelve hundred with whom he started; and upon arriving opposite Quebec, on the 10th of November, three days had been unavoidably spent in collecting boats to pass the river.

Crossing on the night of the 13th, this adventurous soldier and his little command climbed the Heights of Abraham by the same path that had served Wolfe so well sixteen years before. With characteristic audacity he summoned the place. The demand of course was refused; but that Carleton did not fall at once upon the little band of seven hundred that bearded him shows by how feeble a tenure Great Britain then held Canada.

Immediately after the junction Montgomery advanced on Quebec, where he appeared on the 5th of December. Winter having already begun, and neither his numbers nor his equipments being adequate to regular siege operations, he very properly decided to try the desperate chance of an assault upon the strongest fortress in America. This was made on the night of December 31st, 1775. Whatever possibility of success there may have been vanished with the death of Montgomery, who fell at the head of his men.

The American army retired three miles up the river, went into winter-quarters, and established a land blockade of Quebec, which was cut off from the sea by the ice. "For five months," wrote Carleton to the Secretary for War, on the 14th of May, 1776, "this town has been closely invested by the rebels."

From this unpleasant position it was relieved on the 6th of May, when signals were exchanged between it and the *Surprise*, the advance ship of a squadron under Captain Charles Douglas, which had sailed from England on the 11th of March. Arriving off the mouth of the St. Lawrence, on the morning of April 12th, Douglas found ice extending nearly twenty miles to sea, and packed too closely to admit of working through it by dexterous steering.

The urgency of the case not admitting delay, he ran his ship, the *Isis*, with a speed of five knots, against a large piece of ice about ten or twelve feet thick, to test the effect. The ice, probably softened by salt water and salt air, went to pieces.

"Encouraged by this experiment," continues Douglas, somewhat magnificently, "we thought it an enterprise worthy an English ship of the line in our King and country's sacred cause, and an effort due to the gallant defenders of Quebec, to make the attempt of pressing her by force of sail, through the thick, broad, and closely connected fields of ice, to which we saw no bounds towards the western part of our horizon.

"Before night (when blowing a snow-storm, we brought-to, or rather stopped), we had penetrated about eight leagues into it, describing our path all the way with bits of the sheathing of the ship's bottom, and sometimes pieces of the cutwater, but none of the oak plank; and it was pleasant enough at times, when we stuck fast, to see Lord Petersham exercising his troops on the crusted surface of that fluid through which the ship had so recently sailed."

It took nine days of this work to reach Anticosti Island, after which the ice seems to have given no more trouble; but further delay was occasioned by fogs, calms, and head winds.

Upon the arrival of the ships of war, the Americans at once retreated. During the winter, though reinforcements must have been received from time to time, they had wasted from exposure, and from small-pox, which ravaged the camp. On the 1st of May the returns showed nineteen hundred men present, of whom only a thousand were fit for duty. There were then on hand but three days' provisions, and none other nearer than St. John's. The inhabitants would of course render no further assistance to the Americans after the ships arrived. The Navy had again decided the fate of Canada, and was soon also to determine that of Lake Champlain.

When two hundred troops had landed from the ships, Carleton marched out, "to see," he said, "what these mighty boasters were about." The sneer was unworthy a man of his generous character, for the boasters had endured much for faint chances of success; and the smallness of the reinforcement which encouraged him to act shows either an extreme prudence on his part, or the narrow margin by which Quebec escaped. He found the enemy busy with preparations for retreat, and upon his appearance they abandoned their camp.

Their forces on the two sides of the river being now separated by the enemy's shipping, the Americans retired first to Sorel, where the Richelieu enters the St. Lawrence, and thence continued to fall back by gradual stages. It was not until June 15th that Arnold quitted Montreal; and at the end of June the united force was still on the Canadian side of the present border line. On the 3d of July it reached Crown Point, in a pitiable state from small-pox and destitution.

Both parties began at once to prepare for a contest upon Lake Champlain. The Americans, small as their flotilla was, still kept the superiority obtained for them by Arnold's promptitude a year before. On the 25th of June, the American General Schuyler, commanding the Northern Department, wrote: "We have happily such a naval superiority on Lake Champlain, that I have a confident hope the enemy will not appear upon it this campaign, especially as our force is increasing by the addition of gondolas, two nearly finished. Arnold, however"— whose technical knowledge caused him to be intrusted with the naval preparations—"says that 300 carpenters should be employed and a large number of gondolas, row-galleys, be built, twenty or thirty at least. There is great difficulty in getting the carpenters needed."

Arnold's ideas were indeed on a scale worthy of the momentous issues at stake. "To augment our navy on the lake appears to me of the utmost importance. There is water between Crown Point and Pointe au Fer for vessels of the largest size. I am of opinion that row-galleys are the best construction and cheapest for this lake. Perhaps it may be well to have one frigate of 36 guns. She may carry 18-pounders on the Lake, and be superior to any vessel that can be built or floated from St. John's."

Unfortunately for the Americans, their resources in men and means were far inferior to those of their opponents, who were able eventually to carry out, though on a somewhat smaller scale, Arnold's idea of a sailing ship, strictly so called, of force as yet unknown in inland waters. Such a ship, aided as she was by two consorts of somewhat similar character, dominated the Lake as soon as she was afloat, reversing all the conditions. To place and equip her, however, required time, invaluable time, during which Arnold's two schooners exercised control.

Baron Riedesel, the commander of the German contingent with Carleton, after examining the American position at Ticonderoga, wrote, "If we could have begun our expedition four weeks earlier, I am satisfied that everything would have been ended this year (1776); but, not having shelter nor other necessary things, we were unable to remain at the other [southern] end of Champlain."

So delay favors the defence, and changes issues. What would have been the effect upon the American cause if, simultaneously with the loss of New York, August 20th–September 15th, had come news of the fall of Ticonderoga, the repute of which for strength stood high? Nor was this all; for in that event, the plan which was wrecked in 1777 by Sir William Howe's ill-conceived expedition to the Chesapeake would doubtless have been carried out in 1776.

In a contemporary English paper occurs the following significant item: "London, September 26th, 1776. Advices have been received here from Canada, dated August 12th, that General Burgoyne's army has found it impracticable to get across the lakes this season. The naval force of the Provincials is too great for them to contend with at present. They must build larger vessels for this purpose, and these cannot be ready before next summer. The design *was* that the two armies commanded by Generals Howe and Burgoyne should coöperate; that they should both be on the Hudson River at the same time; that they should join about Albany, and thereby cut off all communication between the northern and southern Colonies."

As Arnold's more ambitious scheme could not be realised, he had to content himself with gondolas and galleys, for the force he was to command as well as to build. The precise difference between the two kinds of rowing vessels thus distinguished by name, the writer has not been able to ascertain.

The gondola was a flat-bottomed boat, and inferior in nautical qualities—speed, handiness, and seaworthiness—to the galleys, which probably were keeled. The latter certainly carried sails, and may have been capable of beating to windward. Arnold preferred them, and stopped the building of gondolas. "The galleys," he wrote, "are quick moving, which will give us a great advantage in the open lake."

The complements of the galleys were eighty men, of the gondolas forty-five; from which, and from their batteries, it may be inferred that the latter were between one third and one half the size of the former. The armaments of the two were alike in character, but those of the gondolas much lighter. American accounts agree with Captain Douglas's report of one galley captured by the British. In the bows, an 18 and a 12-pounder; in the stern, two 9s; in broadside, from four to six 6s. There is in this a somewhat droll reminder of the disputed merits of bow, stern, and broadside fire, in a modern iron-clad; and the practical conclusion is much the same. The gondolas had one 12-pounder and two 6s. All the vessels of both parties carried a number of swivel guns.

Amid the many difficulties which lack of resources imposed upon all American undertakings, Arnold succeeded in getting afloat with three schooners, a sloop, and five gondolas, on the 20th of August. He cruised at the upper end of Champlain till the 1st of September, when he moved rapidly north, and on the 3d anchored in the lower narrows, twenty-five miles above St. John's, stretching his line from shore to shore.

Scouts had kept him informed of the progress of the British naval preparations, so that he knew that there was no immediate danger; while an advanced position, maintained with a bold front, would certainly prevent reconnoissances by water, and possibly might impose somewhat upon the enemy. The latter, however, erected batteries on each side of the anchorage, compelling Arnold to fall back to the broader lake. He then had soundings taken about Valcour Island, and between it and the western shore; that being the position in which he intended to make a stand. He retired thither on the 23rd of September.

The British on their side had contended with no less obstacles than their adversaries, though of a somewhat different character. To get carpenters and materials to build, and seamen to man, were the chief difficulties of the Americans, the necessities of the seaboard conceding but partially the demands made upon it; but their vessels were built upon the shores of the Lake, and launched into navigable waters. A large fleet of transports and ships of war in the St. Lawrence supplied the British with adequate resources, which were utilized judiciously and energetically by Captain Douglas; but to get these to the Lake was a long and arduous task.

A great part of the Richelieu River was shoal, and obstructed by rapids. The point where lake navigation began was at St. John's, to which the nearest approach, by a hundred-ton schooner, from the St. Lawrence, was Chambly, ten miles below. Flat-boats and long-boats could be dragged up stream, but vessels of any size had to be transported by land; and the engineers found the roadbed too soft in places to bear the weight of a hundred tons.

Under Douglas's directions, the planking and frames of two schooners were taken down at Chambly, and carried round by road to St. John's, where they were again put together. At Quebec he found building a new hull, of one hundred and eighty tons. This he took apart nearly to the keel, shipping the frames in thirty long-boats, which the transport captains consented to surrender, together with their carpenters, for service on the Lake.

Drafts from the ships of war, and volunteers from the transports, furnished a body of seven hundred seamen for the same employment—a force to which the Americans could oppose nothing equal, commanded as it was by regular naval officers. The largest vessel was ship-rigged, and had a battery of eighteen 12-pounders; she was called the *Inflexible*, and was commanded by Lieutenant John Schanck.

The two schooners, *Maria*, Lieutenant Starke, and *Carleton*, Lieutenant James Richard Dacres, carried respectively fourteen and twelve 6-pounders. These were the backbone of the British flotilla. There were also a radeau, the *Thunderer*, and a large gondola, the *Loyal Convert*, both heavily armed; but, being equally heavy of movement, they do not appear to have played any important part. Besides these, when the expedition started, there were twenty gunboats, each carrying one fieldpiece, from 24s to 9-pounders; or, in some cases, howitzers.

"By all these means," wrote Douglas on July 21st, "our acquiring an absolute dominion over Lake Champlain is not doubted of." The expectation was perfectly sound. With a working breeze, the *Inflexible* alone could sweep the Lake clear of all that floated on it. But the element of time remained. From the day of this writing till that on which he saw the *Inflexible* leave St. John's, October 4th, was over ten weeks; and it was not until the 9th that Carleton was ready to advance with the squadron. By that time the American troops at the head of the Lake had increased to eight or ten thousand. The British land force is reported as thirteen thousand, of which six thousand were in garrison at St. John's and elsewhere.

Arnold's last reinforcements reached him at Valcour on the 6th of October. On that day, and in the action of the 11th, he had with him all the American vessels on the Lake, except one schooner and one galley. His force, thus, was two schooners and a sloop, broadside vessels, besides four galleys and eight gondolas, which may be assumed reasonably to have depended on their bow guns; there, at least, was their heaviest fire. Thus reckoned, his flotilla, disposed to the best advantage, could bring into action at one time, two 18s, thirteen 12s, one 9, two 6s, twelve 4s, and two 2-pounders, independent of swivels; total thirty-two guns, out of eighty-four that were mounted in fifteen vessels.

To this the British had to oppose, in three broadside vessels, nine 12s and thirteen 6s, and in twenty gunboats, twenty other brass guns, "from twenty-four to nines, some with howitzers"; total forty-two guns. In this statement the radeau and gondola have not been included, because of their unmanageableness. Included as broadside vessels, they would raise the British armament—by three 24s, three 12s, four

9s, and a howitzer—to a total of fifty-three guns. Actually, they could be brought into action only under exceptional circumstances, and are more properly omitted.

These minutiæ are necessary for the proper appreciation of what Captain Douglas justly called "a momentous event." It was a strife of pigmies for the prize of a continent, and the leaders are entitled to full credit both for their antecedent energy and for their dispositions in the contest; not least the unhappy man who, having done so much to save his country, afterwards blasted his name by a treason unsurpassed in modern war.

Energy and audacity had so far preserved the Lake to the Americans; Arnold determined to have one more try of the chances. He did not know the full force of the enemy, but he expected that "it would be very formidable, if not equal to ours." The season, however, was so near its end that a severe check would equal a defeat, and would postpone Carleton's further advance to the next spring. Besides, what was the worth of such a force as the American, such a flotilla, under the guns of Ticonderoga, the Lake being lost? It was eminently a case for taking chances, even if the detachment should be sacrificed, as it was.

Arnold's original purpose had been to fight under way; and it was from this point of view that he valued the galleys, because of their mobility. It is uncertain when he first learned of the rig and battery of the *Inflexible*; but a good look-out was kept, and the British squadron was sighted from Valcour when it quitted the narrows. It may have been seen even earlier; for Carleton had been informed, erroneously, that the Americans were near Grand Island, which led him to incline to that side, and so open out Valcour sooner. The British anchored for the night of October 10th, between Grand and Long Islands.

Getting under way next morning, they stood up the Lake with a strong north-east wind, keeping along Grand Island, upon which their attention doubtless was fastened by the intelligence which they had received; but it was a singular negligence thus to run to leeward with a fair wind, without thorough scouting on both hands. The consequence was that the American flotilla was not discovered until Valcour Island, which is from one hundred and twenty to one hundred and eighty feet high throughout its two miles of length, was so far passed that the attack had to be made from the south—from leeward.

When the British were first made out, Arnold's second in command, Waterbury, urged that in view of the enemy's superiority the flotilla should get under way at once, and fight them "on a retreat in the main lake"; the harbour being disadvantageous "to fight a number so much superior, and the enemy being able to surround us on every side, we lying between an island and the main."

Waterbury's advice evidently found its origin in that fruitful source of military errors of design, which reckons the preservation of a force first of objects, making the results of its action secondary. With sounder judgment, Arnold decided to hold on. A retreat before square-rigged sailing vessels having a fair wind, by a heterogeneous force like his own, of unequal speeds and batteries, could result only in disaster. Concerted fire and successful escape were alike improbable; and besides, escape, if feasible, was but throwing up the game.

Better trust to a steady, well-ordered position, developing the utmost fire. If the enemy discovered him, and came in by the northern entrance, there was a five-foot knoll in mid-channel which might fetch the biggest of them up; if, as proved to be the case, the island should be passed, and the attack should be made from leeward, it probably would be partial and in disorder, as also happened. The correctness of Arnold's decision not to chance a retreat was shown in the retreat of two days later.

Valcour is on the west side of the Lake, about three quarters of a mile from the main; but a peninsula projecting from the island at mid-length narrows this interval to a half-mile. From the accounts, it is clear that the American flotilla lay south of this peninsula. Arnold therefore had a reasonable hope that it might be passed undetected. Writing to Gates, the Commander-in-Chief at Ticonderoga, he said: "There is a good harbour, and if the enemy venture up the Lake it will be impossible for them to take advantage of our situation. If we succeed in our attack upon them, it will be impossible for any to escape. If we are worsted, our retreat is open and free. In case of wind, which generally blows fresh at this season, our craft will make good weather, while theirs cannot keep the Lake."

It is apparent from this, written three weeks before the battle, that he then was not expecting a force materially different from his own. Later, he describes his position as being "in a small bay on the west side of the island, as near together as possible, and in such a form that few vessels can attack us at the same time, and those will be exposed to the fire of the whole fleet." Though he unfortunately gives no details, he evidently had sound tactical ideas. The formation of the anchored vessels is described by the British officers as a half-moon.

When the British discovered the enemy, they hauled up for them. Arnold ordered one of his schooners, the *Royal Savage*, and the four galleys, to get under way; the two other schooners and the eight gondolas remaining at their anchors. The *Royal Savage*, dropping to leeward—by bad management, Arnold says—came, apparently unsupported, under the distant fire of the *Inflexible*, as she drew under the lee of Valcour at 11 A.M., followed by the *Carleton*, and at greater distance by the *Maria* and the gunboats.

Three shots from the ship's 12-pounders struck the *Royal Savage*, which then ran ashore on the southern point of the island.

The *Inflexible*, followed closely by the *Carleton*, continued on, but fired only occasionally; showing that Arnold was keeping his galleys in hand, at long bowls—as small vessels with one eighteen should be kept, when confronted with a broadside of nine guns.

Between the island and the main the north-east wind doubtless drew more northerly, adverse to the ship's approach; but, a flaw off the cliffs taking the fore and aft sails of the *Carleton*, she fetched "nearly into the middle of the rebel half-moon, where Lieutenant J. R. Dacres intrepidly anchored with a spring on her cable."

The *Maria*, on board which was Carleton, together with Commander Thomas Pringle, commanding the flotilla, was to leeward when the chase began, and could not get into close action that day. By this time, seventeen of the twenty gunboats had come up, and, after silencing the *Royal Savage*, pulled up to within point-blank range of the American flotilla.

"The cannonade was tremendous," wrote Baron Riedesel. Lieutenant Edward Longcroft, of the radeau *Thunderer*, not being able to get his raft into action, went with a boat's crew on board the *Royal Savage*, and for a time turned her guns upon her former friends; but the fire of the latter forced him again to abandon her, and it seemed so likely that she might be re-taken that she was set on fire by Lieutenant Starke of the *Maria*, when already "two rebel boats were very near her. She soon after blew up."

The American guns converging on the *Carleton* in her central position, she suffered severely. Her commander, Lieutenant Dacres, was knocked senseless; another officer lost an arm; only Mr. Edward Pellew, afterwards Lord Exmouth, remained fit for duty. The spring being shot away, she swung bows on to the enemy, and her fire was thus silenced. Captain Pringle signalled to her to withdraw; but she was unable to obey.

To pay her head off the right way, Pellew himself had to get out on the bowsprit under a heavy fire of musketry, to bear the jib over to windward; but to make sail seems to have been impossible. Two artillery boats were sent to her assistance, "which towed her off through a very thick fire, until out of farther reach, much to the honour of Mr. John Curling and Mr. Patrick Carnegy, master's mate and midshipman of the *Isis*, who conducted them; and of Mr. Edward Pellew, mate of the *Blonde*, who threw the tow-rope from the *Carleton*'s bowsprit."

This service on board the *Carleton* started Pellew on his road to fortune; but, singularly enough, the lieutenancy promised him in consequence, by both the First Lord and Lord Howe, was delayed by the fact that he stayed at the front, instead of going to the rear, where he would have been "within their jurisdiction." The *Carleton* had two feet of water in the hold, and had lost eight killed and six wounded—about half her crew—when she anchored out of fire.

In this small but stirring business, the Americans, in addition to the *Royal Savage*, had lost one gondola. Besides the injuries to the *Carleton*, a British artillery boat, commanded by a German lieutenant, was sunk. Towards evening the *Inflexible* got within point-blank shot of the Americans, "when five broadsides," wrote Douglas, "silenced their whole line." One fresh ship, with scantling for sea-going, and a concentrated battery, has an unquestioned advantage over a dozen light-built craft, carrying one or two guns each, and already several hours engaged.

At nightfall the *Inflexible* dropped out of range, and the British squadron anchored in line of battle across the southern end of the passage between the island and the main; some vessels were extended also to the eastward, into the open Lake.

"The best part of my intelligence," wrote Burgoyne next day from St. John's, to Douglas at Quebec, "is that our whole fleet was formed in line above the enemy, and consequently they must have surrendered this morning, or given us battle on our own terms. The Indians and light troops are abreast with the fleet; they cannot, therefore, escape by land."

The British squadron sharing this confidence, a proper look-out was not kept. The American leader immediately held a conference with his officers, and decided to attempt a retreat, "which was done with such secrecy," writes Waterbury, "that we went through them entirely undiscovered."

The movement began at 7 P.M., a galley leading, the gondolas and schooners following, and Arnold and his second bringing up the rear in the two heaviest galleys. This delicate operation was favoured by a heavy fog, which did not clear till next morning at eight. As the Americans stole by, they could not see any of the hostile ships.

By daylight they were out of sight of the British. Riedesel, speaking of this event, says, "The ships anchored, secure of the enemy, who stole off during the night, and sailing round the left wing, aided by a favourable wind, escaped under darkness." The astonishment next morning, he continues, was great, as was Carleton's rage. The latter started to pursue in such a hurry that he forgot to leave orders for the troops which had been landed; but, failing to discover the fugitives, he returned and remained at Valcour till nightfall, when scouts brought word that the enemy were at Schuyler's Island, eight miles above.

The retreat of the Americans had been embarrassed by their injuries, and by the wind coming out ahead. They were obliged to anchor on the 12th to repair damages, both hulls and sails having suffered severely. Arnold took the precaution to write to Crown Point for bateaux, to tow in case of a southerly wind; but time did not allow these to arrive. Two gondolas had to be sunk on account of their injuries, making three of that class so far lost.

The retreat was resumed at 2 P.M., but the breeze was fresh from the southward, and the gondolas made very little way. At evening the British chased again. That night the wind moderated, and at daybreak the American flotilla was twenty-eight miles from Crown Point—fourteen from Valcour—having still five miles' start. Later, however, by Arnold's report, "the wind again breezed up to the southward, so that we gained very little either by beating or rowing. At the same time the enemy took a fresh breeze from northeast, and, by the time we had reached Split Rock, were alongside of us."

The galleys of Arnold and Waterbury, the *Congress* and the *Washington*, had throughout kept in the rear, and now received the brunt of the attack, made by the *Inflexible* and the two schooners, which had entirely distanced their sluggish consorts. This fight was in the upper narrows, where the Lake is from one to three miles wide; and it lasted, by Arnold's report, for five glasses (two hours and a half), the Americans continually retreating, until about ten miles from Crown Point.

There, the *Washington* having struck some time before, and final escape being impossible, Arnold ran the *Congress* and four gondolas ashore in a small creek on the east side; pulling to windward, with the cool judgment that had marked all his conduct, so that the enemy could not follow him—except in small boats with which he could deal. There he set his vessels on fire, and stood by them until assured that they would blow up with their flags flying. He then retreated to Crown Point through the woods, "despite the savages"; a phrase which concludes this singular aquatic contest with a quaint touch of local colour.

In three days of fighting and retreating the Americans had lost one schooner, two galleys, and seven gondolas—in all, ten vessels out of fifteen. The killed and wounded amounted to over eighty, twenty odd of whom were in Arnold's galley. The original force, numbering seven hundred, had been decimated. Considering its raw material and the recency of its organisation, words can scarcely exaggerate the heroism of the resistance, which undoubtedly depended chiefly upon the personal military qualities of the leader. The British loss in killed and wounded did not exceed forty.

The little American navy on Champlain was wiped out; but never had any force, big or small, lived to better purpose or died more gloriously, for it had saved the Lake for that year. Whatever deductions may be made for blunders, and for circumstances of every character which made the British campaign of 1777 abortive and disastrous, thus leading directly to the American alliance with France in 1778, the delay, with all that it involved, was obtained by the Lake campaign of 1776.

On October 15th, two days after Arnold's final defeat, Carleton dated a letter to Douglas from before Crown Point, whence the American garrison was withdrawn. A week later Riedesel arrived, and wrote that, "were our whole army here it would be an easy matter to drive the enemy from their entrenchments," at Ticonderoga, and—as has been quoted already—four weeks sooner would have insured its fall. It is but a coincidence that just four weeks had been required to set up the *Inflexible* at St. John's; but it typifies the whole story.

Save for Arnold's flotilla, the two British schooners would have settled the business. "Upon the whole, Sir," wrote Douglas in his final letter from Quebec before sailing for England, "I scruple not to say, that had not General Carleton authorized me to take the extraordinary measure of sending up the *Inflexible* from Quebec, things could not this year have been brought to so glorious a conclusion on Lake Champlain."

Douglas further showed the importance attached to this success by men of that day, by sending a special message to the British ambassador at Madrid, "presuming that the early knowledge of this great event in the southern parts of Europe may be of advantage to His

Majesty's service." That the opinion of the government was similar may be inferred from the numerous rewards bestowed. Carleton was made a Knight of the Bath, and Douglas a baronet.

The gallantry shown by both sides upon Lake Champlain in 1776 is evident from the foregoing narrative. With regard to the direction of movements—the skill of the two leaders—the same equal credit cannot be assigned. It was a very serious blunder, on October 11th, to run to leeward, passing a concealed enemy, undetected, upon waters so perfectly well known as those of Champlain were; it having been the scene of frequent British operations in previous wars. Owing to this, "the *Maria*, because of her distant situation (from which the *Inflexible* and *Carleton* had chased by signal) when the rebels were first discovered, and baffling winds, could not get into close action." For the same reason, the *Inflexible* could not support the *Carleton*. The Americans, in the aggregate distinctly inferior, were thus permitted a concentration of superior force upon part of their enemies.

It is needless to enlarge upon the mortifying incident of Arnold's escape that evening. To liken small things to great—always profitable in military analysis—it resembled Hood's slipping away from de Grasse at St. Kitts.

In conduct and courage, Arnold's behavior was excellent throughout. Without enlarging upon the energy which created the flotilla, and the breadth of view which suggested preparations that he could not enforce, admiration is due to his recognition of the fact—implicit in deed, if unexpressed in word—that the one use of the Navy was to contest the control of the water; to impose delay, even if it could not secure ultimate victory.

No words could say more clearly than do his actions that, under the existing conditions, the navy was useless, except as it contributed to that end; valueless, if buried in port. Upon this rests the merit of his bold advance into the lower narrows; upon this his choice of the strong defensive position of Valcour; upon this his refusal to retreat, as urged by Waterbury, when the full force of the enemy was disclosed—a decision justified, or rather, illustrated, by the advantages which the accidents of the day threw into his hands. His personal gallantry was conspicuous there as at all times of his life.

"His countrymen," said a generous enemy of that day, "chiefly gloried in the dangerous attention which he paid to a nice point of honour, in keeping his flag flying, and not quitting his galley till she was in flames, lest the enemy should have boarded, and struck it." It is not the least of the injuries done to his nation in after years, that he should have silenced this boast and effaced this glorious record by so black an infamy.

With the destruction of the flotilla ends the naval story of the Lakes during the War of the American Revolution. Satisfied that it was too late to proceed against Ticonderoga that year, Carleton withdrew to St. John's and went into winter-quarters. The following year the enterprise was resumed under General Burgoyne; but Sir William Howe, instead of coöperating by an advance up the Hudson, which was the plan of 1776, carried his army to Chesapeake Bay, to act thence against Philadelphia.

Burgoyne took Ticonderoga and forced his way as far as Saratoga, sixty miles from Ticonderoga and thirty from Albany, where Howe should have met him. There he was brought to a stand by the army which the Americans had collected, found himself unable to advance or to retreat, and was forced to lay down his arms on October 17th, 1777. The garrison left by him at Ticonderoga and Crown Point retired to Canada, and the posts were re-occupied by the Americans.

No further contest took place on the Lake, though the British vessels remained in control of it, and showed themselves from time to time up to 1781. With the outbreak of war between Great Britain and France, in 1778, the scene of maritime interest shifted to salt water, and there remained till the end.

4

GRANT IN MEXICO

ULYSSES S. GRANT

ADVANCE ON MONTEREY

The advance from Camargo was commenced on the 5th of September. The army was divided into four columns, separated from each other by one day's march. The advance reached Cerralvo in four days and halted for the remainder of the troops to come up.

By the 13th, the rear-guard had arrived, and the same day the advance resumed its march, followed as before, a day separating the divisions. The forward division halted again at Marin, twenty-four miles from Monterey.

Both this place and Cerralvo were nearly deserted, and men, women and children were seen running and scattered over the hills as we approached; but when the people returned they found all their abandoned property safe, which must have given them a favorable opinion of *Los Grengos*—"the Yankees." From Marin the movement was in mass. On the 19th, General Taylor, with his army, was encamped at Walnut Springs, within three miles of Monterey.

The town is on a small stream coming out of the mountain-pass, and is backed by a range of hills of moderate elevation. To the north, between the city and Walnut Springs, stretches an extensive plain. On this plain, and entirely outside of the last houses of the city, stood a strong fort, enclosed on all sides, to which our army gave the name of "Black Fort. Its guns commanded the approaches to the city to the full extent of their range. There were two detached spurs of hills or mountains to the north and northwest of the city, which were also fortified. On one of these stood the Bishop's Palace. The road to Saltillo leaves the upper or western end of the city under the fire of the guns from these heights.

The lower or eastern end was defended by two or three small detached works, armed with artillery and infantry. To the south was the mountain stream before mentioned, and back of that the range of foot-hills. The plaza in the centre of the city was the citadel, properly speaking. All the streets leading from it were swept by artillery, cannon being intrenched behind temporary parapets.

The house-tops near the plaza were converted into infantry fortifications by the use of sand-bags for parapets. Such were the defences of Monterey in September 1847. General Ampudia, with a force of certainly ten thousand men, was in command.

General Taylor's force was about six thousand five hundred strong, in three divisions, under Generals Butler, Twiggs, and Worth. The troops went into camp at Walnut Springs, while the engineer officers, under Major Mansfield—a General in the late war—commenced their reconnoissance.

Major Mansfield found that it would be practicable to get troops around, out of range of the Black Fort and the works on the detached hills to the north-west of the city, to the Saltillo road. With this road in our possession, the enemy would be cut off from receiving further supplies, if not from all communication with the interior. General Worth, with his division somewhat reinforced, was given the task of gaining possession of the Saltillo road, and of carrying the detached works outside the city, in that quarter.

He started on his march early in the afternoon of the 20th. The divisions under Generals Butler and Twiggs were drawn up to threaten the east and north sides of the city and the works on those fronts, in support of the movement under General Worth. Worth's was regarded as the main attack on Monterey, and all other operations were in support of it.

His march this day was uninterrupted; but the enemy was seen to reinforce heavily about the Bishop's Palace and the other outside fortifications on their left. General Worth reached a defensible position just out of range of the enemy's guns on the heights north-west of the city, and bivouacked for the night. The engineer officers with him—Captain Sanders and Lieutenant George G. Meade, afterwards the commander of the victorious National army at the battle of Gettysburg—made a reconnoissance to the Saltillo road under cover of night.

During the night of the 20th, General Taylor had established a battery, consisting of two twenty-four-pounder howitzers and a ten-inch mortar, at a point from which they could play upon Black Fort. A natural depression in the plain, sufficiently deep to protect men standing in it from the fire from the fort, was selected and the battery established on the crest nearest the enemy. The 4th infantry, then consisting of but six reduced companies, was ordered to support the artillerists while they were intrenching themselves and their guns. I was regimental quartermaster at the time and was ordered to remain in charge of camp and the public property at Walnut Springs. It was supposed that the regiment would return to its camp in the morning.

The point for establishing the siege battery was reached and the work performed without attracting the attention of the enemy. At daylight the next morning fire was opened on both sides and continued with, what seemed to me at that day, great fury. My curiosity got the better of my judgment, and I mounted a horse and rode to the front to see what was going on.

I had been there but a short time when an order to charge was given, and lacking the moral courage to return to camp—where I had been ordered to stay—I charged with the regiment. As soon as the troops were out of the depression they came under the fire of Black Fort. As they advanced they got under fire from batteries guarding the east, or lower, end of the city, and of musketry. About one-third of the men engaged in the charge were killed or wounded in the space of a few minutes. We retreated to get out of fire, not backward, but eastward and perpendicular to the direct road running into the city from Walnut Springs.

I was, I believe, the only person in the 4th infantry in the charge who was on horseback. When we got to a place of safety the regiment halted and drew itself together—what was left of it. The adjutant of the regiment, Lieutenant Hoskins, who was not in robust health, found himself very much fatigued from running on foot in the charge and retreat, and, seeing me on horseback, expressed a wish that he could be mounted also. I offered him my horse and he accepted the offer.

A few minutes later I saw a soldier, a quartermaster's man, mounted, not far away. I ran to him, took his horse and was back with the regiment in a few minutes. In a short time we were off again; and the next place of safety from the shots of the enemy that I recollect of being in, was a field of cane or corn to the north-east of the lower batteries. The adjutant to whom I had loaned my horse was killed, and I was designated to act in his place.

This charge was ill-conceived, or badly executed. We belonged to the brigade commanded by Lieutenant-Colonel Garland, and he had received orders to charge the lower batteries of the city, and carry them if he could without too much loss, for the purpose of creating a diversion in favor of Worth, who was conducting the movement which it was intended should be decisive.

By a movement by the left flank, Garland could have led his men beyond the range of the fire from Black Fort and advanced towards the northeast angle of the city, as well covered from fire as could be expected. There was no undue loss of life in reaching the lower end of Monterey, except that sustained by Garland's command.

Meanwhile Quitman's brigade, conducted by an officer of engineers, had reached the eastern end of the city, and was placed under cover of the houses without much loss. Colonel Garland's brigade also arrived at the suburbs, and, by the assistance of some of our troops that had reached house-tops from which they could fire into a little battery covering the approaches to the lower end of the city, the battery was speedily captured and its guns were turned upon another work of the enemy.

An entrance into the east end of the city was now secured, and the houses protected our troops so long as they were inactive. On the west General Worth had reached the Saltillo road after some fighting but without heavy loss. He turned from his new position and captured the forts on both heights in that quarter. This gave him possession of the upper or west end of Monterey. Troops from both Twiggs's and

Butler's divisions were in possession of the east end of the town, but the Black Fort to the north of the town and the plaza in the centre were still in the possession of the enemy. Our camps at Walnut Springs, three miles away, were guarded by a company from each regiment. A regiment of Kentucky volunteers guarded the mortars and howitzers engaged against Black Fort. Practically Monterey was invested.

There was nothing done on the 22d by the United States troops; but the enemy kept up a harmless fire upon us from Black Fort and the batteries still in their possession at the east end of the city. During the night they evacuated these; so that on the morning of the 23d we held undisputed possession of the east end of Monterey.

Twiggs's division was at the lower end of the city, and well covered from the fire of the enemy. But the streets leading to the plaza—all Spanish or Spanish-American towns have near their centres a square called a plaza—were commanded from all directions by artillery. The houses were flat-roofed and but one or two stories high, and about the plaza the roofs were manned with infantry, the troops being protected from our fire by parapets made of sand-bags.

All advances into the city were thus attended with much danger. While moving along streets which did not lead to the plaza, our men were protected from the fire, and from the view, of the enemy except at the crossings; but at these a volley of musketry and a discharge of grape-shot were invariably encountered.

The 3d and 4th regiments of infantry made an advance nearly to the plaza in this way and with heavy loss. The loss of the 3d infantry in commissioned officers was especially severe. There were only five companies of the regiment and not over twelve officers present, and five of these officers were killed.

When within a square of the plaza this small command, ten companies in all, was brought to a halt. Placing themselves under cover from the shots of the enemy, the men would watch to detect a head above the sand-bags on the neighboring houses. The exposure of a single head would bring a volley from our soldiers.

We had not occupied this position long when it was discovered that our ammunition was growing low. I volunteered to go back to the point we had started from, report our position to General Twiggs, and ask for ammunition to be forwarded.

We were at this time occupying ground off from the street, in rear of the houses. My ride back was an exposed one. Before starting I adjusted myself on the side of my horse furthest from the enemy, and with only one foot holding to the cantle of the saddle, and an arm over the neck of the horse exposed, I started at full run. It was only at street crossings that my horse was under fire, but these I crossed at such a flying rate that generally I was past and under cover of the next block of houses before the enemy fired. I got out safely without a scratch.

At one place on my ride, I saw a sentry walking in front of a house, and stopped to inquire what he was doing there. Finding that the house was full of wounded American officers and soldiers, I dismounted and went in. I found there Captain Williams, of the Engineer Corps, wounded in the head, probably fatally, and Lieutenant Territt, also badly wounded, his bowels protruding from his wound. There were quite a number of soldiers also. Promising them to report their situation, I left, readjusted myself to my horse, recommenced the run, and was soon with the troops at the east end.

Before ammunition could be collected, the two regiments I had been with were seen returning, running the same gauntlet in getting out that they had passed in going in, but with comparatively little loss. The movement was countermanded and the troops were withdrawn. The poor wounded officers and men I had found, fell into the hands of the enemy during the night, and died.

While this was going on at the east, General Worth, with a small division of troops, was advancing towards the plaza from the opposite end of the city. He resorted to a better expedient for getting to the plaza—the citadel—than we did on the east. Instead of moving by the open streets, he advanced through the houses, cutting passageways from one to another. Without much loss of life, he got so near the plaza during the night that before morning, Ampudia, the Mexican commander, made overtures for the surrender of the city and garrison. This stopped all further hostilities. The terms of surrender were soon agreed upon. The prisoners were paroled and permitted to take their horses and personal property with them.

My pity was aroused by the sight of the Mexican garrison of Monterey marching out of town as prisoners, and no doubt the same feeling was experienced by most of our army who witnessed it. Many of the prisoners were cavalry, armed with lances, and mounted on miserable little half-starved horses that did not look as if they could carry their riders out of town. The men looked in but little better condition. I thought how little interest the men before me had in the results of the war, and how little knowledge they had of "what it was all about."

After the surrender of the garrison of Monterey a quiet camp life was led until midwinter. As had been the case on the Rio Grande, the people who remained at their homes fraternized with the "Yankees" in the pleasantest manner. In fact, under the humane policy of our commander, I question whether the great majority of the Mexican people did not regret our departure as much as they had regretted our coming. Property and person were thoroughly protected, and a market was afforded for all the products of the country such as the people had never enjoyed before.

The educated and wealthy portion of the population here, as elsewhere, abandoned their homes and remained away from them as long as they were in the possession of the invaders; but this class formed a very small percentage of the whole population.

POLITICAL INTRIGUE

The Mexican war was a political war, and the administration conducting it desired to make party capital out of it. General Scott was at the head of the army, and, being a soldier of acknowledged professional capacity, his claim to the command of the forces in the field was almost indisputable and does not seem to have been denied by President Polk, or Marcy, his Secretary of War. Scott was a Whig, and the administration was democratic. General Scott was also known to have political aspirations, and nothing so popularizes a candidate for high civil positions as military victories. It would not do therefore to give him command of the "army of conquest."

The plans submitted by Scott for a campaign in Mexico were disapproved by the administration, and he replied, in a tone possibly a little disrespectful, to the effect that, if a soldier's plans were not to be supported by the administration, success could not be expected. This was on the 27th of May, 1846. Four days later, General Scott was notified that he need not go to Mexico. General Gaines was next in rank, but he was too old and feeble to take the field.

Colonel Zachary Taylor—a brigadier-general by brevet—was therefore left in command. He, too, was a Whig, but was not supposed to entertain any political ambitions; nor did he; but after the fall of Monterey, his third battle and third complete victory, the Whig papers at home began to speak of him as the candidate of their party for the Presidency.

Something had to be done to neutralize his growing popularity. He could not be relieved from duty in the field where all his battles had been victories: the design would have been too transparent. It was finally decided to send General Scott to Mexico in chief command, and to authorize him to carry out his own original plan: that is, capture Vera Cruz and march upon the capital of the country. It was no doubt supposed that Scott's ambition would lead him to slaughter Taylor or destroy his chances for the Presidency, and yet it was hoped that he would not make sufficient capital himself to secure the prize.

The administration had indeed a most embarrassing problem to solve. It was engaged in a war of conquest which must be carried to a successful issue, or the political object would be unattained. Yet all the capable officers of the requisite rank belonged to the opposition, and the man selected for his lack of political ambition had himself become a prominent candidate for the Presidency. It was necessary to destroy his chances promptly. The problem was to do this without the loss of conquest and without permitting another general of the same political party to acquire like popularity. The fact is, the administration of Mr. Polk made every preparation to disgrace Scott, or, to speak more correctly, to drive him to such desperation that he would disgrace himself.

General Scott had opposed conquest by the way of the Rio Grande, Matamoras and Saltillo from the first. Now that he was in command of all the forces in Mexico, he withdrew from Taylor most of his regular troops and left him only enough volunteers, as he thought, to hold the line then in possession of the invading army. Indeed Scott did not deem it important to hold anything beyond the Rio Grande, and authorized Taylor to fall back to that line if he chose. General Taylor protested against the depletion of his army, and his subsequent movement upon Buena Vista would indicate that he did not share the views of his chief in regard to the unimportance of conquest beyond the Rio Grande.

Scott had estimated the men and material that would be required to capture Vera Cruz and to march on the capital of the country, two hundred and sixty miles in the interior. He was promised all he asked and seemed to have not only the confidence of the President, but his sincere good wishes.

The promises were all broken. Only about half the troops were furnished that had been pledged, other war material was withheld and Scott had scarcely started for Mexico before the President undertook to supersede him by the appointment of Senator Thomas H. Benton as lieutenant-general. This being refused by Congress, the President asked legislative authority to place a junior over a senior of the same grade, with the view of appointing Benton to the rank of major-general and then placing him in command of the army, but Congress failed to accede to this proposition as well, and Scott remained in command: but every general appointed to serve under him was politically opposed to the chief, and several were personally hostile.

General Scott reached Brazos Santiago or Point Isabel, at the mouth of the Rio Grande, late in December 1846, and proceeded at once up the river to Camargo, where he had written General Taylor to meet him. Taylor, however, had gone to, or towards Tampico, for the purpose of establishing a post there. He had started on this march before he was aware of General Scott being in the country. Under these circumstances Scott had to issue his orders designating the troops to be withdrawn from Taylor, without the personal consultation he had expected to hold with his subordinate.

General Taylor's victory at Buena Vista, February 22d, 23d, and 24th, 1847, with an army composed almost entirely of volunteers who had not been in battle before, and over a vastly superior force numerically, made his nomination for the Presidency by the Whigs a foregone conclusion. He was nominated and elected in 1848. I believe that he sincerely regretted this turn in his fortunes, preferring the peace afforded by a quiet life free from abuse to the honor of filling the highest office in the gift of any people, the Presidency of the United States.

When General Scott assumed command of the army of invasion, I was in the division of General David Twiggs, in Taylor's command; but under the new orders my regiment was transferred to the division of General William Worth, in which I served to the close of the war.

The troops withdrawn from Taylor to form part of the forces to operate against Vera Cruz, were assembled at the mouth of the Rio Grande preparatory to embarkation for their destination. I found General Worth a different man from any I had before served directly under. He was nervous, impatient, and restless on the march, or when important or responsible duty confronted him.

There was not the least reason for haste on the march, for it was known that it would take weeks to assemble shipping enough at the point of our embarkation to carry the army, but General Worth moved his division with a rapidity that would have been commendable had he been going to the relief of a beleaguered garrison.

The length of the marches was regulated by the distances between places affording a supply of water for the troops, and these distances were sometimes long and sometimes short. General Worth on one occasion at least, after having made the full distance intended for the day, and after the troops were in camp and preparing their food, ordered tents struck and made the march that night which had been intended for the next day. Some commanders can move troops so as to get the maximum distance out of them without fatigue, while others can wear them out in a few days without accomplishing so much. General Worth belonged to this latter class. He enjoyed, however, a fine reputation for his fighting qualities, and thus attached his officers and men to him.

The army lay in camp upon the sand-beach in the neighborhood of the mouth of the Rio Grande for several weeks, awaiting the arrival of transports to carry it to its new field of operations. The transports were all sailing vessels. The passage was a tedious one, and many of the troops were on shipboard over thirty days from the embarkation at the mouth of the Rio Grande to the time of debarkation south of Vera Cruz. The trip was a comfortless one for officers and men. The transports used were built for carrying freight and possessed but limited accommodations for passengers, and the climate added to the discomfort of all.

The transports with troops were assembled in the harbor of Anton Lizardo, some sixteen miles south of Vera Cruz, as they arrived, and there awaited the remainder of the fleet, bringing artillery, ammunition and supplies of all kinds from the North. With the fleet there was a little steam propeller dispatch-boat—the first vessel of the kind I had ever seen, and probably the first of its kind ever seen by any one then with the army. At that day, ocean steamers were rare, and what there were were sidewheelers. This little vessel, going through the fleet so fast, so noiselessly and with its propeller under water out of view, attracted a great deal of attention. I recollect that Lieutenant Sidney Smith, of the 4th infantry, by whom I happened to be standing on the deck of a vessel when this propeller was passing, exclaimed, "Why, the thing looks as if it was propelled by the force of circumstances."

Finally on the 7th of March, 1847, the little army of ten or twelve thousand men, given Scott to invade a country with a population of seven or eight millions, a mountainous country affording the greatest possible natural advantages for defence, was all assembled and ready to commence the perilous task of landing from vessels lying in the open sea.

The debarkation took place inside of the little island of Sacrificios, some three miles south of Vera Cruz. The vessels could not get anywhere near shore, so that everything had to be landed in lighters or surf-boats; General Scott had provided these before leaving the North. The breakers were sometimes high, so that the landing was tedious.

The men were got ashore rapidly, because they could wade when they came to shallow water; but the camp and garrison equipage, provisions, ammunition and all stores had to be protected from the salt water, and therefore their landing took several days. The Mexicans were very kind to us, however, and threw no obstacles in the way of our landing except an occasional shot from their nearest fort. During the debarkation, one shot took off the head of Major Albertis.

No other, I believe, reached anywhere near the same distance. On the 9th of March the troops were landed and the investment of Vera Cruz, from the Gulf of Mexico south of the city to the Gulf again on the north, was soon and easily effected. The landing of stores was continued until everything was got ashore.

Vera Cruz, at the time of which I write and up to 1880, was a walled city. The wall extended from the water's edge south of the town to the water again on the north. There were fortifications at intervals along the line and at the angles. In front of the city, and on an island half a mile out in the Gulf, stands San Juan de Ulloa, an enclosed fortification of large dimensions and great strength for that period. Against artillery of the present day the land forts and walls would prove elements of weakness rather than strength.

After the invading army had established their camps out of range of the fire from the city, batteries were established, under cover of night, far to the front of the line where the troops lay. These batteries were intrenched and the approaches sufficiently protected. If a sortie had been made at any time by the Mexicans, the men serving the batteries could have been quickly reinforced without great exposure to the fire from the enemy's main line. No serious attempt was made to capture the batteries or to drive our troops away.

The siege continued with brisk firing on our side till the 27th of March, by which time a considerable breach had been made in the wall surrounding the city. Upon this General Morales, who was Governor of both the city and of San Juan de Ulloa, commenced a correspondence with General Scott looking to the surrender of the town, forts and garrison. On the 29th, Vera Cruz and San Juan de Ulloa were occupied by Scott's army. About five thousand prisoners and four hundred pieces of artillery, besides large amounts of small arms and ammunition, fell into the hands of the victorious force. The casualties on our side during the siege amounted to sixty-four officers and men, killed and wounded.

MARCH TO JALAPA

General Scott had less than twelve thousand men at Vera Cruz. He had been promised by the administration a very much larger force, or claimed that he had, and he was a man of veracity. Twelve thousand was a very small army with which to penetrate two hundred and sixty miles into an enemy's country, and to besiege the capital; a city, at that time, of largely over one hundred thousand inhabitants.

Then, too, any line of march that could be selected led through mountain passes easily defended. In fact, there were at that time but two roads from Vera Cruz to the City of Mexico that could be taken by an army; one by Jalapa and Perote, the other by Cordova and Orizaba, the two coming together on the great plain which extends to the City of Mexico after the range of mountains is passed.

It was very important to get the army away from Vera Cruz as soon as possible, in order to avoid the yellow fever, or vomito, which usually visits that city early in the year, and is very fatal to persons not acclimated; but transportation, which was expected from the North, was arriving very slowly. It was absolutely necessary to have enough to supply the army to Jalapa, sixty-five miles in the interior and above the fevers of the coast. At that point the country is fertile, and an army of the size of General Scott's could subsist there for an indefinite period. Not counting the sick, the weak and the garrisons for the captured city and fort, the moving column was now less than ten thousand strong. This force was composed of three divisions, under Generals Twiggs, Patterson, and Worth.

The importance of escaping the vomito was so great that as soon as transportation enough could be got together to move a division the advance was commenced. On the 8th of April, Twiggs's division started for Jalapa. He was followed very soon by Patterson, with his division. General Worth was to bring up the rear with his command as soon as transportation enough was assembled to carry six days' rations for his troops with the necessary ammunition and camp and garrison equipage. It was the 13th of April before this division left Vera Cruz.

The leading division ran against the enemy at Cerro Gordo, some fifty miles west, on the road to Jalapa, and went into camp at Plan del Rio, about three miles from the fortifications. General Patterson reached Plan del Rio with his division soon after Twiggs arrived. The two were then secure against an attack from Santa Anna, who commanded the Mexican forces. At all events they confronted the enemy without reinforcements and without molestation, until the 18th of April. General Scott had remained at Vera Cruz to hasten preparations for the field; but on the 12th, learning the situation at the front, he hastened on to take personal supervision. He at once commenced his preparations for the capture of the position held by Santa Anna and of the troops holding it.

Cerro Gordo is one of the higher spurs of the mountains some twelve to fifteen miles east of Jalapa, and Santa Anna had selected this point as the easiest to defend against an invading army. The road, said to have been built by Cortez, zigzags around the mountain-side and was defended at every turn by artillery. On either side were deep chasms or mountain walls. A direct attack along the road was an impossibility. A flank movement seemed equally impossible. After the arrival of the commanding-general upon the scene, reconnoissances were sent out to find, or to make, a road by which the rear of the enemy's works might be reached without a front attack.

These reconnoissances were made under the supervision of Captain Robert E. Lee, assisted by Lieutenants P. G. T. Beauregard, Isaac I. Stevens, Z. B. Tower, G. W. Smith, George B. McClellan, and J. G. Foster, of the corps of engineers, all officers who attained rank and fame, on one side or the other, in the great conflict for the preservation of the unity of the nation. The reconnoissance was completed, and the labor of cutting out and making roads by the flank of the enemy was effected by the 17th of the month. This was accomplished without the knowledge of Santa Anna or his army, and over ground where he supposed it impossible. On the same day, General Scott issued his order for the attack on the 18th.

The attack was made as ordered, and perhaps there was not a battle of the Mexican war, or of any other, where orders issued before an engagement were nearer being a correct report of what afterwards took place. Under the supervision of the engineers, roadways had been opened over chasms to the right where the walls were so steep that men could barely climb them. Animals could not. These had been opened under cover of night, without attracting the notice of the enemy. The engineers, who had directed the opening, led the way and the troops followed. Artillery was let down the steep slopes by hand, the men engaged attaching a strong rope to the rear axle and letting the guns down, a piece at a time, while the men at the ropes kept their ground on top, paying out gradually, while a few at the front directed the course of the piece. In like manner the guns were drawn by hand up the opposite slopes.

In this way, Scott's troops reached their assigned position in rear of most of the intrenchments of the enemy, unobserved. The attack was made, the Mexican reserves behind the works beat a hasty retreat, and those occupying them surrendered.

On the left, General Pillow's command made a formidable demonstration, which doubtless held a part of the enemy in his front and contributed to the victory. I am not pretending to give full details of all the battles fought, but of the portion that I saw. There were troops engaged on both sides at other points in which both sustained losses; but the battle was won as here narrated.

The surprise of the enemy was complete, the victory overwhelming; some three thousand prisoners fell into Scott's hands, also a large amount of ordnance and ordnance stores. The prisoners were paroled, the artillery parked and the small arms and ammunition destroyed. The battle of Buena Vista was probably very important to the success of General Scott at Cerro Gordo and in his entire campaign from Vera Cruz to the great plains reaching to the City of Mexico. The only army Santa Anna had to protect his capital and the mountain passes west of Vera Cruz, was the one he had with him confronting General Taylor.

It is not likely that he would have gone as far north as Monterey to attack the United States troops when he knew his country was threatened with invasion further south. When Taylor moved to Saltillo and then advanced on to Buena Vista, Santa Anna crossed the desert confronting the invading army, hoping no doubt to crush it and get back in time to meet General Scott in the mountain passes west of Vera Cruz.

His attack on Taylor was disastrous to the Mexican army, but, notwithstanding this, he marched his army to Cerro Gordo, a distance not much short of one thousand miles by the line he had to travel, in time to intrench himself well before Scott got there. If he had been successful at Buena Vista his troops would no doubt have made a more stubborn resistance at Cerro Gordo. Had the battle of Buena Vista not been fought Santa Anna would have had time to move leisurely to meet the invader further south and with an army not demoralized nor depleted by defeat.

After the battle the victorious army moved on to Jalapa, where it was in a beautiful, productive and healthy country, far above the fevers of the coast. Jalapa, however, is still in the mountains, and between there and the great plain the whole line of the road is easy of defence. It was important, therefore, to get possession of the great highway between the sea-coast and the capital up to the point where it leaves the mountains, before the enemy could have time to re-organize and fortify in our front.

Worth's division was selected to go forward to secure this result. The division marched to Perote on the great plain, not far from where the road debouches from the mountains. There is a low, strong fort on the plain in front of the town, known as the Castle of Perote. This, however, offered no resistance and fell into our hands, with its armament.

General Scott having now only nine or ten thousand men west of Vera Cruz, and the time of some four thousand of them being about to expire, a long delay was the consequence. The troops were in a healthy climate, and where they could subsist for an indefinite period even if their line back to Vera Cruz should be cut off. It being ascertained that the men whose time would expire before the City of Mexico could possibly fall into the hands of the American army, would not remain beyond the term for which they had volunteered, the commanding-general determined to discharge them at once, for a delay until the expiration of their time would have compelled them to pass through Vera Cruz during the season of the vomito. This reduced Scott's force in the field to about five thousand men.

Early in May, Worth, with his division, left Perote and marched on to Puebla. The roads were wide and the country open except through one pass in a spur of mountains coming up from the south, through which the road runs. Notwithstanding this the small column was divided into two bodies, moving a day apart. Nothing occurred on the march of special note, except that while lying at the town of Amozoque—an easy day's march east of Puebla—a body of the enemy's cavalry, two or three thousand strong, was seen to our right, not more than a mile away. A battery or two, with two or three infantry regiments, was sent against them and they soon disappeared. On the 15th of May we entered the city of Puebla.

General Worth was in command at Puebla until the latter end of May, when General Scott arrived. Here, as well as on the march up, his restlessness, particularly under responsibilities, showed itself. During his brief command he had the enemy hovering around near the city, in vastly superior numbers to his own. The brigade to which I was attached changed quarters three different times in about a week, occupying at first quarters near the plaza, in the heart of the city; then at the western entrance; then at the extreme east.

On one occasion General Worth had the troops in line, under arms, all day, with three days' cooked rations in their haversacks. He galloped from one command to another proclaiming the near proximity of Santa Anna with an army vastly superior to his own. General Scott arrived upon the scene the latter part of the month, and nothing more was heard of Santa Anna and his myriads.

There were, of course, bodies of mounted Mexicans hovering around to watch our movements and to pick up stragglers, or small bodies of troops, if they ventured too far out. These always withdrew on the approach of any considerable number of our soldiers. After the arrival of General Scott I was sent, as quartermaster, with a large train of wagons, back two days' march at least, to procure forage. We had less than a thousand men as escort, and never thought of danger. We procured full loads for our entire train at two plantations, which could easily have furnished as much more.

There had been great delay in obtaining the authority of Congress for the raising of the troops asked for by the administration. A bill was before the National Legislature from early in the session of 1846-7, authorizing the creation of ten additional regiments for the war to be attached to the regular army, but it was the middle of February before it became a law.

Appointments of commissioned officers had then to be made; men had to be enlisted, the regiments equipped and the whole transported to Mexico. It was August before General Scott received reinforcement sufficient to warrant an advance. His moving column, not even now more than ten thousand strong, was in four divisions, commanded by Generals Twiggs, Worth, Pillow, and Quitman. There was also a cavalry corps under General Harney, composed of detachments of the 1st, 2d, and 3d dragoons. The advance commenced on the 7th of August with Twiggs's division in front. The remaining three divisions followed, with an interval of a day between. The marches were short, to make concentration easier in case of attack.

I had now been in battle with the two leading commanders conducting armies in a foreign land. The contrast between the two was very marked. General Taylor never wore uniform, but dressed himself entirely for comfort. He moved about the field in which he was operating to see through his own eyes the situation. Often he would be without staff officers, and when he was accompanied by them there was no prescribed order in which they followed. He was very much given to sit his horse side-ways—with both feet on one side—particularly on the battlefield.

General Scott was the reverse in all these particulars. He always wore all the uniform prescribed or allowed by law when he inspected his lines; word would be sent to all division and brigade commanders in advance, notifying them of the hour when the commanding general might be expected. This was done so that all the army might be under arms to salute their chief as he passed. On these occasions he wore his dress uniform, cocked hat, aiguillettes, sabre and spurs. His staff proper, besides all officers constructively on his staff—engineers, inspectors, quartermasters, etc., that could be spared—followed, also in uniform and in prescribed order. Orders were prepared with great care and evidently with the view that they should be a history of what followed.

In their modes of expressing thought, these two generals contrasted quite as strongly as in their other characteristics. General Scott was precise in language, cultivated a style peculiarly his own; was proud of his rhetoric; not averse to speaking of himself, often in the third person, and he could bestow praise upon the person he was talking about without the least embarrassment. Taylor was not a conversationalist, but on paper he could put his meaning so plainly that there could be no mistaking it. He knew how to express what he wanted to say in the fewest well-chosen words, but would not sacrifice meaning to the construction of high-sounding sentences.

But with their opposite characteristics both were great and successful soldiers; both were true, patriotic, and upright in all their dealings.

Both were pleasant to serve under—Taylor was pleasant to serve with. Scott saw more through the eyes of his staff officers than through his own. His plans were deliberately prepared, and fully expressed in orders. Taylor saw for himself, and gave orders to meet the emergency without reference to how they would read in history.

ADVANCE ON THE CITY OF MEXICO

The route followed by the army from Puebla to the City of Mexico was over Rio Frio mountain, the road leading over which, at the highest point, is about eleven thousand feet above tide water. The pass through this mountain might have been easily defended, but it was not; and the advanced division reached the summit in three days after leaving Puebla.

The City of Mexico lies west of Rio Frio mountain, on a plain backed by another mountain six miles farther west, with others still nearer on the north and south. Between the western base of Rio Frio and the City of Mexico there are three lakes, Chalco and Xochimilco on the left and Texcoco on the right, extending to the east end of the City of Mexico. Chalco and Texcoco are divided by a narrow strip of land over which the direct road to the city runs. Xochimilco is also to the left of the road, but at a considerable distance south of it, and is connected with Lake Chalco by a narrow channel. There is a high rocky mound, called El Penon, on the right of the road, springing up from the low flat ground dividing the lakes. This mound was strengthened by intrenchments at its base and summit, and rendered a direct attack impracticable.

Scott's army was rapidly concentrated about Ayotla and other points near the eastern end of Lake Chalco. Reconnoissances were made up to within gun-shot of El Penon, while engineers were seeking a route by the south side of Lake Chalco to flank the city, and come upon it from the south and south-west.

A way was found around the lake, and by the 18th of August troops were in St. Augustin Tlalpam, a town about eleven miles due south from the plaza of the capital. Between St. Augustin Tlalpam and the city lie the hacienda of San Antonio and the village of Churubusco, and south-west of them is Contreras. All these points, except St. Augustin Tlalpam, were intrenched and strongly garrisoned. Contreras is situated on the side of a mountain, near its base, where volcanic rocks are piled in great confusion, reaching nearly to San Antonio. This made the approach to the city from the south very difficult.

The brigade to which I was attached—Garland's, of Worth's division—was sent to confront San Antonio, two or three miles from St. Augustin Tlalpam, on the road to Churubusco and the City of Mexico. The ground on which San Antonio stands is completely in the valley, and the surface of the land is only a little above the level of the lakes, and, except to the south-west, it was cut up by deep ditches filled with water. To the south-west is the Pedregal—the volcanic rock before spoken of—over which cavalry or artillery could not be passed, and infantry would make but poor progress if confronted by an enemy.

From the position occupied by Garland's brigade, therefore, no movement could be made against the defences of San Antonio except to the front, and by a narrow causeway, over perfectly level ground, every inch of which was commanded by the enemy's artillery and infantry. If Contreras, some three miles west and south, should fall into our hands, troops from there could move to the right flank of all the positions held by the enemy between us and the city. Under these circumstances General Scott directed the holding of the front of the enemy without making an attack until further orders.

On the 18th of August, the day of reaching San Augustin Tlalpam, Garland's brigade secured a position within easy range of the advanced intrenchments of San Antonio, but where his troops were protected by an artificial embankment that had been thrown up for some other purpose than defense. General Scott at once set his engineers reconnoitring the works about Contreras, and on the 19th, movements were commenced to get troops into positions from which an assault could be made upon the force occupying that place. The Pedregal on the north and north-east, and the mountain on the south, made the passage by either flank of the enemy's defences difficult, for their work stood exactly between those natural bulwarks; but a road was completed during the day and night of the 19th, and troops were got to the north and west of the enemy.

This affair, like that of Cerro Gordo, was an engagement in which the officers of the engineer corps won special distinction. In fact, in both cases, tasks which seemed difficult at first sight were made easier for the troops that had to execute them than they would have been on an ordinary field. The very strength of each of these positions was, by the skill of the engineers, converted into a defence for the assaulting parties while securing their positions for final attack. All the troops with General Scott in the valley of Mexico, except a part of the division of General Quitman at San Augustin Tlalpam and the brigade of Garland (Worth's division) at San Antonio, were engaged at the battle of Contreras, or were on their way, in obedience to the orders of their chief, to reinforce those who were engaged.

The assault was made on the morning of the 20th, and in less than half an hour from the sound of the advance the position was in our hands, with many prisoners and large quantities of ordnance and other stores. The brigade commanded by General Riley was from its position the most conspicuous in the final assault, but all did well, volunteers and regulars.

From the point occupied by Garland's brigade we could see the progress made at Contreras and the movement of troops toward the flank and rear of the enemy opposing us. The Mexicans all the way back to the city could see the same thing, and their conduct showed plainly that they did not enjoy the sight.

We moved out at once, and found them gone from our immediate front. Clarke's brigade of Worth's division now moved west over the point of the Pedregal, and after having passed to the north sufficiently to clear San Antonio, turned east and got on the causeway leading to Churubusco and the City of Mexico. When he approached Churubusco his left, under Colonel Hoffman, attacked a tête-de-pont at that place and brought on an engagement. About an hour after, Garland was ordered to advance directly along the causeway, and got up in time to take part in the engagement. San Antonio was found evacuated, the evacuation having probably taken place immediately upon the enemy seeing the stars and stripes waving over Contreras.

The troops that had been engaged at Contreras, and even then on their way to that battle-field, were moved by a causeway west of, and parallel to the one by way of San Antonio and Churubusco. It was expected by the commanding general that these troops would move north sufficiently far to flank the enemy out of his position at Churubusco, before turning east to reach the San Antonio road, but they did not succeed in this, and Churubusco proved to be about the severest battle fought in the valley of Mexico.

General Scott coming upon the battle-field about this juncture, ordered two brigades, under Shields, to move north and turn the right of the enemy. This Shields did, but not without hard fighting and heavy loss. The enemy finally gave way, leaving in our hands prisoners, artillery and small arms. The balance of the causeway held by the enemy, up to the very gates of the city, fell in like manner. I recollect at this place that some of the gunners who had stood their ground, were deserters from General Taylor's army on the Rio Grande.

Both the strategy and tactics displayed by General Scott in these various engagements of the 20th of August, 1847, were faultless as I look upon them now, after the lapse of so many years. As before stated, the work of the engineer officers who made the reconnoissances and led the different commands to their destinations, was so perfect that the chief was able to give his orders to his various subordinates with all the precision he could use on an ordinary march.

I mean, up to the points from which the attack was to commence. After that point is reached the enemy often induces a change of orders not before contemplated. The enemy outside the city outnumbered our soldiery quite three to one, but they had become so demoralized by the succession of defeats this day, that the City of Mexico could have been entered without much further bloodshed.

In fact, Captain Philip Kearney—afterwards a general in the war of the rebellion—rode with a squadron of cavalry to the very gates of the city, and would no doubt have entered with his little force, only at that point he was badly wounded, as were several of his officers. He had not heard the call for a halt.

General Franklin Pierce had joined the army in Mexico, at Puebla, a short time before the advance upon the capital commenced. He had consequently not been in any of the engagements of the war up to the battle of Contreras. By an unfortunate fall of his horse on the afternoon of the 19th, he was painfully injured. The next day, when his brigade, with the other troops engaged on the same field, was ordered against the flank and rear of the enemy guarding the different points of the road from San Augustin Tlalpam to the city, General Pierce attempted to accompany them. He was not sufficiently recovered to do so, and fainted. This circumstance gave rise to exceedingly unfair and unjust criticisms of him when he became a candidate for the Presidency.

Whatever General Pierce's qualifications may have been for the Presidency, he was a gentleman and a man of courage. I was not a supporter of him politically, but I knew him more intimately than I did any other of the volunteer generals.

General Scott abstained from entering the city at this time, because Mr. Nicholas P. Trist, the commissioner on the part of the United States to negotiate a treaty of peace with Mexico, was with the army, and either he or General Scott thought—probably both of them—that a treaty would be more possible while the Mexican government was in possession of the capital than if it was scattered and the capital in the hands of an invader. Be this as it may, we did not enter at that time. The army took up positions along the slopes of the mountains south of the city, as far west as Tacubaya.

Negotiations were at once entered into with Santa Anna, who was then practically *the Government* and the immediate commander of all the troops engaged in defence of the country. A truce was signed which denied to either party the right to strengthen its position, or to receive reinforcements during the continuance of the armistices, but authorized General Scott to draw supplies for his army from the city in the meantime.

Negotiations were commenced at once and were kept up vigorously between Mr. Trist and the commissioners appointed on the part of Mexico, until the 2d of September. At that time Mr. Trist handed in his ultimatum. Texas was to be given up absolutely by Mexico, and New Mexico and California ceded to the United States for a stipulated sum to be afterwards determined. I do not suppose Mr. Trist had any discretion whatever in regard to boundaries. The war was one of conquest, in the interest of an institution, and the probabilities are that private instructions were for the acquisition of territory out of which new States might be carved.

At all events the Mexicans felt so outraged at the terms proposed that they commenced preparations for defence, without giving notice of the termination of the armistice. The terms of the truce had been violated before, when teams had been sent into the city to bring out supplies for the army. The first train entering the city was very severely threatened by a mob. This, however, was apologized for by the authorities and all responsibility for it denied; and thereafter, to avoid exciting the Mexican people and soldiery, our teams with their escorts were sent in at night, when the troops were in barracks and the citizens in bed.

The circumstance was overlooked and negotiations continued. As soon as the news reached General Scott of the second violation of the armistice, about the 4th of September, he wrote a vigorous note to President Santa Anna, calling his attention to it, and, receiving an unsatisfactory reply, declared the armistice at an end.

General Scott, with Worth's division, was now occupying Tacubaya, a village some four miles south-west of the City of Mexico, and extending from the base up the mountain-side for the distance of half a mile. More than a mile west, and also a little above the plain, stands Molino del Rey. The mill is a long stone structure, one story high and several hundred feet in length. At the period of which I speak General Scott supposed a portion of the mill to be used as a foundry for the casting of guns. This, however, proved to be a mistake. It was valuable to the Mexicans because of the quantity of grain it contained.

The building is flat roofed, and a line of sand-bags over the outer walls rendered the top quite a formidable defence for infantry.

Chapultepec is a mound springing up from the plain to the height of probably three hundred feet, and almost in a direct line between Molino del Rey and the western part of the city. It was fortified both on the top and on the rocky and precipitous sides.

The City of Mexico is supplied with water by two aqueducts, resting on strong stone arches. One of these aqueducts draws its supply of water from a mountain stream coming into it at or near Molino del Rey, and runs north close to the west base of Chapultepec; thence along the centre of a wide road, until it reaches the road running east into the city by the Garita San Cosme; from which point the aqueduct and road both run east to the city.

The second aqueduct starts from the east base of Chapultepec, where it is fed by a spring, and runs north-east to the city. This aqueduct, like the other, runs in the middle of a broad road-way, thus leaving a space on each side. The arches supporting the aqueduct afforded protection for advancing troops as well as to those engaged defensively. At points on the San Cosme road parapets were thrown across, with an embrasure for a single piece of artillery in each.

At the point where both road and aqueduct turn at right angles from north to east, there was not only one of these parapets supplied by one gun and infantry supports, but the houses to the north of the San Cosme road, facing south and commanding a view of the road back to Chapultepec, were covered with infantry, protected by parapets made of sandbags. The roads leading to garitas (the gates) San Cosme and Belen, by which these aqueducts enter the city, were strongly intrenched. Deep, wide ditches, filled with water, lined the sides of both roads. Such were the defences of the City of Mexico in September 1847, on the routes over which General Scott entered.

Prior to the Mexican war General Scott had been very partial to General Worth—indeed he continued so up to the close of hostilities—but, for some reason, Worth had become estranged from his chief. Scott evidently took this coldness somewhat to heart. He did not retaliate, however, but on the contrary showed every disposition to appease his subordinate. It was understood at the time that he gave Worth authority to plan and execute the battle of Molino del Rey without dictation or interference from any one, for the very purpose of restoring their former relations. The effort failed, and the two generals remained ever after cold and indifferent towards each other, if not actually hostile.

The battle of Molino del Rey was fought on the 8th of September. The night of the 7th, Worth sent for his brigade and regimental commanders, with their staffs, to come to his quarters to receive instructions for the morrow. These orders contemplated a movement up to within striking distance of the Mills before daylight. The engineers had reconnoitred the ground as well as possible, and had acquired all the information necessary to base proper orders both for approach and attack.

By daylight on the morning of the 8th, the troops to be engaged at Molino were all at the places designated. The ground in front of the Mills, to the south, was commanded by the artillery from the summit of Chapultepec as well as by the lighter batteries at hand; but a charge was made, and soon all was over. Worth's troops entered the Mills by every door, and the enemy beat a hasty retreat back to Chapultepec.

Had this victory been followed up promptly, no doubt Americans and Mexicans would have gone over the defences of Chapultepec so near together that the place would have fallen into our hands without further loss. The defenders of the works could not have fired upon us without endangering their own men. This was not done, and five days later more valuable lives were sacrificed to carry works which had been so nearly in our possession on the 8th.

I do not criticise the failure to capture Chapultepec at this time. The result that followed the first assault could not possibly have been foreseen, and to profit by the unexpected advantage, the commanding general must have been on the spot and given the necessary instructions at the moment, or the troops must have kept on without orders. It is always, however, in order to follow a retreating foe, unless stopped or otherwise directed. The loss on our side at Molino del Rey was severe for the numbers engaged. It was especially so among commissioned officers.

I was with the earliest of the troops to enter the Mills. In passing through to the north side, looking towards Chapultepec, I happened to notice that there were armed Mexicans still on top of the building, only a few feet from many of our men. Not seeing any stairway or ladder reaching to the top of the building, I took a few soldiers, and had a cart that happened to be standing near brought up, and, placing the shafts against the wall and chocking the wheels so that the cart could not back, used the shafts as a sort of ladder extending to within three or four feet of the top. By this I climbed to the roof of the building, followed by a few men, but found a private soldier had preceded me by some other way.

There were still quite a number of Mexicans on the roof, among them a major and five or six officers of lower grades, who had not succeeded in getting away before our troops occupied the building. They still had their arms, while the soldier before mentioned was walking as sentry, guarding the prisoners he had *surrounded*, all by himself. I halted the sentinel, received the swords from the commissioned officers, and proceeded, with the assistance of the soldiers now with me, to disable the muskets by striking them against the edge of the wall, and throw them to the ground below.

Molino del Rey was now captured, and the troops engaged, with the exception of an appropriate guard over the captured position and property, were marched back to their quarters in Tacubaya. The engagement did not last many minutes, but the killed and wounded were numerous for the number of troops engaged.

During the night of the 11th batteries were established which could play upon the fortifications of Chapultepec. The bombardment commenced early on the morning of the 12th, but there was no further engagement during this day than that of the artillery. General Scott assigned the capture of Chapultepec to General Pillow, but did not leave the details to his judgment. Two assaulting columns, two hundred and fifty men each, composed of volunteers for the occasion, were formed. They were commanded by Captains McKinzie and Casey respectively. The assault was successful, but bloody.

In later years, if not at the time, the battles of Molino del Rey and Chapultepec have seemed to me to have been wholly unnecessary. When the assaults upon the garitas of San Cosme and Belen were determined upon, the road running east to the former gate could have been reached easily, without an engagement, by moving along south of the Mills until west of them sufficiently far to be out of range, thence north to the road above mentioned; or, if desirable to keep the two attacking columns nearer together, the troops could have been turned east so as to come on the aqueduct road out of range of the guns from Chapultepec. In like manner, the troops designated to act against Belen could have kept east of Chapultepec, out of range, and come on to the aqueduct, also out of range of Chapultepec. Molino del Rey and Chapultepec would both have been necessarily evacuated if this course had been pursued, for they would have been turned.

General Quitman, a volunteer from the State of Mississippi, who stood well with the army both as a soldier and as a man, commanded the column acting against Belen. General Worth commanded the column against San Cosme. When Chapultepec fell, the advance commenced along the two aqueduct roads. I was on the road to San Cosme, and witnessed most that took place on that route. When opposition was encountered, our troops sheltered themselves by keeping under the arches supporting the aqueduct, advancing an arch at a time. We encountered no serious obstruction until within gun-shot of the point where the road we were on intersects that running east to the city, the point where the aqueduct turns at a right angle.

I have described the defences of this position before. There were but three commissioned officers besides myself, that I can now call to mind, with the advance when the above position was reached. One of these officers was a Lieutenant Semmes, of the Marine Corps. I think Captain Gore, and Lieutenant Judah, of the 4th infantry, were the others. Our progress was stopped for the time by the single piece of artillery at the angle of the roads and the infantry occupying the house-tops back from it.

West of the road from where we were stood a house occupying the south-west angle made by the San Cosme road and the road we were moving upon. A stone wall ran from the house along each of these roads for a considerable distance and thence back until it joined, enclosing quite a yard about the house. I watched my opportunity and skipped across the road and behind the south wall. Proceeding cautiously to the west corner of the enclosure, I peeped around and, seeing nobody, continued, still cautiously, until the road running east and west was reached. I then returned to the troops, and called for volunteers.

All that were close to me, or that heard me, about a dozen, offered their services. Commanding them to carry their arms at a trail, I watched our opportunity and got them across the road and under cover of the wall beyond, before the enemy had a shot at us. Our men under cover of the arches kept a close watch on the intrenchments that crossed our path and the house-tops beyond, and whenever a head showed itself above the parapets they would fire at it. Our crossing was thus made practicable without loss.

When we reached a safe position I instructed my little command again to carry their arms at a trail, not to fire at the enemy until they were ordered, and to move very cautiously following me until the San Cosme road was reached; we would then be on the flank of the men serving the gun on the road, and with no obstruction between us and them. When we reached the south-west corner of the enclosure before described, I saw some United States troops pushing north through a shallow ditch near by, who had come up since my reconnaissance.

This was the company of Captain Horace Brooks, of the artillery, acting as infantry. I explained to Brooks briefly what I had discovered and what I was about to do. He said, as I knew the ground and he did not, I might go on and he would follow. As soon as we got on the road leading to the city, the troops serving the gun on the parapet retreated, and those on the house-tops near by followed; our men went after them in such close pursuit—the troops we had left under the arches joining—that a second line across the road, about half-way between the first and the garita, was carried. No reinforcements had yet come up except Brooks's company, and the position we had taken was too advanced to be held by so small a force. It was given up, but retaken later in the day, with some loss.

Worth's command gradually advanced to the front now open to it. Later in the day in reconnoitring I found a church off to the south of the road, which looked to me as if the belfry would command the ground back of the garita San Cosme. I got an officer of the voltigeurs, with a mountain howitzer and men to work it, to go with me. The road being in possession of the enemy, we had to take the field to the south to reach the church. This took us over several ditches breast deep in water and grown up with water plants. These ditches, how-ever, were not over eight or ten feet in width. The howitzer was taken to pieces and carried by the men to its destination.

When I knocked for admission a priest came to the door who, while extremely polite, declined to admit us. With the little Spanish then at my command, I explained to him that he might save property by open-ing the door, and he certainly would save himself from becoming a prisoner, for a time at least; and besides, I intended to go in whether he consented or not. He began to see his duty in the same light that I did, and opened the door, though he did not look as if it gave him special pleasure to do so.

The gun was carried to the belfry and put together. We were not more than two or three hundred yards from San Cosme. The shots from our little gun dropped in upon the enemy and created great con-fusion. Why they did not send out a small party and capture us, I do not know. We had no infantry or other defences besides our one gun.

The effect of this gun upon the troops about the gate of the city was so marked that General Worth saw it from his position. He was so pleased that he sent a staff officer, Lieutenant Pemberton—later Lieutenant-General commanding the defences of Vicksburg—to bring me to him. He expressed his gratification at the services the howitzer in the church steeple was doing, saying that every shot was effective, and ordered a captain of voltigeurs to report to me with another how-itzer to be placed along with the one already rendering so much ser-vice. I could not tell the General that there was not room enough in the steeple for another gun, because he probably would have looked upon such a statement as a contradiction from a second lieutenant. I took the captain with me, but did not use his gun.

The night of the 13th of September was spent by the troops under General Worth in the houses near San Cosme, and in line confronting the general line of the enemy across to Belen. The troops that I was with were in the houses north of the road leading into the city, and were engaged during the night in cutting passage-ways from one house to another towards the town. During the night Santa Anna, with his army—except the deserters—left the city.

He liberated all the convicts confined in the town, hoping, no doubt, that they would inflict upon us some injury before daylight; but several hours after Santa Anna was out of the way, the city authorities sent a delegation to General Scott to ask—if not demand—an armistice, respecting church property, the rights of citizens and the supremacy of the city government in the management of municipal affairs. General Scott declined to trammel himself with conditions, but gave assurances that those who chose to remain within our lines would be protected so long as they behaved themselves properly.

General Quitman had advanced along his line very successfully on the 13th, so that at night his command occupied nearly the same position at Belen that Worth's troops did about San Cosme. After the interview above related between General Scott and the city council, orders were issued for the cautious entry of both columns in the morning.

The troops under Worth were to stop at the Alameda, a park near the west end of the city. Quitman was to go directly to the Plaza, and take possession of the Palace—a mass of buildings on the east side in which Congress has its sessions, the national courts are held, the public offices are all located, the President resides, and much room is left for museums, receptions, etc. This is the building generally designated as the "Halls of the Montezumas."

5

STONE RIVER

MILO S. HASCALL

In setting out it will be well to give a brief account of the history of the Army of the Cumberland, and its commanders, so far as I know, up to the time of the memorable battle.

My having been a cadet at West Point from June 1848 to June 1852, when I graduated in the same class with Sheridan, Stanly, Slocum, Crook, Bonaparte and others, whose names have since become so distinguished, and my service in the regular army subsequently till the fall of 1853, threw me in contact with, and was the means of my knowing personally, or by reputation, most, if not all the prominent characters on both sides, that were brought to the knowledge of the public by the War of the Rebellion.

This knowledge of the men in the army of those times served me well all through the war, as it was seldom I came in contact with an officer on the other side, but what I knew all his peculiar characteristics, and idiosyncrasies.

For illustration of this idea, as we were approaching Atlanta, my division had the advance of the Army of the Ohio the morning we came in sight of the city. My advance guard captured a rebel picket post, and one of the men captured had a morning paper from Atlanta, in which was Johnston's farewell order to his troops, and Hood's order assuming command.

I had been three years at West Point with Hood, he having graduated in 1853, in Schofield's class. I knew Hood to be a great, large hearted, large sized man, noted a great deal more for his fine social and fighting qualities, than for any particular scholastic acquirements, and inferred (correctly as the result showed) that Johnston had been removed because Davis, and his admirers, had had enough of the Fabian policy, and wanted a man that would take the offensive.

I immediately sent word to Gen. Sherman, who, with his staff, was not far off, and when he came to the front, informed him of the news I had, and the construction I put upon it, and in consequence, an immediate concentration to resist an attack was made in the vicinity, where we were.

It was none too soon, as Hood, upon taking command immediately moved out to Decatur with nearly his entire army, fell upon McPherson's corps, with the besom of destruction, killing the gallant McPherson early in the engagement, and with his vastly superior force, beating back the Army of the Tennessee so fast, that there is no telling what might have happened, had we not made the concentration we did, and been prepared to give them a tremendous enfilading fire as soon as they came opposite the flanks of the Army of the Ohio.

It was my fortune to be stationed at Ft. Adams, Newport, Rhode Island, as soon as my furlough expired after graduating at the Military

Academy, and there found Lieut. W. S. Rosecrans (afterward the commanding general at Stone River), and from being stationed some ten months at the same post, became somewhat familiarly acquainted with him and his peculiarities.

I had never met Gen. Don Carlos Buel, and knew but little of him, although he was a regular army man, until the fall of '61, upon my return from service in West Virginia, during the first summer of the war. I was then Colonel of the 17th Indiana, and was assigned to the command of a brigade in Nelson's Division of Buel's Army, which was then in and around Louisville, Ky., and whose purpose was a forward move against Nashville.

While Buel's Army, the Army of the Cumberland, was concentrating in and about Louisville, preparing for the forward movement, Gov. Morton, of Indiana, was frequently in Louisville, consulting with Gen. Buel, and offering suggestions as to army movements etc., and these, after a time, came to be regarded by Gen. Buel as meddlesome, and uncalled for, so much so that he finally intimated to Gov. Morton that it would be as well for him to attend to his duties as Governor of Indiana, while he would attend to his as Commanding General of the forces in the field.

It is important to mention this circumstance here, as it will be seen further on, that this matter had an important bearing upon Gen. Buel's subsequent career. It will not be necessary, nor appropriate in this paper, to enter into a detailed account of the operations of the Army of the Cumberland in its march upon, and capture of Nashville—in its subsequent march to Shiloh, and the part it took in that most unfortunate, not to say (in many respects) disgraceful battle to our army—in its subsequent advance upon Corinth, and its operations there—in its subsequent march into northern Alabama and the vicinity of Chattanooga, and the forced march back to Louisville, made necessary by Bragg's advance upon that city through the Sequatchie Valley, from Chattanooga.

All this is known to the public, and the public has arrived at its own conclusions as to the merits or demerits of these various operations. It is not too much to say, however, that those of us who accompanied Gen. Buel in this remarkable march and counter-march, and particularly those who had important commands during the same, had ample opportunity to arrive at intelligent conclusions as to the merits and demerits of the man.

It may be inferred from what has already been said, that Gen. Buel was not particularly popular with political soldiers, newspaper correspondents, and others who were carrying on the war from safe distances in the rear. He was eminently and emphatically a soldier, with no ambition or expectations outside the line of his duty, and with honor and integrity so entirely above suspicion, that the camp follower and money getter did not presume to even enter into his presence.

Notwithstanding all this, by the time of the return of the Army of the Cumberland to Louisville, though that army had then performed services that justly entitled it to the lasting gratitude of the country, and notwithstanding its eminent commander enjoyed, so far as I knew, the entire confidence of the officers and men in regard to his loyalty, patriotism and ability, yet there had sprung up a fire in the rear party that was constantly impugning his loyalty, his ability, and his fitness to command, and demanding his removal. In the light of what has already been said, it can now be seen whence, and from what source this hue and cry proceeded.

On account of a contemporaneous popularity that Gen. Rosecrans had achieved about that time, at the battle of Iuka, there arose a demand in the press that Gen. Buel be superseded in the command of the Army of the Cumberland by that officer. As I have said, my acquaintance with Gen. Rosecrans previous to his assuming command of the Army of the Cumberland, had been confined to the ten months I had been stationed with him at Newport, R.I., in '52–3.

My recollections of him were not such as to inspire me with confidence in him as the proper person to be placed in command of an army. At that time he seemed to be a great enthusiast in regard to the Catholic Church; seemed to want to think of nothing else, talk of nothing else, and in fact do nothing else, except to proselyte for it and attend upon its ministrations. No night was ever so dark and tempestuous, that he would not brave the boisterous seas of Newport Harbor to attend mass, and no occasion, however inappropriate, was ever lost sight of to advocate its cause; in fact, he was what would nowadays be called most emphatically a crank on that subject, and might not inappropriately be considered a one-ideaed man lacking in the breadth and poise, so necessary to success in the commander of an army in the field.

While Buel's Army was in Louisville getting reinforcements and preparing to renew operations against Bragg, I obtained a few days leave of absence and had no end of inquiries on my way home and after arriving there, as to what I thought of the propriety and necessity of relieving Buel. I uniformly replied that as far as the Army was concerned there was not, that I knew of, any want of confidence in Buel, but on the other hand, nothing but the most sincere confidence and respect. That the only reason that could be assigned was the want of confidence that the fire in the rear might have caused in the country at large, and that even if this was thought to be necessary, it would be very bad policy to substitute Rosecrans in his stead. How near correct I was in this estimate the public is now prepared to judge.

Of course the possibility of Buel's removal dispirited him, and perhaps inspired some of the officers under him, that might by possibility be selected to succeed him, with a desire that such might be the case. At all events, shortly after the army again took the offensive, the notorious and disastrous affair at Perryville took place, in regard to which it was charged at the time by Gen. Buel, and believed by others, that it was brought on by Gen. A. McD. McCook separating himself more from the body of the army than his orders justified, and beyond supporting distance, in order that an engagement might be brought on, in which, if successful, he might claim the sole credit, and thereby supersede Buel in command.

However this may be, this engagement was the culminating affair in Buel's career. The blame was (as I think) unjustly attached to him, and he was relieved of his command, and Gen. W. S. Rosecrans appointed in his place. After this battle, the Army resumed offensive operations against Bragg and in due time arrived in Nashville, when offensive operations were for a time suspended, in order to get supplies forward, and put the army in shape for active, and if possible, decisive operations.

During the weeks that we thus lay encamped about Nashville I had frequent opportunities to see Gen. Rosecrans and observe his manner, characteristics and surroundings and had hoped to be enabled to form a more favorable opinion of the man and his fitness for the high position to which he had been called than I had theretofore entertained. I was sorry, however, to be forced to the conclusion that my estimate of the man had been even more favorable than the facts would justify. His head seemed to have been completely turned by the greatness of his promotion. Instead of the quiet dignity, orderly and business methods that had formerly obtained at the headquarters of the Army, the very reverse seemed to be the rule.

Having by this time surrounded himself, in addition to the usual staff and appliances ordinarily to be found at the headquarters of an army in the field, with a numerous coterie of newspaper correspondents, and Catholic priests, who seemed in his estimation to be vastly more important than anyone else about him, and laid in a good supply of crucifixes, holy water, *spiritus frumenti*, Chinese gongs, flambeaux, jobbing presses, printers' devils, javelins, white elephants, and other cabalistic emblems and evidences that a holy crusade was about to be entered upon, and having daily announced through his various newspaper correspondents, jobbing presses, and other means of reaching the public and the Confederate Army lying immediately in our front, exactly what was going on, one could but wonder at the sublime indifference of Bragg, and his Army remaining in the State of Tennessee, in the midst of preparations for their destruction such as these.

As this magnificent and resplendent cavalcade of Holy, Oriental, and gorgeous splendor moved about from camp to camp during the weeks that we lay at Nashville making these gigantic and awe-inspiring preparations for the advance, every knee was bowed, and every tongue confessed, that Allah was great, and thrice illustriously great was this Savior that had been sent to us.

All things though, however grand and glorious, must have an end, and it was finally announced during the last days of December 1862, that the army was ready for a forward move. You will not be surprised to be informed after what has preceded, that it was my opinion that the Catholic officers having command in that army would fare well when the honors of the campaign came to be distributed. Accordingly, I made a prediction in writing that every one of these, consisting of Brig. Gen. Philip H. Sheridan, Brig. Gen. D. S. Stanly, Brig. Gen. James S. Negley, and Capt. James St. Claire Morton, would all be promoted entirely regardless of what the fortunes of war might have in store for them. This I did without the slightest feeling of unkindness or jealousy towards these officers, but simply on account of my belief that the

Commanding General was such a narrow-minded bigot in regard to Catholicism, that it was impossible for him not to allow considerations of this kind to control his estimate of men.

We shall see how nearly correct I was in this estimate further on. At the time this campaign was entered upon the National Forces had not been divided into Army Corps and numbered. Each Army commander divided his army as to him seemed best. Rosecrans divided his into three grand divisions called the Right, Center, and Left, and each of these into three ordinary divisions of four brigades each, the Right, Center and Left commanded respectively by Generals A. McD. McCook, George H. Thomas, and Thos. L. Crittenden.

At the time of this advance and for a long time previous thereto, I was commanding a brigade in Gen. Thos. J. Wood's division of the left wing. The advance movement all along the line finally commenced about the 26th day of December, 1862. The first day Palmer's division of the left wing had the advance and on the evening of that day, had reached the vicinity of Lavergne, having had some pretty sharp skirmishing in so doing.

The next day by rotation Wood's division had the advance. It was not the place of my brigade to lead the division that day, but I was specially requested to take the advance, however, as the progress made the day before had not been satisfactory. I consented to do so upon condition that the cavalry, which had been in advance the day before, should be retired to the rear of my brigade ready to be brought into use should we succeed in routing the enemy, and should the topography of the country admit of the successful use of cavalry.

I had seen so many disastrous results ensue from the use of squadrons of cavalry in advance of an army under such circumstances as we were advancing, that I did not want to run any such risks in addition to the ordinary and inevitable risks of such advances against an army in the field. The cavalry necessarily has to retire before any effective work can be done, and usually comes back pell mell with a lot of riderless horses, and creates infinitely more confusion, consternation, and even danger to the advancing army, than anything the enemy would be likely to do at that stage of the operations.

Having thus arrived at the front and got the cavalry out of the way to the rear, I found the enemy securely lodged in the town of Lavergne, and masked from our view by the buildings, shrubbery, and fences. My orders contemplated an immediate advance along the main pike toward Murfreesboro. Thus no opportunity was given for flanking them, and so compelling them to abandon the town. The country was open between my command and the town, and afforded no shelter whatever for the troops. I formed the brigade in two lines about 200 yards apart, with a strong line of skirmishers about the same distance in advance of the first line, with a section of artillery in the interval between the infantry lines.

As these dispositions were about completed preparatory to ordering an advance of the line a heavy infantry fire was opened upon us from the buildings and cover the town afforded to the enemy, and their fire was taking effect even upon the first line of infantry back of the skirmish line. At this juncture I ordered the infantry to lie down, the artillery to open with shot and shell upon the town, and the heavy line of skirmishers to fix bayonets and on double quick to make the distance between them and the town; to be immediately followed by the main lines of infantry as soon as the skirmishers had reached the town. This movement was entirely successful; we soon had routed the enemy from the town, but had left some forty or fifty dead comrades behind us to be cared for by those in our rear.

As soon as we had driven the enemy beyond the town, we continued the same order with two regiments in line of battle about 200 yards apart to the left of the main pike, and two to the right in like manner, all preceded by a heavy line of skirmishers, and pushed forward with all possible dispatch. A heavy rain set in about the time we commenced the advance beyond the town, which continued all day, so the corn-fields and other plowed fields soon became ankle deep with mud. Nevertheless we pressed forward continuously.

If we encountered the enemy in any considerable force, the skirmish line gradually slackened their progress until the main line came up with them. Artillery was brought forward and fired advancing along the road. In this manner we kept up an almost continuous advance, our dead and wounded being cared for by those in our rear. By nightfall we had made an advance of nearly eight miles, to Stewart's Creek.

As we approached Stewart's Creek we discovered that the enemy had set the bridge over the same on fire. I immediately concentrated four pieces of artillery on a little eminence to the right of the road, and commenced shelling the enemy beyond the creek. Under the cover of this fire the infantry was ordered forward at double quick, and succeeded in subduing the flames before sufficient damage had been done to prevent the use of the bridge by our army. So rapid had been our advance that three companies of rebel cavalry that had been hovering on our left flank during the advance, were cut off before they reached the bridge, and were captured by us with all their horses and accoutrements. In the evening we were congratulated by all our superior officers for having accomplished a very satisfactory day's work.

This brought us up to the evening of the 27th of December. During the time between this and the afternoon of the 30th of the same month, all portions of our army had pressed forward along the different lines of march laid out for them, encountering the usual incidents of driving in the enemy's cavalry and outposts, until finally at that time our entire army had arrived along the left bank of Stone River, opposite the city of Murfreesboro, some two or three miles further on. Here we encountered the enemy in force and their fortifications were plainly visible all along opposite us on the right bank of the river, between it and the city of Murfreesboro, and here it was very evident Bragg intended to make his stand and accept the gauge of battle.

There was desultory firing all along the line during that memorable afternoon, but during that time our army was finally concentrated, McCook, with his three divisions on the right, Thomas, with his three in the center, and Crittenden, with his three on the left. The whole line, with the intervals for artillery and cavalry, occupying a distance of two or three miles, more or less. Crittenden's three divisions were formed, two divisions in line of battle, and one in reserve, as follows: Palmer's division on the right, Wood's on the left, and Van Cleve in reserve opposite the interval between Palmer's and Wood's, and each division consisting likewise of three brigades, were formed in like manner, two in line and one in reserve.

In Wood's division, Wagner's brigade was on the right, my own on the left, and Harker in reserve. This arrangement brought my brigade on the extreme left of the entire army. During that evening we were made acquainted with the plan of the attack which was to be made by our army under cover of the gray of the morning the following day, the memorable 31st day of December, 1862. This was for the left wing (Crittenden's) to cross Stone River—which was at that time fordable at all points for all arms of the service—and deliver a furious attack on the enemy's extreme right, this to be followed up by a wheel to the right by other portions of our army in case Crittenden was successful in his attack, until all portions of our army should become engaged and the battle become general all along the line.

This plan was well conceived, and might have worked well enough perhaps, if the enemy had waited for us. The same mistake (or a similar one rather) was made here that was made by Grant at Shiloh, only the latter was much more faulty.

In that case, Grant was moving his army up the Tennessee River to Savannah, the object being to attack Beauregard, then at Corinth, some twenty miles from Savannah, as soon as he should have made a junction with Buell's army, then at Nashville, Tenn., and which was to march from that place to Savannah. Grant's army, proceeding by boats, arrived at Savannah by detachments first, and should have all been landed on the side of the river toward Grant's reinforcements, instead of on the side toward the enemy—unless he considered from the time he landed, anything more than a picket force of cavalry to keep him advised of the enemy's movements on the side toward them—that he had enough to successfully cope with him.

If he thought the latter, he should have been with his troops on the side of the river toward the enemy instead of eight miles below on the other side. Thus the most elementary principles of grand tactics and military science, that, in case two armies are endeavoring to concentrate with a view of delivering an attack on a superior force of the enemy, the inferior force nearest the enemy, should be careful to oppose all natural obstructions, such as rivers, mountains, heavy forests, impassable marshes, between it and the enemy until a junction can be made. In this case the detachments of Grant's army were allowed to land on the side toward the enemy, select their locations as best they could without instructions or concert of action of any kind, and this within fifteen to eighteen miles of the enemy in force, in the enemy's country, where it was known to all that he had daily and hourly opportunity from the citizens who fell back before our forces, to find out all the time the exact locations and strength of Grant's and Buel's armies, respectively.

Under circumstances like these, the merest tyro in military knowledge ought to have known that an experienced, able officer, such as Beauregard was known to be, would not wait for the concentration, before anticipating the attack. So it was no surprise to any one except the troops on that side the river towards Corinth, and possibly to Grant, then at Savannah, that on that fatal Sunday morning in April, 1862, when Grant had got sufficient troops on that side of the river to make it an object for Beauregard to destroy or capture them, and when Buel's advance had approached within twenty to twenty-five miles of Savannah, that Beauregard determined upon an attack, and declared he would crush or capture the troops on that side, and water his horse in the Tennessee River that night, and that but for the timely arrival by forced marches of Buel's advance of two divisions on the field about four o'clock that afternoon, he would undoubtedly have executed his purpose.

If Buel had been guilty of such blundering (not to call it by any worse name than this) it would have been impossible to make the country at the North believe that he did not meditate its destruction. For this blunder Grant was promptly relieved of his command, by the proper authorities, and it was many years afterwards, before anyone was found, who did not think this was very moderate punishment, under such circumstances. The fault in the case under consideration differs in kind, but not in its disastrous effects upon our cause and our army.

The right of our army at Murfreesboro, judging from what happened (and as I said at the outset, when I don't know personally what happened, I speak from necessary inference) seemed to think that inasmuch as our plan of battle contemplated an attack by the extreme left, to be followed up by them subsequently during the day, that they had nothing to do at that early hour in the morning, but to keep a picket force out, send their artillery horses to a distant point for water, stack their arms, and get breakfast. They did not seem to think possibly Bragg might have plans of his own, and that our attack might be anticipated, and that our right might receive a desperate attack while our left was preparing to deliver one. This, as you all know, was what happened, and you all know its disastrous results.

Current reports at the time were to the effect that the right was found when the attack came upon them in the condition already described, and the prompt manner in which they were hurled from the field, corroborates this view of the case. This, of course, caused the troops to their left to be immediately out-flanked, and no resistance, to amount to anything, from that portion of our line could be expected under such circumstances.

How much Gen. Rosecrans and his staff are properly to blame for the state of things existing on the right at the time of the attack, I have no means of knowing, and do not undertake to say but that it was the prime cause of the very serious disaster to our arms, and to the prestige of our army that happened at that battle, there can be no doubt or chance for two opinions. How the battle raged, and what happened, so far as I then knew, I cannot better describe than by extracting from my official report of that day's proceedings, made on the 6th of January, following, and which I do as follows:

HEADQUARTERS 1ST BRIGADE, 1ST DIV'N, LEFT WING, NEAR MURFREESBORO, TENN., Jan. 6, 1863.
Capt. M. P. Bestow, A.A.A.G.:

Sir: I have the honor to submit the following report of the operations of my brigade, (formerly the 15th Brigade, 6th Division, but under the new nomenclature, 1st Brigade, 1st Division, left wing) on the eventful 31st of December, 1862.—During the night of the 30th I had received notice through Gen. Wood, our division commander, that the left wing, Crittenden's corps, would cross Stone river and attack the enemy on their right. My brigade was posted on the extreme left of our entire line of battle and was guarding and overlooking the ford over which we were to cross. On the morning of the 31st heavy firing was heard on the extreme right of our line, (McCook's corps) but as they had been fighting their way all the distance from Nolensville as we had from Lavergne, no particular importance was attached to this, and I was getting my brigade into position, ready to cross as soon as Gen. Van Cleve's division, which was then crossing, was over. All this time the firing on the right became heavier, and apparently nearer to us, and our fears began to be aroused that the right wing was being rapidly driven back upon us.

At this juncture Gen. Van Cleve halted his division and the most terrible state of suspense pervaded the entire line, as it became more and more evident that the right was being driven rapidly back upon us. On and on they came till the heaviest fire was getting nearly around to the pike leading to Nashville, when General Rosecrans appeared in person, and ordered me to go with my brigade at once to the support of the right, pointing toward our rear, where the heaviest fire was raging. Gen. Van Cleve's division and Col. Harker's brigade of our division received the same order.

I at once changed the front of my brigade to the rear, preparatory to starting in the same direction, but had not proceeded more than 200 yards in the new direction before the fugitives from the right became so numerous, and the fleeing mule-teams and horsemen so thick, that it was impossible for me to go forward with my command without its becoming a confused mass. I therefore halted, and awaited developments.

Gen. Van Cleve and Col. Harker not meeting with so much opposition pressed forward and got into position beyond the railroad, ready to open on the enemy as soon as our fugitives were out of the way. They soon opened fire, joined by some batteries and troops belonging to the center (Gen. Thomas' corps) and Estep's battery of my brigade, and after about an hour's fighting along this new line, during which time I was moving my command from point to point, ready to support any troops that most needed it, the onslaught of the enemy seemed to be in a great measure checked, and we had reasonable probability of maintaining this line.

During all this time my men were exposed to a severe fire of shot and shell from a battery on the other side of the river, and several men were killed. About this time an aid of Gen. Palmer's came galloping up to me, and said that unless he could be supported his division would give way. Palmer's division formed the right of Gen. Crittenden's line of battle on the morning of the 31st. After consulting with Gen. Wood he ordered me to send a regiment to support Gen. Palmer. Accordingly I sent the 3d Kentucky regiment, commanded by Lieut. Col. Sam'l McKee. Before the regiment had been ten minutes in its new position, Capt. Kerstetter, my Adjutant General, reported to me that Col. McKee had been killed and the regiment badly cut up.

I therefore moved with the other three regiments of my command to their relief. The line they were trying to hold was that port of our original line of battle lying immediately to the right of the railroad, and forming an acute angle with the same. This portion of our original line, about two regimental fronts, together with two fronts to the left held by Colonel Wagner's brigade, was all of our original line of battle but what our troops had been driven from; and if they succeeded in carrying this they would have turned our left, and a total route of our forces could not then have been avoided.

Seeing the importance of the position, I told my men that it must be held even if it cost the last man we had. I immediately sent in the 26th Ohio, commanded by the gallant Major Wm. H. Squires, to take position on the right of the 3d Kentucky, and support it, and dispatched an aid for the 18th Indiana battery to come to this point and open on the enemy. No sooner had the 26th Ohio got in position than they became hotly engaged, and the numerous dead and wounded that were immediately brought to the rear told how desperate was the contest.

The gallant Lieut. McClellan of that regiment was brought to the rear mortally wounded, and expired by my side in less than five minutes from the time the regiment took position. Still the fight went on, and still brave men went down. The 3d Kentucky, now reduced to less than one-half its original number, with ten officers out of its fourteen remaining ones badly wounded, was still bravely at work.

In less than ten minutes after the fall of Lieut. Col. McKee, the gallant Major Daniel R. Collier, of that regiment, received two severe wounds, one in the leg and one in the breast. Adjutant Bullitt had his horse shot from under him, but nothing could induce either of them to leave the field. Equally conspicuous and meritorious was the conduct of Major Squires and Adjutant Franklin, of the 26th Ohio. Major Squires' horse was three times shot through the neck; nevertheless, he and all his officers stood by throughout and most gallantly sustained and encouraged their men.

Estep's battery came up in due time, and taking a position on a little rise of ground in the rear of the 26th Ohio, and 3d Kentucky, opened a terrific fire of shot and shell over the heads of our infantry. About one hour after the 26th Ohio got into position, this terrible attack of the enemy was repulsed, and they drew back into the woods, and under cover of an intervening hill, to reform their shattered columns and renew the attack.

I now took a survey of the situation, and found that along the entire line to the right and left of the railroad, which had not yet been carried by the enemy, I was the only general officer present, and was therefore in command, and responsible for the conduct of affairs. Col. Hazen, commanding a brigade in Gen. Palmer's division, was present with his brigade to the left of the railroad. Col. Gross, commanding another brigade in the same division, was also present with what there was left of his brigade, and most nobly did he co-operate with me, with the 6th and 25th Ohio to the right of the railroad, while Col. Wagner, commanding the 2d brigade, 1st division, (left wing) nobly sustained his front, assisted by Col. Hazen to the left of the railroad. I now relieved the 3d Kentucky regiment, who were nearly annihilated, and out of ammunition, with the 58th Indiana regiment of my brigade, commanded by Col. Geo. P. Buell; and this being a much larger regiment than the 3d Kentucky, filled up the entire space from where the right of the 3d Kentucky rested, to the railroad.

I then threw forward the right of the 6th Ohio regiment of Col. Gross' brigade, which was on the right of the 26th Ohio, so that its line of battle was more nearly perpendicular to the railroad, and so its fire would sweep the front of the 26th Ohio, and 58th Indiana, and supported the 6th Ohio with Estep's battery on a little eminence to its right, and brought the 97th Ohio, Col. Lane, from Wagner's brigade, to still further strengthen the right. These dispositions being made, I galloped a little to the rear, and found Gen. Rosecrans, and called his attention to the importance of the position I was holding, and the necessity of keeping it well supported. He rode to the front with me, approved of the dispositions I had made, spoke a few words of encouragement to the men, cautioning them to hold their fire until the enemy had got well up, and had no sooner retired than the enemy emerged from the woods over the hill, and were moving upon us again in splendid style, and in great force.

As soon as they came in sight, the 6th and 26th Ohio, and Estep's battery opened on them, and did splendid execution; but on they came, until within 100 yards of our line, when Col. Buell, of the 58th Indiana, who had lost three men, but had not fired a gun, ordered his men to fire. The effect was indescribable; the enemy fell in winrows, and went staggering back from the effects of this unexpected volley. Soon, however, they came up again and assaulted us furiously for about one and a half hours, but the men all stood their ground nobly, and at the end of that time compelled the enemy to retire as before.

During the heat of this attack a heavy cross fire was brought to bear on the position I occupied, and Corporal Frank Mayer, of the 3d Ohio Volunteer Cavalry, in command of my escort, was shot through the leg, and my Adjt. General, Capt. Ed. R. Kerstetter, was shot through his coat, grazing his back. The regiments all behaved splendidly again, and the 58th Indiana won immortal honors. Lieut. Blackford, of that regiment, was shot dead, and several of the officers, including Capts. Downey and Alexander, badly wounded. Estep's battery was compelled to retire from the position assigned to it after firing a half dozen rounds, but it did terrible execution while there. The 6th and 26th Ohio did noble service, as did the 97th, but their own immediate commanders will no doubt allude to them more particularly.

Thus ended the third assault upon our position. I should have remarked that the 100th Illinois, the other regiment composing my brigade, which was in reserve during the first engagement described above, had, under instruction of Col. Hazen, moved to the front on the left of the railroad, and taken up a position at right angles with the railroad, where they fought splendidly in all the actions that took place on the left of the road. There was no formidable attack made upon them, though they were almost constantly under fire of greater or less severity, particularly from shot and shell, and suffered quite severely in killed and wounded. Lieut. Morrison Worthington, of that regiment, was killed while gallantly sustaining his men, and six other commissioned officers, including Major Hammond, were wounded. Their operations being to the left of the railroad, in a wood, did not come so immediately under my personal observation, but their conduct, from Col. Bartleson down, was such as leaves nothing to be desired.

The 58th Indiana having now been over three hours in action, and the 26th Ohio about four hours, were exhausted and very near out of ammunition. I therefore relieved the 58th Indiana with the 40th Indiana from Col. Wagner's brigade, and the 26th Ohio was relieved by the 23d Kentucky. There was now not more than an hour of the day left, and though the enemy was constantly maneuvering in our front, no formidable attack was made upon us, except with artillery.

The enemy having been three several times repulsed in their attack on that position, seemed satisfied to keep at a respectful distance, and the sun set upon us, masters of the situation. We had sustained ourselves *and held the only portion of the original line of battle that was held throughout by any portion of our army.* To have lost this position would have been to lose everything, as our left would then have been turned also, and utter rout or capture inevitable.

During the evening of the 31st, I was officially notified that in consequence of the indisposition of Gen. Wood, and a wound received by him during the forenoon of that day, he was relieved of the command of the division, and that the same would devolve upon myself. I therefore turned over the command of the brigade to Col. Geo. P. Buell, of the 58th Indiana, and assumed command of the division. All of which is respectfully submitted.

Milo S. Hascall, Brig. Gen. Vols., Com's Brigade.

Ed. R. Kerstetter, Capt. & A.A.G. (Official.)

After the battle was over, during the evening, Colonel Harker's brigade that had gone to the assistance of the right, returned to where we had been in action during the day, and thus the division was once more together, and on this ground we did the best we could towards getting something to eat, and prepared to bivouac on the same ground for the night.

About eleven o'clock that night, I was visited by Capt. John Mendenhall, Chief of Artillery on Gen. Crittenden's staff, and who belonged to the Regular Army of the United States, and a gentleman of first-class intelligence, and purity of character, and informed that since the cessation of hostilities for the night, a council of war had been held at Gen. Rosecrans' headquarters, by himself and his Grand Division Commanders, and that a general retreat to Nashville had been decided upon, and that all except Gen. Crittenden concurred in the advisability of such movement, and he was overruled by the others, and that in pursuance of such determination, I was forthwith to send all the transportation of my division, except one wagon for each brigade, to the rear, and when the transportation was all under way, this was to be followed by a general retreat of our army to Nashville.

Mendenhall said that Crittenden was very much incensed at the proposition for retreat; said his army was in position and on hand, and that if he were overruled and if a retreat was decided upon, that he would cross the river and retreat by way of Gallatin to Nashville. However, the retreat was decided upon, and the baggage had been sent to the rear as above directed, and we were laying on our arms awaiting the further order to retreat, when a very singular circumstance caused Rosecrans to change his mind, and conclude to fight it out where we were.

A large number of our straggling, demoralized detachments in the rear of our army, being hungry and thirsty, had concluded to disobey orders, and make fire and try and get something to eat. One party would make a fire, another would go there to get a fire brand to start another, and when this became general along our rear, Rosecrans concluded the enemy had got in our rear, and were forming line of battle by torch lights, and hence withdrew the order for a general retreat. After this, about one o'clock, I was informed also by Capt. Mendenhall, that the retreat had been given up, and that I was ordered to fall back with my division about half a mile, and take up a position that would there be assigned me.

Accordingly I did so, and in the morning found myself occupying a position with no advantages for offensive or defensive operations, and very much exposed to the enemy's fire, with no chance for returning it with any effect. The enemy were occupying the position I had fallen back from, and at that point concentrated a large number of pieces of artillery, with which, about nine o'clock in the morning, they opened upon us a tremendous artillery fire, under the cover of which I supposed their infantry would charge upon us, but for some strange reason or other, they did not do so. Desultory firing afterwards was kept up during the day, until about three o'clock in the afternoon.

In the meantime we had sent a division across the river to the left, which was occupying the high ground near where the enemy's right was resting originally. About three o'clock, Breckenridge's troops, of the rebel army, fell furiously upon this division, and drove them rapidly from their position, on account of their superior numbers. At this juncture Crittenden ordered Mendenhall to concentrate his artillery on the bank of the river to our front and left, which he promptly did, and ordered me, with my division, to promptly cross the river in support of the division already there in retreat.

Upon our arrival on the other side of the river, the furious fire from Mendenhall's artillery had checked the rebel advance, and the division over there turned upon their assailants, and with the assistance of my division, drove Breckenridge back to the position he had occupied before making the assault. The latter part of these operations were carried on in the darkness, and we slept upon our arms, amidst the dead and wounded. It had been raining hard all the night, and the river was rising very rapidly, so much so that if we had remained there until morning, there would have been danger that the river would become impassable, and the divisions been left there by themselves in the presence of the whole rebel army.

Accordingly, about two o'clock at night, we were ordered to recross the river, and take up positions where we had been during the previous day. We arrived back there between that time and morning, thoroughly wet through, and completely jaded out, having had no sleep, and but little to eat during the previous forty-eight hours. Both armies continued after this during the third day, to occupy the positions they had on that morning. It was cold, wet, and very disagreeable weather; both armies were completely tired out, and seemed content to do nothing more than to engage in some desultory firing, and watch each other closely.

On the morning of the fourth day, January 3, or rather, during the forenoon of that day, the stragglers from the right, during the first day's battle, who had not stopped in their flight until they reached Nashville, began to return in large numbers, in companies, and even regiments, and Bragg, observing this, concluded we were receiving large bodies of reinforcements from the north, and therefore concluded to fall back and give up the contest. He accordingly did so, and on the fourth day, January 4, he took possession of Murfreesboro without the firing of a gun.

Thus ended the great battle of Stone River. We had not made a single attack during the whole time; were badly beaten and well nigh driven from the field the first day, and only saved from an ignominious retreat upon Nashville by the ridiculous misconception on the part of Rosecrans, already alluded to on the first night after the battle commenced. As it was, we lost all our transportation, by sending it to the rear, that night, preparatory for the retreat, the whole having been burned by the rebels at Lavergne, notwithstanding we were supposed to have some cavalry in our rear, under Gen. Stanley. Where it was at the time our transportation was being burned by the rebel cavalry, I have never heard.

Finally our fugitives from the first day's battle began to return, thereupon Bragg became very much frightened and beat a retreat, and we thus gained Murfreesboro. After reports were written up to praise the men it had been determined upon in advance to promote, and these identical men that I had predicted would be favored, were promoted; one of them, St. Claire Morton, from Captain to Brigadier-General, while others, upon whom rested the heat and burden of the day, and who saved the army from utter annihilation, were not only not promoted, but in many instances not even mentioned.

It was, for instance, Sheridan's fate to be early driven from the field, whether from his fault or not, it is not necessary to inquire. Enough for this occasion that it was so, and the facts of his subsequent career no more justify what was done for him on this occasion, than would the subsequent illustrious career of Gen. Grant justify his promotion for the terrible blunders committed by him concerning the most unfortunate battle of Shiloh.

In regard to the Catholic Church, I do not wish to be understood as having any desire to say anything against that church, but simply to condemn the idea of making membership in that, or any other particular church, a necessary concomitant to advancement, either in a military or civil capacity, under our government.

Farther, in all that I have said nothing has been said in malice towards any officer or person, but simply that that criticism so necessary to the establishment of right and justice in regard to the late war may be freely indulged in, whether it affect the highest officer, or the lowest private that offered his life in defense of his country.

It will be seen that my estimate of the fitness of Gen. Rosecrans to command an army was not enhanced by his career during and preceding the battle of Stone River. When disaster came to the right, he should have given his attention personally to that, and lent the magic of his personal presence to rallying the fleeing troops from that division, in place of going to the extreme left himself—instead of by a staff officer—for ordering the movement of troops in that direction.

When the whole affair was over, and quiet restored, I made an application to be transferred to another army on account of want of confidence in him as the commander of an army in the field. This I supposed would cause my arrest, and give an opportunity for me to demonstrate the great cause that existed for my apprehensions, but instead of doing this, he returned my application endorsed that he could not spare the services of so useful an officer as myself, and that there would be no forward movement of the army for six months, and detailed me to proceed to Indianapolis, Ind., to superintend the work of returning deserters from Ohio, Indiana, and Illinois.

Just before my leaving Murfreesboro for Indianapolis we saw Bragg's telegraphic account to Richmond, of the first day's proceedings. It was as follows: "This morning, under cover of the darkness, we attacked the enemy on his extreme right, and have routed him from every portion of his line except upon his extreme left, where he has successfully resisted us."

As I left there was a proposition started in Crittenden's command to raise money to present Bragg a sword for making the above truthful statement of the first day's operations.

While at Indianapolis, I was, at the request of Gen. Burnside, transferred by the War Department, to the army of the Ohio and given the command of a division in that army. The next that we heard of Gen. Rosecrans was at the battle of Chickamauga, and that was the last we heard of him in a military way, and all can now see how much cause there was for the apprehensions I entertained. This was not the first instance that great unfitness achieved high rank in our armies and it was quite common for great merit to be entirely unrewarded, and indeed entirely unknown. But time is a great healer, and let us hope that honest merit will in the end get its recognition, trusting in the truthfulness of the idea that

> "Ever the world goes round and round,
> And ever the truth comes uppermost,
> And justice shall be done."

6

VICKSBURG DURING THE TROUBLE

MARK TWAIN

We used to plow past the lofty hill-city, Vicksburg, down-stream; but we cannot do that now. A cut-off has made a country town of it, like Osceola, St. Genevieve, and several others. There is currentless water—also a big island—in front of Vicksburg now. You come down the river the other side of the island, then turn and come up to the town; that is, in high water: in low water you can't come up, but must land some distance below it.

Signs and scars still remain, as reminders of Vicksburg's tremendous war experiences; earthworks, trees crippled by the cannon balls, cave-refuges in the clay precipices, etc. The caves did good service during the six weeks' bombardment of the city—May 8 to July 4, 1863. They were used by the non-combatants—mainly by the women and children; not to live in constantly, but to fly to for safety on occasion. They were mere holes, tunnels, driven into the perpendicular clay bank, then branched Y shape, within the hill. Life in Vicksburg, during the six weeks was perhaps—but wait; here are some materials out of which to reproduce it:

Population, twenty-seven thousand soldiers and three thousand non-combatants; the city utterly cut off from the world—walled solidly in, the frontage by gunboats, the rear by soldiers and batteries; hence, no buying and selling with the outside; no passing to and fro; no God-speeding a parting guest, no welcoming a coming one; no printed acres of world-wide news to be read at breakfast, mornings—a tedious dull absence of such matter, instead; hence, also, no running to see steamboats smoking into view in the distance up or down, and plowing toward the town—for none came, the river lay vacant and undisturbed; no rush and turmoil around the railway station, no struggling over bewildered swarms of passengers by noisy mobs of hackmen—all quiet there; flour two hundred dollars a barrel, sugar thirty, corn ten dollars a bushel, bacon five dollars a pound, rum a hundred dollars a gallon; other things in proportion: consequently, no roar and racket of drays and carriages tearing along the streets; nothing for them to do, among that handful of non-combatants of exhausted means; at three o'clock in the morning, silence—silence so dead that the measured tramp of a sentinel can be heard a seemingly impossible distance; out of hearing of this lonely sound, perhaps the stillness is absolute: all in a moment come ground-shaking thunder-crashes of artillery, the sky is cobwebbed with the crisscrossing red lines streaming from soaring bomb-shells, and a rain of iron fragments descends upon the city; descends upon the empty streets: streets which are not empty a moment later, but mottled with dim figures of frantic women and children scurrying from home and bed toward the cave dungeons—encouraged by the humorous grim soldiery, who shout "Rats, to your holes!" and laugh.

The cannon-thunder rages, shells scream and crash overhead, the iron rain pours down, one hour, two hours, three, possibly six, then stops; silence follows, but the streets are still empty; the silence continues; by-and-bye a head projects from a cave here and there and yonder, and reconnoitres, cautiously; the silence still continuing, bodies follow heads, and jaded, half smothered creatures group themselves about, stretch their cramped limbs, draw in deep draughts of the grateful fresh air, gossip with the neighbors from the next cave; maybe straggle off home presently, or take a lounge through the town, if the stillness continues; and will scurry to the holes again, by-and-bye, when the war-tempest breaks forth once more.

There being but three thousand of these cave-dwellers—merely the population of a village—would they not come to know each other, after a week or two, and familiarly; insomuch that the fortunate or unfortunate experiences of one would be of interest to all?

Those are the materials furnished by history. From them might not almost anybody reproduce for himself the life of that time in Vicksburg? Could you, who did not experience it, come nearer to reproducing it to the imagination of another non-participant than could a Vicksburger who *did* experience it? It seems impossible; and yet there are reasons why it might not really be. When one makes his first voyage in a ship, it is an experience which multitudinously bristles with striking novelties; novelties which are in such sharp contrast with all this person's former experiences that they take a seemingly deathless grip upon his imagination and memory. By tongue or pen he can make a landsman live that strange and stirring voyage over with him; make him see it all and feel it all. But if he wait? If he make ten voyages in succession—what then? Why, the thing has lost color, snap, surprise;

and has become commonplace. The man would have nothing to tell that would quicken a landsman's pulse.

Years ago, I talked with a couple of the Vicksburg non-combatants—a man and his wife. Left to tell their story in their own way, those people told it without fire, almost without interest.

A week of their wonderful life there would have made their tongues eloquent forever perhaps; but they had six weeks of it, and that wore the novelty all out; they got used to being bomb-shelled out of home and into the ground; the matter became commonplace. After that, the possibility of their ever being startlingly interesting in their talks about it was gone. What the man said was to this effect:

It got to be Sunday all the time. Seven Sundays in the week—to us, anyway. We hadn't anything to do, and time hung heavy. Seven Sundays, and all of them broken up at one time or another, in the day or in the night, by a few hours of the awful storm of fire and thunder and iron. At first we used to shin for the holes a good deal faster than we did afterwards. The first time, I forgot the children, and Maria fetched them both along. When she was all safe in the cave she fainted. Two or three weeks afterwards, when she was running for the holes, one morning, through a shell-shower, a big shell burst near her, and covered her all over with dirt, and a piece of the iron carried away her game-bag of false hair from the back of her head. Well, she stopped to get that game-bag before she shoved along again! Was getting used to things already, you see. We all got so that we could tell a good deal about shells; and after that we didn't always go under shelter if it was a light shower. Us men would loaf around and talk; and a man would say, "There she goes!" and name the kind of shell it was from the sound of it, and go on talking—if there wasn't any danger from it. If a shell was bursting close over us, we stopped talking and stood still; uncomfortable, yes, but it wasn't safe to move. When it let go, we went on talking again, if nobody hurt—maybe saying, "That was a ripper!" or some such commonplace comment before we resumed; or, maybe, we would see a shell poising itself away high in the air overhead. In that case, every fellow just whipped out a sudden, "See you again, gents!" and shoved. Often and often I saw gangs of ladies promenading the streets, looking as cheerful as you please, and keeping an eye canted up watching the shells; and I've seen them stop still when they were uncertain about what a shell was going to do, and wait and make certain; and after that they sa'ntered along again, or lit out for shelter, according to the verdict. Streets in some towns have a litter of pieces of paper, and odds and ends of one sort or another lying around. Ours hadn't; they had *iron* litter. Sometimes a man would gather up all the iron fragments and unbursted shells in his neighborhood, and pile them into a kind of monument in his front yard—a ton of it, sometimes. No glass left; glass couldn't stand such a bombardment; it was all shivered out. Windows of the houses vacant—looked like eye-holes in a skull. *Whole* panes were as scarce as news.

We had church Sundays. Not many there, along at first; but by-and-bye pretty good turnouts. I've seen service stop a minute, and everybody sit quiet—no voice heard, pretty funeral-like then—and all the more so on account of the awful boom and crash going on outside and overhead; and pretty soon, when a body could be heard, service would go on again. Organs and church-music mixed up with a bombardment is a powerful queer combination—along at first. Coming out of church, one morning, we had an accident—the only one that happened around me on a Sunday. I was just having a hearty handshake with a friend I hadn't seen for a while, and saying, "Drop into our cave to-night, after bombardment; we've got hold of a pint of prime wh—" Whiskey, I was going to say, you know, but a shell interrupted. A chunk of it cut the man's arm off, and left it dangling in my hand. And do you know the thing that is going to stick the longest in my memory, and outlast everything else, little and big, I reckon, is the mean thought I had then? It was "the whiskey *is saved*." And yet, don't you know, it was kind of excusable; because it was as scarce as diamonds, and we had only just that little; never had another taste during the siege.

Sometimes the caves were desperately crowded, and always hot and close. Sometimes a cave had twenty or twenty-five people packed into it; no turning-room for anybody; air so foul, sometimes, you couldn't have made a candle burn in it. A child was born in one of those caves one night. Think of that; why, it was like having it born in a trunk.

Twice we had sixteen people in our cave; and a number of times we had a dozen. Pretty suffocating in there. We always had eight; eight belonged there. Hunger and misery and sickness and fright and sorrow, and I don't know what all, got so loaded into them that none of them were ever rightly their old selves after the siege. They all died but three of us within a couple of years. One night a shell burst in front of the hole and caved it in and stopped it up. It was lively times, for a while, digging out. Some of us came near smothering. After that we made two openings—ought to have thought of it at first.

Mule meat. No, we only got down to that the last day or two. Of course it was good; anything is good when you are starving.

This man had kept a diary during—six weeks? No, only the first six days. The first day, eight close pages; the second, five; the third, one—loosely written; the fourth, three or four lines; a line or two the fifth and sixth days; seventh day, diary abandoned; life in terrific Vicksburg having now become commonplace and matter of course.

The war history of Vicksburg has more about it to interest the general reader than that of any other of the river-towns. It is full of variety, full of incident, full of the picturesque. Vicksburg held out longer than any other important river-town, and saw warfare in all its phases, both land and water—the siege, the mine, the assault, the repulse, the bombardment, sickness, captivity, famine.

The most beautiful of all the national cemeteries is here. Over the great gateway is this inscription:

"Here Rest in Peace 16,600 Who Died for Their
Country in the Years 1861 to 1865"

7

STEALING THE GENERAL

WILLIAM PITTENGER

The greater number of us arranged to pass the night at a small hotel adjoining the Marietta depot. Before retiring we left orders with the hotel clerk to rouse us in time for the northward bound train, due not long after daylight. Notwithstanding our novel situation, I never slept more soundly. Good health, extreme fatigue, and the feeling that the die was now cast and further thought useless, made me sink into slumber almost as soon as I touched the bed. Others equally brave and determined were affected in a different way.

Our doom might be fixed before the setting of another sun. We might be hanging to the limbs of some of the trees along the railroad, with an enraged populace jeering and shouting vengeance because we had no more lives to give up; or we might leave a trail of fire and destruction behind us, and come triumphantly rolling into Chatta-nooga and Huntsville, within the Federal lines, to receive the welcome plaudits of comrades left behind, and the thanks of our general, and the praises of a grateful people.

Such thoughts as these passed in swift review, and were not calculated to make one sleep soundly.

As the hotel was much crowded, we obtained a few rooms in close proximity, and crowded them to their utmost capacity. Andrews noted our rooms before retiring, that he might, if necessary, seek any one of us out for consultation before we rose. Porter and Hawkins were unfortunately overlooked; they had arrived on an earlier train and obtained lodging at some distance from the depot. The clerk failed to have them called in time for the morning train, as they had ordered, and, greatly to their regret and chagrin, they were left behind. This was a serious loss, as they were both cool, brave men, and Hawkins was the most experienced railway engineer of our company. W. F. Brown, who took his place in this work, was, however, fully competent, though possibly somewhat less cautious.

Long before the train was due, Andrews, who had slept little, if at all, that night, glided from room to room silently as a ghost, the doors being purposely left unfastened, and aroused the slumberers. It seemed to some of us scarcely a moment from the time of retiring until he came thus to the bedside of each sleeper in turn, and cautiously wakening him, asked his name, to prevent the possibility of mistake, and then told each one exactly the part he was expected to take in the enterprise of the day. There was hasty dressing, and afterwards an informal meeting held in Andrews' room, at which nearly one-half of the whole number were present, and plans were more fully discussed.

Then Marion A. Ross, one of the most determined of the whole number, took the bold step of advising and even urging the abandonment, for the present, of the whole enterprise. He reasoned with great force that under present circumstances, with the rebel vigilance fully aroused by Mitchel's rapid advance, with guards stationed around the train we were to capture, as we had learned would be the case at Big Shanty, and with the road itself obstructed by numerous trains, the enterprise was sure to fail, and would cost the life of every man engaged in it.

Andrews very gently answered his arguments and strove to show that the objections urged really weighed in favor of the original plan. No such attempt as we purposed had ever been made, and consequently would not be guarded against; the presence of a line of sentinels and of so many troops at Big Shanty would only tend to relax vigilance still further; and the great amount of business done on the road, with the running of many unscheduled trains, would screen us from too close inquiry when we ran our train ahead of time.

This reasoning was not altogether satisfactory, and some of the others joined Ross in a respectful but firm protest against persisting in such a hopeless undertaking. But Andrews, speaking very low, as was his wont when thoroughly in earnest, declared that he had once before postponed the attempt, and returned to camp disgraced.

"Now," he continued, "I will accomplish my purpose or leave my bones to bleach in Dixie. But I do not wish to control any one against his own judgment. If any of you think it too hazardous, you are perfectly at liberty to take the train in the opposite direction and work your way back to camp as you can."

This inflexible determination closed the discussion, and as no man was willing to desert his leader, we all assured him of our willingness to obey his orders to the death. I had taken no part in the discussion, as I was not in possession of sufficient facts to judge of the chance of success, and I wished the responsibility to rest upon the leader, where it properly belonged.

The train was now nearly due, and we proceeded to the station for the purchase of tickets. By the time they had been procured—not all for one place, as we wished to lessen the risk of suspicion—the train swept up to the platform. Hastily glancing at it in the early morning light, and seeing only that it was very long and apparently well filled, the twenty adventurers entered by different doors, but finally took their places in one car.

From Marietta to Big Shanty, the railroad sweeps in a long bend of eight miles around the foot of Kenesaw Mountain, which lies directly between the two stations. This elevation is now scarred all over with rebel intrenchments, and was the scene of one of the severest contests of the war. This, however, as well as the whole of the three months' struggle from Chattanooga to Atlanta, came a year and a half later. At this time the nearest Federal soldiers were more than two hundred miles away.

When the train moved on and the conductor came to take our tickets we observed him carefully, as we knew not how closely his fate and ours might be linked together in the approaching struggle. The most vivid anticipation fell far short of the reality. Upon the qualities of that one man our success or failure hinged. He was quite young—not more than twenty-three or four—and looked like a man of resolution and energy. We noticed that he was also scrutinizing us and the other passengers very closely, and naturally feared that he had in some manner been put on his guard.

In fact, as we learned long afterwards, he had been warned that some of the new conscripts who were reluctant to fight for the Confederacy were contemplating an escape and might try to get a ride on the cars. His orders were to watch for all such and arrest them at once. But he did not think that any of the men who got on at Marietta looked in the least like conscripts or deserters.

The train ran slowly, stopping at several intervening points, and did not reach Big Shanty until it was fully daylight. This station had been selected for the seizure, because the train breakfasted there, and it was probable that many of the employees and passengers would leave it for their meal, thus diminishing the opposition we might expect. Another most important reason for the selection was the absence of any telegraph office. But, on the other hand, Camp McDonald had been lately located here, and a large body of soldiers—some accounts said as many as ten thousand men—were already assembled. Their camp included the station within the guard-line.

When Andrews and the first party had been at Atlanta, three weeks earlier, few troops had yet arrived at this point. The capture of a train in the midst of a camp of the enemy was not a part of the original plan, but subsequently became necessary. It was certainly a great additional element of danger, but it was not now possible to substitute any other point.

The decisive hour had arrived. It is scarcely boastful to say that the annals of history record few enterprises more bold and novel than that witnessed by the rising sun of Saturday morning, April 12, 1862. Here was a train, with several hundred passengers, with a full complement of hands, lying inside a line of sentinels, who were distinctly seen pacing back and forth in close proximity, to be seized by a mere score of men, and to be carried away before the track could be obstructed, or the intruding engineer shot down at his post.

Only the most careful calculation and prompt execution, concentrating the power of the whole band into a single lightning-like stroke, could afford the slightest prospect of success. In the bedroom conference every action was predetermined with the nicest accuracy. Our engineer and his assistant knew the signal at which to start; the brakesmen had their work assigned; the man who was to uncouple the cars knew just the place at which to make the separation; the remainder of the number constituted a guard, in two divisions, who were to stand with ready revolvers abreast of the cars to be seized, and shoot down without hesitation any one who attempted to interfere with the work.

Andrews was to command the whole, and do any part of the work not otherwise provided for. Should there be any unexpected hindrance, we were to fight until we either overcame all opposition and captured the train or perished in a body. If we failed to carry off our prize we were inevitably lost; if any man failed to be on board when the signal was given, his fate also was sealed. A delay of thirty seconds after our designs became clearly known would have resulted in the slaughter of the whole party.

When our train rolled up to the platform the usual announcement was shouted, "Big Shanty; twenty minutes for breakfast!" Most fortunately for us, the conductor, engineer, firemen, and train-hands generally, with many of the passengers, poured out, and hurried to the long, low eating-room which gave its name to the station. The engine was utterly unguarded. This uncommon carelessness was the result of perfect security, and greatly favored our design.

Yet it was a thrilling moment! Victory or death hung on the next minute! There was no chance for drawing back, and I do not think any of us had the disposition. A little while before, a sense of shrinking came over the writer like that preceding a plunge into ice-water; but with the next breath it passed away, and left me as calm and quiet as if no enemy had been within a hundred miles.

Still, for a moment, we kept our seats. Andrews went forward to examine the track and see if there was any hindrance to a rapid rush ahead. Almost immediately he returned, and said, very quietly, "All right, boys; let us go now." There was nothing in this to attract special observation; but whether it did or not was now a matter of indifference. The time of concealment was past.

We rose, left the cars, and walked briskly to the head of the train. With the precision of machinery, every man took his appointed place. Three cars back from the tender the coupling-pin was drawn out, as the load of passenger-cars would only have been an incumbrance. Wilson W. Brown, who acted as engineer, William Knight as assistant, Alfred Wilson as fireman, together with Andrews, mounted the engine, Knight grasping the lever, and waiting the word for starting. The appointed brakesmen threw themselves flat on the top of the cars.

At a signal from Andrews, the remainder of the band, who had kept watch, climbed with surprising quickness into a box-car which stood open. All was well! Knight, at Andrews' orders, jerked open the steam-valve, and we were off! Before the camp-guards or the bystanders could do more than turn a curious eye upon our proceedings, the train was under way, and we were safe from interruption.

The writer was stationed in the box-car, and as soon as all were in, we pulled the door shut to guard against any stray musket-balls. For a moment of most intense suspense after we were thus shut in all was still. In that moment a thousand conflicting thoughts swept through our minds. Then came a pull, ajar, a clang, and we were flying away on our perilous journey.

Those who were on the engine caught a glimpse of the excited crowd, soldiers and citizens, swarming and running about in the wildest confusion. It has been said that a number of shots were fired after us, but those in the box-car knew nothing of it, and it is certain that no one was injured. A widely-circulated picture represented us as waving our hats and shouting in triumph. Nothing so melodramatic took place. The moment was too deep and earnest, and we had too many perils still to encounter for any such childish demonstration.

Yet it was a grand triumph, and having nothing of a more practical character for the moment to do, I realized it to the fullest extent. There are times in life when whole years of enjoyment are condensed into a single experience. It was so with me then. I could comprehend the emotion of Columbus when he first beheld through the dim dawn the long-dreamed-of shores of America, or the less innocent but no less fervent joy of Cortez when he planted the Cross of Spain on the halls of Montezuma.

My breast throbbed fast with emotions of joy and gladness that words labor in vain to express. A sense of ethereal lightness ran through my veins, and I seemed ascending higher, higher, with each pulsation of the engine. Remember, I was but twenty-two then, full of hope and ambition. Not a dream of failure shadowed my rapture. We had always been told that the greatest difficulty was to reach and take possession of the engine, after which success was certain. But for unforeseen contingencies it would have been.

Away we rush, scouring past field and village and woodland. At each leap of the engine our hearts rose higher, and we talked merrily of the welcome that would greet us when we dashed into Huntsville a few hours later, our enterprise done, and the brightest laurels of the war eclipsed!

We found the railroad, however, to be of the roughest and most difficult character. The grades were very heavy and the curves numerous and sharp. We seemed to be running towards every point of the compass. The deep valleys and steep hills of this part of the country had rendered the building of the road difficult and costly. There were numerous high embankments where an accident would be of deadly character. The track was also uneven and in generally bad condition, for the war had rendered railroad iron scarce and high-priced, besides diverting all attention and resources into other channels.

This unfavorable character of the road very greatly increased the difficulty experienced by an engineer unfamiliar with the route in making rapid time, or in avoiding the varied difficulties incident to our progress. But we trusted implicitly that the far-sighted plans of Andrews, the skill of our engineers, and our own willing efforts would overcome all hindrances.

Our first run was short. There was a sudden checking of speed and a halt. When those of us who were in the box-car pushed open our door and asked the reason for stopping so soon, we were told that the fire was low and the steam exhausted. This was startling intelligence, and caused a moment of consternation. If our "General"—the name of the locomotive we had captured—failed us at the beginning of the race, we too well knew what the end would be. For hundreds of miles on every side of us were desperate and daring foes. A hundred times our number of horse and foot could be gathered against us in a few hours.

The most timid bird pursued by hounds feels safe, for its wings can bear it above their jaws. But if those wings should be broken! This engine gave us wings; but if it should be disabled no valor of ours could beat back the hosts about us, no skill elude their rage.

But we found a less threatening explanation of our premature halt. The schedule time of our train was very slow—only about sixteen miles an hour—and the fires had been allowed to run down because of the expected stop of twenty minutes for breakfast at Big Shanty—a stop that we had reduced to less than two minutes. Then the valve being thrown wide open, the little steam in the boiler was soon exhausted. But this difficulty was of short duration. A rest of three minutes, with plenty of wood thrown into the furnace, wrought a change, and we again glided rapidly forward.

But when viewed soberly, and in the light of all the facts since developed, what were the chances of success and escape possessed by the flying party? Was the whole attempt, as has been frequently asserted, rash and foolhardy? Or had it that character of practicability which is ever the stamp of true genius?

Historical accuracy, as well as justice to the memory of a brave but unfortunate man, compels me to pronounce the scheme almost faultless. In this estimate I have the full concurrence of all who were engaged on the opposite side. It is hard to see how the plan could have been improved without allowing its projector to have had a knowledge of the precise condition of the enemy such as no commander at the beginning of an important enterprise ever has. No one of the plans by which Generals Grant and Sherman finally overthrew the Rebellion presented a clearer prospect of success.

These are the elements of the problem upon which Andrews based his hopes. Big Shanty is twenty-eight miles north of Atlanta and thirty-two south of Kingston. Short of these places he was convinced that no engine could be obtained for pursuit. He could obstruct the road so that no train would reach Big Shanty for hours. Pinch-bars and other instruments for lifting track might be found on the captured engine, or obtained from some station or working-party. His force of twenty men was counted ample to overcome resistance at any switch or passing train.

One irregular train only was expected to be on the road, and that would soon be met—certainly at Kingston or before—after which it would be safe to run at the highest speed to the first bridge, burn it, and pass on to the next, which, with all other large bridges, could be served in the same manner. Each bridge burnt would be an insuperable barrier to pursuit by an engine beyond that point. Thus every part of the scheme was fair and promising. Only those critics who are wise after the event can pronounce the attempt rash and hopeless.

The destruction of the telegraph would also be necessary; but this was not difficult. It seemed as if every contingency was provided for, and then there was the additional fighting power of twenty chosen men to guard against any possible emergency. We were now embarked on this most perilous but hopeful voyage. Coolness, precision of work, and calm effort could scarcely fail to sever the chief military communications of the enemy before the setting of the sun, and convince him that no enterprise was too audacious for the Union arms.

After the fire had been made to burn briskly, Andrews jumped off the engine, ran back to the box-car, about the door of which we were standing, and clasped our hands in an ecstasy of congratulation. He declared that all our really hard work was done and that our difficulties were nearly passed; that we had the enemy at such a disadvantage that he could not harm us; and exhibited every sign of joy. Said he, "Only one train to meet, and then we will put our engine to full speed, burn the bridges that I have marked out, dash through Chattanooga, and on to Mitchel at Huntsville. We've got the upper hand of the rebels now, and they can't help themselves!"

How glad we all were! When, three years later, the capture of Richmond set all the bells of the North ringing out peals of triumph, the sensation of joy was more diffused but less intense than we then experienced. Almost everything mankind values seemed within our grasp. Oh, if we had met but one unscheduled train!

This reference of Andrews to one train which he expected to meet before we began to burn bridges has been quoted in many public sketches, and has led to some misapprehension. He did expect to meet three trains before reaching Chattanooga; but two of these were regular trains, and being also farther up the road, were not supposed to present any serious difficulty. Their position at any given time could be definitely ascertained, and we could avoid collision with them, no matter how far we ran ahead of time. But so long as there were any irregular trains on the road before us, our only safety was in keeping the regular time of the captured train. This was, unfortunately, very slow; but if we exceeded it we lost the right of way, and were liable to a collision at any moment.

This risk was greatly increased by our inability to send ahead telegraphic notifications of our position. The order of southward-bound trains, according to the information we then had, was as follows: First, a way-freight, which was very uncertain as to time, but which we expected to meet early in the morning, and felt sure that it would be at Kingston or south of that point. This was the only real hindrance according to our programme, and it was to this train that Andrews referred. Behind this were the regular freight train, and still farther north the regular passenger train. As a matter of fact, we did meet these trains at Adairsville and Calhoun, the latter being somewhat behind time; but we might have met them farther north had it not been for unforeseen hindrances.

There is considerable discrepancy in the many published accounts of the following chase, which the writer has not in every case been able to perfectly reconcile. In the intense excitement and novel situations involved, men were not likely to observe or remember every event accurately. But no pains have been spared to combine fulness and completeness in the following account. Using the best of my own recollections, consulting my comrades, reading carefully all published accounts, and especially going over the whole route years after, with Fuller and Murphy, two of the pursuing party, who kindly gave me all the information in their power, it is hoped that substantial accuracy has been obtained. Some of the incidents of the chase, such as the number of times the track was torn up, and whether we were fired upon by pursuing soldiers, allow some room for a conflict of memory. But the variations are not material.

Side by side with the road ran the telegraph-wires, which were able, by the flashing of a single lightning message ahead, to arrest our progress and dissipate our fondest hopes. There was no telegraph station where we had captured the train, but we knew not how soon our enemies might reach one, or whether they might not have a portable battery at command. Therefore we ran but a short distance, after replenishing the furnace, before again stopping to cut the wire.

John Scott, an active young man of the Twenty-first Ohio, scrambled up the pole with the agility of a cat, and tried to break the wire by swinging upon it; but failing in this, he knocked off the insulating box at the top of the pole and swung with it down to the ground. Fortunately, a small saw was found on the engine, with which the wire was severed in two places, and the included portion, many yards in length, was taken away with us, in order that the ends might not be readily joined.

While one or two of the party were thus engaged others worked with equal diligence in taking up a rail from the track. No good track-raising instruments had been found on the train, and we had not yet procured them from any other source. A smooth iron bar, about four feet long, was the only instrument yet found, and with this some of the spikes were slowly and painfully battered out. After a few had thus been extracted, a lever was got under the rail and the remainder were pried loose. This occupied much more time than cutting the wire, and it required no prophet to foretell that if we did not procure better tools rail-lifting would have to be used very sparingly in our program. In the present instance, however, the loss of time was no misfortune, as we were ahead of the schedule time, which we still felt bound to observe.

After another rapid but brief run, we paused long enough to chop down a telegraph-pole, cut the wire again, and place the pole, with many other obstructions, on the track. We did not here try to lift a rail; indeed, we had little serious fear of any pursuit at this time, and merely threw on these obstructions because of having spare time to employ.

We thus continued—running a little ahead of time, then stopping to obstruct the track and cut the wire—until Cass Station was reached, where we took on a good supply of wood and water. At this place we also obtained a complete time schedule of the road. Andrews told the tank-tender that we were running a powder-train through to the army of General Beauregard at Corinth, which was almost out of ammunition, and that the greatest haste was necessary. He further claimed to be a Confederate officer of high rank, and said that he had impressed this train for the purpose in hand, and that Fuller, with the regular passenger train, would be along shortly.

The whole story was none too plausible, as General Mitchel was now interposed between our present position and Beauregard, and we would never have been able to get a train to the army of the latter on this route; but the tender was not critical and gave us his schedule, adding that he would willingly send his shirt to Beauregard if that general needed it. When this man was afterwards asked if he did not suspect the character of the enemy he thus aided, he answered that he would as soon have suspected the President of the Confederacy himself as one who talked so coolly and confidently as Andrews did!

Keeping exactly on regular time, we proceeded without any striking adventures until Kingston was reached. This place—thirty-two miles from Big Shanty—we regarded as marking the first stage of our journey. Two hours had elapsed since the capture of the train, and hitherto we had been fairly prosperous. No track-lifting instruments had yet been obtained, notwithstanding inquiries for them at several stations. We had secured no inflammable materials for more readily firing the bridges, and the road was not yet clear before us. But, on the other hand, no serious hindrance had yet occurred, and we believed ourselves far ahead of any possible pursuit.

But at Kingston we had some grounds for apprehending difficulty. This little town is at the junction with the road to Rome, Georgia. Cars and engines were standing on the side track. Here we fully expected to meet our first train, and it would be necessary for us to get the switches properly adjusted before we could pass it to go on our way.

When we drew up at the station there was handed to Andrews our first and last communication from the management of the road, in the shape of a telegram, ordering Fuller's train—now ours—to wait at Kingston for the local freight, which was considerably behind time. The order was not very welcome, but we drew out on the side track, and watched eagerly for the train.

Many persons gathered around Andrews, who here, as always, personated the conductor of our train, and showered upon him many curious and somewhat suspicious questions. Ours was an irregular train, but the engine was recognized as Fuller's. The best answers possible were given. A red flag had been placed on our engine, and the announcement was made that Fuller, with another engine, was but a short way behind. The powder story was emphasized, and every means employed to avoid suspicion. Andrews only, and the usual complement of train-hands, were visible, the remainder of the party being tightly shut up in the car, which was designated as containing Beauregard's ammunition.

The striking personal appearance of Andrews greatly aided him in carrying through his deception, which was never more difficult than at this station. His commanding presence, and firm but graceful address, marked him as a Southern gentleman—a member of the class from which a great proportion of the rebel officers were drawn.

His declarations and orders were therefore received with the greater respect on this account. But all these resources were here strained to the utmost.

At length the anxiously expected local freight train arrived, and took its place on another side track. We were about to start on our way, with the glad consciousness that our greatest obstacle was safely passed, when a red flag was noticed on the hindmost freight-car. This elicited immediate inquiry, and we were informed that another very long freight train was just behind, and that we would be obliged to wait its arrival also. This was most unfortunate, as we had been already detained at Kingston much longer than was pleasant.

There were many disagreeable elements in the situation. A crowd of persons was rapidly assembling. The train from Rome was also nearly due, and though it only came to the station and returned on its own branch, yet it was not agreeable to notice the constant increase of force that our enemies were gaining. If any word from the southward arrived, or if our true character was revealed in any other way, the peril would be imminent. But we trusted that this second delay would be brief. Slowly the minutes passed by. To us, who were shut up in the box-car, it appeared as if they would never be gone.

Our soldier comrades on the outside kept in the background as much as possible, remaining at their posts on the engine and the cars, while Andrews occupied attention by complaining of the delay, and declaring that the road ought to be kept clear of freight trains when so much needed for the transportation of army supplies, and when the fate of the whole army of the West might depend upon the celerity with which it received its ammunition.

There was plausibility enough in his words to lull suspicion in all minds except that of the old switch-tender of the place, who grumbled out his conviction "that something was wrong with that stylish-looking fellow, who ordered everybody around as if the whole road belonged to him." But no one paid any attention to this man's complaints, and not many minutes after a distant whistle sounded from the northward, and we felt that the crisis had passed. As there was no more room on the side track, Andrews ordered the switch-tender to let this train run by on the main track. That worthy was still grumbling, but he reluctantly obeyed, and the long succession of cars soon glided by us.

This meant release from a suspense more intolerable than the most perilous action. To calmly wait where we could do nothing, while our destiny was being wrought out by forces operating in the darkness, was a terrible trial of nerve. But it was well borne. Brown, Knight, and Wilson, who were exposed to view, exhibited no more impatience than was to be expected of men in their assumed situation. Those of us in the box-car talked in whispers only, and examined the priming of our pistols. We understood that we were waiting for a delayed train, and well knew the fearful possibilities of an obstructed track, with the speedy detection, and fight against overwhelming odds that would follow, if the train for which we waited did not arrive sooner than pursuers from Big Shanty.

When we recognized the whistle of the coming train it was almost as welcome as the boom of Mitchel's cannon, which we expected to hear that evening after all our work was done. As it rumbled by us we fully expected an instant start, a swift run of a few miles, and then the hard work but pleasant excitement of bridge-burning. Alas!

Swift and frequent are the mutations of war. Success can never be assured to any enterprise in advance. The train for which we had waited with so much anxiety had no sooner stopped than we beheld on it an emblem more terrible than any comet that ever frighted a superstitious continent. Another red flag! Another train close behind! This was terrible, but what could be done?

With admirable presence of mind Andrews moderated his impatience, and asked the conductor of the newly-arrived train the meaning of such an unusual obstruction of the road. His tone was commanding, and without reserve the conductor gave the full explanation. To Andrews it had a thrilling interest. The commander at Chattanooga had received information that the Yankee General Mitchel was coming by forced marches and in full strength against that town; therefore all the rolling-stock of the road had been ordered to Atlanta. This train was the first instalment, but another and still longer section was behind. It was to start a few minutes after he did, and would probably not be more than ten or fifteen minutes behind.

In turn, the conductor asked Andrews who he was, and received the information that he was an agent of General Beauregard, and that he had impressed a train into military service in Atlanta, which he was running through with powder, of which Beauregard was in extreme need. Under such circumstances he greatly regretted this unfortunate detention. The conductor did not suspect the falsity of these pretences, but told Andrews that it was very doubtful if he could get to Beauregard at Corinth by going through Chattanooga, as it was certain that Mitchel had captured Huntsville, directly on the line between them.

Andrews replied that this made no difference, as he had his orders, and should press on until they were countermanded, adding that Mitchel was probably only paying a flying visit to Huntsville, and would have to be gone soon, or find Beauregard upon him. Andrews also ordered the conductor to run far enough down the main track to allow the next train to draw in behind him, and for both trains there to wait the coming of Fuller with the regular mail.

His orders were implicitly obeyed; and then to our party recommenced the awful trial of quiet waiting. One of the men outside was directed to give notice to those in the box-car of the nature of the detention, and warn them to be ready for any emergency. Either Brown or Knight, I think, executed this commission. Leaning against our car, but without turning his eyes towards it, and speaking in a low voice, he said, "We are waiting for one of the trains the rebels are running off from Mitchel. If we are detected before it comes, we will have to fight. Be ready." We *were* ready; and so intolerable is suspense that most of us would have felt as a welcome relief the command to throw open our door and spring into deadly conflict.

Slowly the leaden moments dragged themselves away. It seems scarcely creditable, but it is literally true, that for twenty-five minutes more we lay on that side track and waited—waited with minds absorbed, pulses leaping, and ears strained for the faintest sound which might give a hint as to our destiny. One precious hour had we wasted at Kingston—time enough to have burned every bridge between that place and Dalton! The whole margin of time on which we had allowed ourselves to count was two hours; now half of that was thrown away at one station, and nothing accomplished.

We dared wait no longer. Andrews decided to rush ahead with the intention of meeting this extra train wherever it might be found, and forcing it to back before him to the next siding, where he could pass it. The resolution was in every way dangerous, but the danger would at least be of an active character.

Just at this moment the long-expected whistle was heard, and soon the train came into plain view, bringing with it an almost interminable string of cars. The weight and length of its train had caused the long delay. Obedient to direction, it followed the first extra down the main track, and its locomotive was a long way removed from the depot when the last car cleared the upper end of the side track on which we lay. At length it had got far enough down, and it was possible for us to push on. Andrews instantly ordered the switch-tender to arrange the track so as to let us out.

But here a new difficulty presented itself. This man had been in an ill humor from the first, and was now fully convinced that something was wrong. Possibly the tone in which he was addressed irritated him still more. He therefore responded to Andrews' order by a surly refusal, and hung up the keys in the station-house. When we in the box-car overheard his denial, we were sure that the time for fighting had come. There was no more reason for dreading the issue of a conflict at this station than at any other point, and we waited the signal with the confident expectation of victory.

But even a victory at that moment would have been most undesirable. We had no wish to shed blood unnecessarily. A telegraph office was at hand, and it was possible that before the wire could be cut a message might be flashed ahead. There were also engines in readiness for prompt pursuit, and while we might have overcome immediate opposition by the use of our firearms, our triumph would have been the signal for a close and terrible chase.

The daring coolness of Andrews removed all embarrassments. While men are hesitating and in doubt, boldness and promptness on the part of an opponent are almost sure to carry the day. Ceasing to address the switch-tender, Andrews walked hurriedly into the station, and with the truthful remark that he had no more time to waste, took down the key and began to unlock the switch.

The tender cursed him terribly, and called for some to arrest him. The crowd around also disliked the action, and began to hoot and yell; but before any one had decided as to what ought to be done Andrews had unlocked and changed the switch, and waved his hand for the engineer to come on. It was an inexpressible relief when the cars moved forward and the sounds of strife died out.

As soon as the locomotive passed to the main track, Andrews tossed the keys to the ruffled owner of them, saying, in his blandest manner, "Pardon me, sir, for being in such a hurry, but the Confederacy can't wait for every man's notions. You'll find it is all right," and stepped on board his engine. The excitement gradually ceased, and no thought of pursuit was entertained until startling intelligence was received a few moments later from Big Shanty.

Before describing the terrible struggle above Kingston, it will be well to narrate the operations of the persons whose train had been so unceremoniously snatched from them at Big Shanty. From printed accounts published contemporaneously by several of those engaged in the pursuit, as well as from personal responses to inquiries made regarding the most material points, the writer is confident that he can tell the strange story without essential error. It is a striking commentary on the promptness of the seizure, that the bystanders generally reported that only eight men, instead of twenty, had been observed to mount the train.

William A. Fuller, conductor, Anthony Murphy, manager of the State railroad shops at Atlanta, and Jefferson Cain, engineer, stepped off their locomotive, leaving it unguarded save by the surrounding sentinels, and in perfect confidence took their seats at the breakfast-table at Big Shanty. But before they had tasted a morsel of food the quick ear of Murphy, who was seated with his back towards the window, caught the sound of escaping steam, and he exclaimed, "Fuller, who's moving your train?" Almost simultaneously the latter, who was somewhat of a ladies' man, and was bestowing polite attentions upon two or three fair passengers, saw the same movement, and sprang up, shouting, "Somebody's running off with our train!"

No breakfast was eaten then. Everybody rushed through the door to the platform. The train was then fully under way, just sweeping out of sight around the first curve. With quick decision Fuller shouted to Murphy and Cain, "Come on!" and started at a full run after the flying train! This attempt to run down and catch a locomotive by a foot-race seemed so absurd that as the three, at the top of their speed, passed around the same curve, they were greeted with loud laughter and ironical cheers by the excited multitude. To all appearances it was a foolish and hopeless chase.

Yet, paradoxical as the statement may seem, this chase on foot was the wisest course possible for Fuller and his companions. What else could they do? Had they remained quietly in camp, with no show of zeal, they would have been reproached with negligence in not guarding their train more carefully, even if they were not accused with being in league with its captors.

As they ran, Fuller explained the situation and his purposes to his companions. They had neither electric battery nor engine. Had they obtained horses, they would necessarily have followed the common road, instead of the railroad, and if they thought of that expedient at all, it would be as distasteful to railroad men as abandoning their ship to sailors, and they preferred leaving that course for others. It would have been wise for those who could think of nothing else to do to ride as mounted couriers to the stations ahead; but whether this was done or not I have never learned. Certainly it was not done so promptly as to influence the fortunes of the day.

But the truth is that Fuller and Murphy were at first completely deceived as to the nature of the event which had taken place. They had been warned to guard against the escape of conscript deserters from that very camp; and although they would never have suspected an attempt on the part of the conscripts to escape by capturing their engine, yet when it was seen to dash off, the thought of this warning was naturally uppermost.

Even then Fuller conjectured that they would use his engine only to get a mile or two beyond the guard line, and then abandon it. He was therefore anxious to follow closely in order to find the engine and return for his passengers at the earliest moment possible. Little did he anticipate the full magnitude of the work and the danger before him. That any Federal soldiers were within a hundred miles of Big Shanty never entered his mind or that of any other person.

For a mile or two the three footmen ran at the top of their speed, straining their eyes forward for any trace of the lost engine which they expected to see halted and abandoned at almost any point on the road. But they were soon partially undeceived as to the character of their enemies. About two miles from the place of starting they found the telegraph wire severed and a portion of it carried away. The fugitives were also reported as quietly oiling and inspecting their engine. No mere deserters would be likely to think of this. The two actions combined clearly indicated the intention of making a long run, but who the men were still remained a mystery. A few hundred yards from this place a party of workmen with a hand-car was found, and these most welcome reinforcements were at once pressed into the service.

Fuller's plans now became more definite and determined. He had a good hand-car and abundance of willing muscle to work it. By desperate exertions, by running behind the car and pushing it up the steep grades, and then mounting and driving it furiously down-hill and on the levels, it was possible to make seven or eight miles an hour; at the same time, Fuller knew that the captive engine, if held back to run on schedule time, as the reports of the workmen indicated, would make but sixteen miles per hour. Fuller bent all his thoughts and energies towards Kingston, thirty miles distant.

He had been informed of the extra trains to be met at that point, and was justified in supposing that the adventurers would be greatly perplexed and hindered by them, even if they were not totally stopped. Had the seizure taken place on the preceding day, as originally planned, he might well have despaired, for then the road would have been clear. Yet he had one other resource, as will appear in due time, of which his enemies knew nothing.

Fuller did not pause to consider how he should defeat the fugitives when he had overtaken them, and he might have paid dearly for this rashness. But he could rely on help at any station, and when he had obtained the means of conveyance, as he would be sure to do at Kingston, he could easily find an overwhelming force to take with him. This Saturday was appointed as a general muster of volunteers, State militia, and conscripts, and armed soldiers were abundant in every village. But Fuller's dominant thought was that his property—the property with which he had been intrusted—was wrested from his grasp, and it was his duty to recover it, at whatever of personal hazard. That any serious harm was intended to the railroad itself he probably did not yet suspect.

Talking and wearying themselves with idle conjectures, but never ceasing to work, Fuller and his party pressed swiftly on. But suddenly there was a crash, a sense of falling, and when the shock allowed them to realize what had happened, they found themselves floundering in a ditch half filled with water, and their hand-car imbedded in the mud beside them! They had reached the place where the first rail had been torn from the track, and had suffered accordingly. But the bank was, fortunately for them, not very high at that spot, and a few bruises were all the damage they sustained. Their hand-car, which was also uninjured, was lifted on the track and driven on again. This incident increased both their caution and their respect for the men before them.

Without further mishap they reached Etowah Station, on the northern bank of the river of the same name. Here was a large bridge, which the Andrews party might have burned without loss of time had they foreseen the long detention at Kingston; but its destruction was not a part of their plan, and it was suffered to stand. The mind of Fuller grew very anxious as he approached this station. On what he should find there depended, in all probability, his power to overtake the fugitives, whose intentions seemed more formidable with each report he received of their actions. Andrews had firmly believed that no engine for pursuit could be found south of Kingston; but Fuller had a different expectation.

Extensive iron-furnaces were located on the Etowah River, about five miles above the station. These works were connected with the railroad by a private track, which was the property of Major Cooper, as well as the works themselves. Murphy knew that Major Cooper had also bought an engine called the "Yonah." It had been built in the shop over which Murphy presided, and was one of the best locomotives in the State.

"But where," Fuller and Murphy asked themselves, "is this engine now?" If it was in view of the adventurers as they passed, they had doubtless destroyed it, ran it off the track, or carried it away with them. They could not afford to neglect such an element in the terrible game they were playing. But if it was now at the upper end of the branch at the mines, as was most probable, it would take the pursuers five miles out of their way to go for it, and even then it might not be ready to start. This diversion could not be afforded.

Fuller and Murphy had come nineteen miles, and had already consumed two hours and three-quarters. The adventurers were reported as passing each station on time, and if this continued they must have reached Kingston forty-five minutes before Fuller and his companions arrived at Etowah, thirteen miles behind them. One hour and a half more to Kingston—this was the very best that could be done with the hand-car. It was clear that if the "Yonah" did not come to their assistance, they were as effectually out of the race as if on the other side of the ocean. Everything now hinged on the position of that one engine.

Here we may pause to note how all coincidences, we might almost say providences, seemed to work against the bridge-burning enterprise. We were at Kingston three-quarters of an hour before our pursuers reached Etowah, thirteen miles distant. If there had been no extra trains, or if they had been sharply on time, so that we could have passed the three with a delay not exceeding fifteen or twenty minutes, which ought to have been an abundant allowance, every bridge above Kingston would have been in ashes before sundown! Or if the delay had been as great as it actually was, even then, if the locomotive "Yonah" had occupied any position excepting one, the same result would have followed.

The pursuers seized their inestimable prize, called for all the volunteers who could snatch guns at a moment's notice, and were soon swiftly but cautiously rushing with the power of steam towards Kingston. The speed of nearly a mile a minute was in refreshing contrast to the slow and laborious progress of the hand-car, and they were naturally jubilant. But what lay before them at Kingston?

The frequent obstructions of the track, the continued cutting of the telegraph, and especially the cool assumption of the leader of the adventurers in calling himself a Confederate officer of high rank in charge of an impressed powder train, all conspired to deepen their conviction that some desperate scheme was on foot. But they did not pause long to listen to reports. Their eyes and their thoughts were bent towards Kingston. Had the adventurers been stopped there, or had they surprised and destroyed the trains met? The pursuers could scarcely form a conjecture as to what was before them; but the speed with which they were flying past station after station would soon end their suspense.

Even the number of men on the flying train was a matter of uncertainty. At the stations passed observers reported that only four or five were seen; but the track-layers and others who had observed them at work were confident of a much larger number—twenty-five or thirty at the least. Besides, it was by no means sure that they had not confederates in large numbers to co-operate with them at the various stations along the road. Fuller knew about how many persons had entered the train at Marietta; but it was not sure that these were all. A hundred more might be scattered along the way, at various points, ready to join in whatever strange plan was now being worked out.

Fuller reached Kingston at least an hour earlier than would have been possible with the hand-car, and a single glance showed that the adventurers were gone, and his hopes of arresting them at that point were ended. They were, however, barely out of sight, and all their start had been reduced to minutes. But here again the pursuit was checked. The foresight of Andrews had blockaded the road as much as possible with the trains which had so long hindered his own movements. Two large and heavy trains stood on the main road; one of the two side tracks was occupied by the third freight, and the other by the engine of the Rome branch.

What Fuller and his friends learned at Kingston left no doubt on their minds that some deliberate and far-reaching military movement was on foot. While its precise nature was yet concealed, the probability that the road itself, and possibly Confederate towns and stores, were to be destroyed, was freely conceded. All agreed that the one thing to be done was to follow their enemies closely, and thus compel them to turn and fight or abandon their enterprise. A large force—one or two hundred well-armed men—was taken on board, and instructions left that as soon as the track could be cleared another armed train was to follow for the purpose of rendering any needed assistance.

We will now resume the direct narrative.

When Kingston was left behind, it was believed by our leader that, notwithstanding all our vexatious delays, we still had a margin of at least an hour's time. Our movements were arranged on that supposition. Our speed was increased to about forty miles an hour, and this swift running, after our long halt at Kingston, was exquisitely delightful.

While we were actually under way our prospects did not yet seem very unfavorable. There were yet one freight and one passenger train to meet, which we would now encounter an hour farther south, because of our long hindrance; but we felt confident of our power to deceive or overpower them, and they did not embarrass our running because they were on the regular schedule.

A short distance south of Adairsville we again stopped, and Andrews called us to come forth and work with a will. No exhortation was needed. John Scott, as usual, climbed the telegraph-pole, and the wire was soon severed. Two or three rails were slowly and painfully battered loose with our iron bar, which still constituted our only instrument for track-lifting. These were loaded on the car to carry away with us. There happened to be a large number of cross-ties lying near, and these we also loaded up for future use. When all was done we moved on, feeling that we had provided for the delay or destruction of any train that might pursue.

We reached Adairsville before the expected freight, but had only just taken our place on the side track when its whistle was heard. When it came up, Andrews, who still personated a Confederate officer, and exacted and received the obedience which in those days of conscription and impressment was readily yielded to military authority, ordered the train to be run past the station and back again on the side track behind his own, to wait for the expected passenger train.

The usual explanations about the powder train were repeated to credulous ears. Then came five minutes of suspense and waiting. The train was behind time—a trifling matter in itself, but, in our situation, each minute might turn the scale between death and life. We could not afford to repeat the experience of Kingston. Not one bridge had yet been burned, and all we could show for our hazard, beside our captured train, were a few cross-ties and lifted rails. After a whispered word of consultation with his engineer, who was willing to assume the most deadly risks rather than to lie still, Andrews remarked to the bystanders that a government powder express must not be detained by any number of passenger trains, and then gave the word, "Go ahead!"

We started quite moderately, but, as soon as the station was out of sight, we noticed a wonderful acceleration of speed. The cars seemed almost to leap from the track, and we whirled from side to side at a bewildering rate. No one of us had ever rode at such a rate before. Though we had no means of measuring the speed, none of us estimated it at less than a mile a minute.

At any rate, the moments were rapidly carrying us towards our own lines, and a very few hours of such running would see us delivered from the series of perils which had so long environed us. We had learned that just beyond Calhoun, a station only ten miles from Adairsville, there was a large bridge, which we knew was marked for destruction. If that was passed without stopping, we would be convinced that an enemy was on our track, and that the race was simply for life. A few minutes would decide. But in the mean time, as an enemy might be following us, it occurred to the writer that it would be well to continue obstructing the track.

This was accomplished by breaking open the hind end of the last box-car, and shoving out one by one the ties previously loaded. A part only of the ties on board were thus employed, as we thought it possible that the remainder might be more useful in other directions. Many of those sprinkled on the track showed a perverse disposition to jump off, but we felt sure that enough remained to make a pursuer cautious. Nothing more impressed us with the fearful speed of our train than the manner in which these ties seemed instantly to vanish when they touched the ground.

We reached Calhoun before any train was met. When we slackened speed, just before arriving at the station, we shoved out one more cross-tie, and then carefully concealed the hole in the car by piling other ties across it. As we drew nearer, great was the satisfaction of Andrews and his engineer when they saw the belated passenger train—our last obstacle—lying quietly at the station. It had been just starting, but, on hearing our whistle, it awaited our arrival. We ran down almost against it; and, without getting off his locomotive, Andrews shouted his orders to have the road cleared for an impressed powder train. The news from the north and west—the panic caused by the rumored approach of General Mitchel—made this sudden demand seem less unreasonable, and it was unhesitatingly obeyed.

The passenger train was switched out of the way, and we glided smoothly by the last train we were to meet. Thus, at length, we had reached the ground where bridge-burning was to begin, and all obstacles were out of the way; what could hinder full and decisive success?

With no thought of our deadly peril we had stopped a short distance above Calhoun to cut the telegraph and oil the engine. Several of us were also engaged in battering out the spikes preparatory to lifting another rail. As we expected to spend ten or fifteen minutes in burning the large bridge which spanned the Oostenaula River, a little distance from us, Andrews thought it better that we should have a rail up in order to guard against the possibility of the train we had just passed being turned back after us in time to interrupt our work. It might have been better, as we were tempted to think afterwards, if we had begun on the bridge directly; but it was absolutely necessary to cut the wire, and the lifting of the rail would not take an additional minute.

The engine was inspected, and found to be still in perfect condition, though both wood and water were running low; the wire was severed; and eight of us had just taken hold of the loose end of a rail, out of which the spikes had been battered, and were trying to pull the other end loose also. But it was too firmly fixed, and we were about to release it, and wait the taking out of a few more spikes, when, away in the distance, we heard the whistle of an engine in pursuit! The effect was magical. With one convulsive effort the rail was broken asunder, and the whole party pitched in a heap over the low embankment. No one was hurt, and we were on our feet in a moment.

It did not require many moments to realize the situation. Our enemies were upon us at last! Their train was in plain sight. We could even see that they were well armed. There seemed to be no resource but flight.

A train was bearing down upon us at full speed. "Shall we stand and fight? Shall we attack them now?" were questions eagerly asked.

But Andrews still hesitated to depart from the course pursued so far. We had the rail broken which would arrest the enemy, and probably give us time to fire the bridge ahead. Then all might yet be well— that is if the stations ahead were not warned, and the track obstructed before us. Should that prove the case, then to stand and sell our lives as dearly as possible, or, abandoning our engine, to fly on foot across the country, were all the alternatives. The crisis of our fate drew near, and our hardest and sharpest work lay just ahead.

Influenced by such considerations, which were then mainly confined to his own mind, Andrews, without a moment's hesitation, gave the signal, which was as quickly obeyed, for mounting the train. The engineer threw the valve wide open, and, with a spring that threw us from our feet, the noble steed was once more careering forward. To his companions on the locomotive Andrews said, quietly, as he ever spoke in times of deepest excitement, "Push her, boys; let her do her best. We must lose no time in getting to the bridge above."

Some of the engine oil was thrown into the furnace, and the already fiery pace sensibly quickened. The problem seemed perfectly simple. If we could reach the bridge, and get it well on fire in less time than our enemies could piece out the broken rail, we had still a chance of life and success. If not, more desperate means became necessary. The speed of the engine might save us a precious half-minute, and on such a narrow margin everything turned.

Nobly did our good old locomotive respond to the call! Rocking, whirling, bounding—it seemed a marvel that some of the box-cars were not hurled from the track. Inside these cars all was action. Though we could scarcely keep one position a moment, idleness could not now be indulged. We knew that the time for concealment had passed, and we wrought with flying fingers in preparation for our incendiary work.

The forward end of our box-car, and both ends of the others, were knocked out by employing one of the heavy cross-ties as a battering-ram, and the greater part of the sides were loosened in the same manner, and torn into fragments for kindling. This destruction of barriers also opened a way of communication with the engine. Andrews approved what we had done, and told us frankly that our lives probably depended on the number of seconds we consumed in getting the bridge on fire.

Just then an exclamation of wonder and dismay from our keen-sighted fireman, Alfred Wilson, drew attention. He declared positively that he saw the smoke of the pursuing engine still following us! It

was scarcely credible, but he was so positive, and it was so important to know the truth, that our speed was slackened to ascertain. In
a moment a whistle, clear and unmistakable, rang out from beyond a
curve we had just passed. All doubt was at an end; but our surprise and
consternation were as great as when the train was first discovered in
pursuit. There had been no time to lay again the rail we had taken up,
and the broken half of which we still had with us. It seemed a miracle
wrought against us.

But Andrews' resources were not yet exhausted. He ordered
another effort, which might yet give us time to fire the bridge ahead,
that he was most unwilling to pass without destroying. The locomotive was reversed, and our kindling-wood, with most of the ties,
carried forward, and the moment we began to move backward the
hindmost car was uncoupled. The pursuing locomotive was then in
fearful proximity. We could see that it was running backward, and that
a number of men were crowded on it. Almost at the same moment its
machinery was reversed and ours turned forward. As we left them at
lightning speed we could just see that their velocity was well checked
before they touched our abandoned car.

But this was not yet sufficient. As we came to the next slight up-
grade the same manœuvre was repeated, and our second car flung
back at the enemy in like manner. The time lost in doing this brought
them again near us, and we saw that they were pushing our first car
before them.

Fuller saw the car we dropped, and by promptly having his engine
reversed, reduced the collision to merely a smart shock. It was dex-
trously coupled fast and driven forward at full speed. The second car
we dropped was treated in the same manner, and the enemy's speed
was scarcely diminished. The time lost in dropping the cars was about
as long as that lost in coupling to them.

Thus in the short space between Calhoun and the Oostenaula River three hindrances or perils, the greatness of which will be best appreciated by railroad men, were overcome by the skill and daring of Fuller's band, and in spite of them they attained a rate of running on this crooked and irregular road which would have been most remarkable on a perfectly smooth and unobstructed track.

Now the Oostenaula bridge was in sight, and we slackened speed for a desperate attempt to burn it. But before we could come to a full stop the pursuer was close upon us, and very reluctantly we steamed over the bridge and continued our flight. The prospect was rapidly darkening before us. It was certain that one of the trains we had met at Adairsville or Calhoun was turned back after us and driven with the utmost determination.

Of all conjectures to account for this pursuit, that of a telegram by the way of Richmond was most probable and most portentous. If this was really the case, our fate was sealed.

With a relentless pursuer hanging upon our heels, and the towns ahead warned and ready to dispute our passage, human bravery and foresight would avail nothing. I have no doubt the mind of Andrews was weighed down and perplexed by the uncertainty of our situation. Could we have known even as much of the number and plans of our foes as they knew of ours—above all, could we have known whether the road was open before us—the problem would have been simpler. Yet we had but two hopes: to wreck the train behind us, a task of no small difficulty now they were on their guard; or, failing in this, to distance them in running far enough to lift some rails or burn one of the bridges still ahead. If only one bridge could be burned, it would stop the pursuit for the time and leave us free to encounter the opposition before us.

Accordingly the jaded "General" was spurred to full speed. The load was now lighter, and as much of the kindling as we thought it prudent to spare was used in putting the furnace into a fiercer blaze.

Mile after mile the terrible chase continued. Station after station was passed without the least lessening of speed. But swift running alone could not save us.

The pursuing train was heard as expected. Before our foes came near enough to reveal our character everything was arranged, and taking the left-hand road, that which led directly to Chattanooga, we again darted forward. This was, however, a decisive point in the race. When we thus passed Dalton without having destroyed our pursuers, we knew that all hope of passing through Chattanooga with our engine must be abandoned.

Our original hope had been to get so far ahead of all pursuit as to pass Chattanooga before the pursuers had reached Dalton. Then the junction of roads at the latter point would not have been an embarrassment to us, as will be made clear by a reference to the map.

The Confederate whistle sounded. There was no time for reflection now.

One object only could now be attained by clinging longer to the train, the speedy abandonment of which was inevitable. Andrews wished to shorten the distance to our own lines as much as possible, so that the slender chance of escaping through the woods and mountains might be increased. It was far easier to travel on the engine than to run or skulk through the country on foot. It was better to continue this mode of locomotion as long as possible, or until we were carried as near Chattanooga as it was prudent to venture.

Andrews had always kept with him from the time we first met him at the midnight consultation a mysterious and well-filled pair of saddle-bags. These, of which he had been very careful, and which were supposed to contain important and compromising documents, were now added to the fire. It was a signal, if any were needed, that the time had now come to prepare for the worst. Andrews and three others—Brown, Knight, and Alfred Wilson—were now on the engine, and the remaining sixteen were huddled together on the tender.

But another decision was arrived at on the engine against which some of us on the tender would have protested with all our energy had the opportunity been offered. Alfred Wilson, whose opinion was directly opposite to that of George D. Wilson and the writer, says—

"A few minutes before we came to the final halt, Andrews, Brown, Knight, and myself hastily discussed as to the best thing to be done, and it was concluded that the best course was to separate and scatter in all directions.

"Andrews now told us all that it was 'every man for himself'; that we must scatter and do the best we could to escape to the Federal lines."

This, then, was the formal dissolution of the expedition by the order of its leader. When we were brought together again under widely different circumstances, we were simply a collection of soldiers, and while we respected the judgment and advice of Andrews, we no longer considered that we owed him military obedience.

A few minutes before we came to the final halt, Andrews, Brown, Knight, and myself hastily discussed as to the best thing to be done, and it was concluded that the best course was to separate and scatter in all directions.

Editor's note: Eight of the raiders, including Andrews, would be captured, tried, and executed as spies. The others escaped to the North and eventual safety. Six would become the first in history to be awarded the Medal of Honor.

8

CUSTER'S LAST BATTLE

FRANCES FULLER VICTOR

General Terry left Fort Abraham Lincoln on the Missouri River, May 17th, 1876, with his division, consisting of the 7th Cavalry under Lieut. Col. George A. Custer, three companies of infantry, a battery of Gatling guns, and 45 enlisted scouts. His whole force, exclusive of the wagon-train drivers, numbered about 1,000 men. His march was westerly, over the route taken by the Stanley expedition in 1873.

On the 11th of June, Terry reached the south bank of the Yellowstone at the mouth of Powder River, where by appointment he met steamboats, and established his supply camp. A scouting party of six companies of the 7th Cavalry under Major M. A. Reno was sent out June 10th, which ascended Powder River to its forks, crossed westerly to Tongue River and beyond, and discovered, near Rosebud River, a heavy Indian trail about ten days old leading westward toward Little Big Horn River. After following this trail a short distance Reno returned to the Yellowstone and rejoined his regiments, which then marched, accompanied by steamboats, to the mouth of Rosebud River where it encamped June 21st. Communication by steamboats and scouts had previously been opened with Col. John Gibbon, whose column was at this time encamped on the north side of the Yellowstone, near by.

Col. Gibbon of the 7th Infantry had left Fort Ellis in Montana about the middle of May, with a force consisting of six companies of his regiment, and four companies of the 2d Cavalry under Major J. S. Brisbin. He had marched eastward down the north bank of the Yellowstone to the mouth of the Rosebud, where he encamped about June 1st.

Gen. Terry now consulted with Gibbon and Custer, and decided upon a plan for attacking the Indians who were believed to be assembled in large numbers near Big Horn River. Custer with his regiment was to ascend the valley of the Rosebud, and then turn towards Little Big Horn River, keeping well to the south. Gibbon's troops were to cross the Yellowstone at the mouth of Big Horn River, and march up the Big Horn to its junction with the Little Big Horn, to co-operate with Custer. It was hoped that the Indians would thus be brought between the two forces so that their escape would be impossible.

Col. Gibbon's column was immediately put in motion for the mouth of the Big Horn. On the next day, June 22d, at noon, Custer announced himself ready to start, and drew out his regiment. It consisted of 12 companies, numbering 28 officers and 747 soldiers. There were also a strong detachment of scouts and guides, several civilians, and a supply train of 185 pack mules. Gen. Terry reviewed the column in the presence of Gibbon and Brisbon and it was pronounced in splendid condition. "The officers clustered around Terry for a final shake of the hand, the last good-bye was said, and in the best of spirits, filled with high hopes, they galloped away—many of them to their death."

Gen. Terry's orders to Custer were as follows:

Camp at the mouth of Rosebud River,
June 22d, 1876.
Lieut. Col. Custer, 7th Cavalry.

Colonel: The Brigadier General Commanding directs that as soon as your regiment can be made ready for the march, you proceed up the Rosebud in pursuit of the Indians whose trail was discovered by Major Reno a few days ago. It is, of course, impossible to give any definite instructions in regard to this movement, and, were it not impossible to do so, the Department Commander places too much confidence in your zeal, energy, and ability to wish to impose upon you precise orders which might hamper your action when nearly in contact with the enemy. He will, however, indicate to you his own views of what your action should be, and he desires that you should conform to them unless you shall see sufficient reason for departing from them.

He thinks that you should proceed up the Rosebud until you ascertain definitely the direction in which the trail above spoken of leads. Should it be found (as it appears to be almost certain that it will be found) to turn towards the Little Big Horn, he thinks that you should still proceed southward perhaps as far as the head waters of the Tongue, and then turn toward the Little Big Horn, feeling constantly, however, to your left, so as to preclude the possibility of the escape of the Indians to the south or south-east by passing around your left flank.

The column of Col. Gibbon is now in motion for the mouth of the Big Horn. As soon as it reaches that point it will cross the

Yellowstone, and move up at least as far as the forks of the Big and Little Big Horn.

Of course its future movements must be controlled by circumstances as they arise; but it is hoped that the Indians, if up on the Little Big Horn, may be so nearly inclosed by the two columns that their escape will be impossible. The Department Commander desires that on your way up the Rosebud you should thoroughly examine the upper part of Tulloch's Creek, and that you should endeavor to send a scout through to Col. Gibbon's column with information of the result of your examination. The lower part of this creek will be examined by a detachment from Col. Gibbon's command.

The supply steamer will be pushed up the Big Horn as far as the forks of the river are found to be navigable for that space, and the Department Commander, who will accompany the column of Col. Gibbon, desires you to report to him there not later than the expiration of the time for which your troops are rationed, unless in the meantime you receive further orders.

Respectfully, &c.,
E. W. Smith, Captain 18th Infantry,
Acting Assistant Adjutant General.

After proceeding southerly up the Rosebud for about seventy miles, Custer, at 11 p.m. on the night of the 24th, turned westerly towards Little Big Horn River. The next morning while crossing the elevated land between the two rivers, a large Indian village was discovered about fifteen miles distant, just across Little Big Horn River. Custer with characteristic promptness decided to attack the village at once.

One company was escorting the train at the rear. The balance of the force was divided into three columns. The trail they were on led down to the stream at a point some distance south of the village. Major Reno, with three companies under Capt. T. H. French, Capt. Myles Moylan, and Lieut. Donald McIntosh, was ordered to follow the trail, cross the stream, and charge down its north bank. Capt. F. W. Benteen, with his own company and two others under Capt. T. B. Weir and Lieut. E. S. Godfrey, was sent to make a detour to the south of Reno. The other five companies of the regiment, under the immediate command of Custer, formed the right of the little army.

On reaching the river, Reno crossed it as ordered, and Custer with his five companies turned northerly into a ravine running behind the bluffs on the east side of the stream.

The supply steamer *Far West* with Gen. Terry and Col. Gibbon on board, which steamed up the Yellowstone on the evening of June 23d, overtook Gibbon's troops near the mouth of the Big Horn early on the morning of the 24th; and by 4 o'clock P.M. of the same day, the entire command with the animals and supplies had been ferried over to the south side of the Yellowstone. An hour later the column marched out to and across Tulloch's Creek, and then encamped for the night.

At 5 o'clock on the morning of the 25th, (Sunday) the column was again in motion; and after marching 22 miles over a country so rugged as to task the endurance of the men to the utmost, the infantry halted for the night. Gen. Terry, however, with the cavalry and the battery pushed on 14 miles further in hopes of opening communication with Custer, and camped at midnight near the mouth of the Little Big Horn.

Scouts sent out from Terry's camp early on the morning of the 26th discovered three Indians, who proved to be Crows who had accompanied Custer's regiment. They reported that a battle had been fought and that the Indians were killing white men in great numbers. Their story was not fully credited, as it was not expected that a conflict would occur so soon, or believed that serious disaster could have overtaken so large a force.

The infantry, which had broken camp very early, now came up, and the whole column crossed the Little Big Horn and moved up its western valley. It was soon reported that a dense heavy smoke was resting over the southern horizon far ahead, and in a short time it became visible to all. This was hailed as a sign that Custer had met the Indians, defeated them, and burned their village. The weary foot soldiers were elated and freshened by the sight, and pressed on with increased spirit and speed.

Custer's position was believed to be not far ahead, and efforts were repeatedly made during the afternoon to open communication with him; but the scouts who attempted to go through were met and driven back by hostile Indians who were hovering in the front. As evening came on, their numbers increased and large parties could be seen on the bluffs hurrying from place to place and watching every movement of the advancing soldiers.

At 8:40 in the evening the infantry had marched that day about 30 miles. The forks of the Big Horn, the place where Terry had requested Custer to report to him, were many miles behind and the expected messenger from Custer had not arrived. Daylight was fading, the men were fatigued, and the column was therefore halted for the night. The animals were picketed, guards were set, and the weary men, wrapped in their blankets and with their weapons beside them, were soon asleep on the ground.

Early on the morning of the 27th, the march up the Little Big Horn was resumed. The smoke cloud was still visible and apparently but a short distance ahead. Soon a dense grove of trees was reached and passed through cautiously, and then the head of the column entered a beautiful level meadow about a mile in width, extending along the west side of the stream and overshadowed east and west by high bluffs.

It soon became apparent that this meadow had recently been the site of an immense Indian village, and the great number of temporary brushwood and willow huts indicated that many Indians beside the usual inhabitants had rendezvoused there. It was also evident that it had been hastily deserted. Hundreds of lodge-poles, with finely-dressed buffalo-robes and other hides, dried meat, stores, axes, utensils, and Indian trinkets were left behind; and in two tepees or lodges still standing, were the bodies of nine Indians who had gone to the "happy hunting-grounds."

Every step of the march now revealed some evidence that a conflict had taken place not far away. The dead bodies of Indian horses were seen, and cavalry equipments and weapons, bullet-pierced clothing, and blood-stained gloves were picked up; and at last the bodies of soldiers and their horses gave positive proof that a disastrous battle had taken place. The Crow Indians had told the truth.

The head of the column was now met by a breathless scout, who came running up with the intelligence that Major Reno with a body of troops was intrenched on a bluff further on, awaiting relief. The soldiers pushed ahead in the direction pointed out, and soon came in sight of men and horses intrenched on top of a hill on the opposite or east side of the river. Terry and Gibbon immediately forded the stream and rode toward the group. As they approached the top of the hill, they were welcomed by hearty cheers from a swarm of soldiers who came out of their intrenchments to meet their deliverers. The scene was a touching one. Stout-hearted soldiers who had kept bravely up during the hours of conflict and danger now cried like children, and the pale faces of the wounded lighted up as hope revived within them.

The story of the relieved men briefly told was as follows: After separating from Custer about noon, June 25th, Reno proceeded to the river, forded it, and charged down its west bank toward the village, meeting at first with but little resistance. Soon however he was attacked by such numbers as to be obliged to dismount his men, shelter his horses in a strip of woods, and fight on foot. Finding that they would soon be surrounded and defeated, he again mounted his men, and charging upon such of the enemy as obstructed his way, retreated across the river, and reached the top of a bluff followed closely by Indians.

Just then Benteen, returning from his detour southward, discovered Reno's perilous position, drove back the Indians, and joined him on the hill. Shortly afterward, the company which was escorting the mule train also joined Reno. The seven companies thus brought together had been subsequently assailed by Indians; many of the men had been killed and wounded, and it was only by obstinate resistance that they had been enabled to defend themselves in an entrenched position. The enemy had retired on the evening of the 26th.

After congratulations to Reno and his brave men for their successful defence, enquiries were made respecting Custer, but no one could tell where he was. Neither he or any of his men had been seen since the fight commenced, and the musketry heard from the direction he took had ceased on the afternoon of the 25th. It was supposed by Reno and Benteen that he had been repulsed, and retreated northerly towards Terry's troops.

A search for Custer and his men was immediately began, and it revealed a scene calculated to appall the stoutest heart. Although neither Custer or any of that part of his regiment which he led to combat were found alive to tell the tale, an examination of their trail and the scene of conflict enabled their comrades to form some idea of the engagement in which they perished.

General Custer's trail, from the place where he left Reno's and turned northward, passed along and in the rear of the crest of hills on the east bank of the stream for nearly three miles, and then led, through an opening in the bluff, down to the river. Here Custer had evidently attempted to cross over to attack the village. The trail then turned back on itself, as if Custer had been repulsed and obliged to retreat, and branched to the northward, as if he had been prevented from returning southerly by the way he came, or had determined to retreat in the direction from which Terry's troops were advancing.

Several theories as to the subsequent movements of the troops have been entertained by persons who visited the grounds. One is, that the soldiers in retreating took advantage of two ravines; that two companies under Capt. T. W. Custer and Lieut. A. E. Smith, were led by Gen. Custer up the ravine nearest the river, while the upper ravine furnished a line of retreat for the three companies of Capt. G. W. Yates, Capt. M. W. Keogh, and Lieut. James Calhoun.

At the head of this upper ravine, a mile from the river, a stand had been made by Calhoun's company; the skirmish lines were marked by rows of the slain with heaps of empty cartridge shells before them, and Lieuts. Calhoun and Crittenden lay dead just behind the files. Further on, Capt. Keogh had fallen surrounded by his men; and still further on, upon a hill, Capt. Yates' company took its final stand. Here, according to this theory, Yates was joined by what remained of the other two companies, who had been furiously assailed in the lower ravine; and here Gen. Custer and the last survivors of the five companies met their death, fighting bravely to the end.

Another theory of the engagement is, that Custer attempted to retreat up the lower ravine in columns of companies; that the companies of Custer and Smith being first in the advance and last in the retreat, fell first in the slaughter which followed the retrograde movement; that Yates' company took the position on the hill, and perished there with Custer and other officers; and that the two other companies, Keogh's and Calhoun's, perished while fighting their way back towards Reno—a few reaching the place where Custer first struck the high banks of the river.

Still another theory is, that the main line of retreat was by the upper ravine; that Calhoun's company was thrown across to check the Indians, and was the first annihilated. That the two companies of Capt. Custer and Lieut. Smith retreated from the place where Gen. Custer was killed into the lower ravine, and were the last survivors of the conflict.

Near the highest point of the hill lay the body of General Custer, and near by were those of his brother Captain Custer, Lieut. Smith, Capt. Yates, Lieut. W. V. Riley of Yates' company, and Lieut. W. W. Cooke. Some distance away, close together, were found another brother of Gen. Custer—Boston Custer, a civilian, who had accompanied the expedition as forage master of the 7th Cavalry—and his nephew Armstrong Reed, a youth of nineteen, who was visiting the General at the time the expedition started, and accompanied it as a driver of the herd of cattle taken along. The wife of Lieut. Calhoun was a sister of the Custers and she here lost her husband, three brothers, and a nephew.

Other officers of Custer's battalion killed but not already mentioned, were Asst. Surgeon L. W. Lord, and Lieuts. H. M. Harrington, J. E. Porter, and J. G. Sturgis. The last named was a West Point graduate of 1875, and a son of General S. D. Sturgis, the Colonel of the 7th

Cavalry, who had been detained by other duties when his regiment started on this expedition.

The bodies of the slain were rifled of valuables and all were mutilated excepting Gen. Custer, and Mark Kellogg—a correspondent of the *New York Herald*. Gen. Custer was clad in a buckskin suit; and a Canadian—Mr. Macdonald—was subsequently informed by Indians who were in the fight, that for this reason he was not mangled, as they took him to be some brave hunter accidentally with the troops. Others believe that Custer was passed by from respect for the heroism of one whom the Indians had learned to fear and admire.

The dead were buried June 28th, where they fell, Major Reno and the survivors of his regiment performing the last sad rites over their comrades.

A retreat to the mouth of Big Horn River was now ordered and successfully effected, the wounded being comfortably transported on mule litters to the mouth of the Little Big Horn, where they were placed on a steamboat and taken to Fort Lincoln. Gibbon's Cavalry followed the Indians for about ten miles, and ascertained that they had moved to the south and west by several trails. A good deal of property had been thrown away by them to lighten their march, and was found scattered about. Many of their dead were also discovered secreted in ravines a long distance from the battle field.

At the boat was found one of Custer's scouts, who had been in the fight—a Crow named Curley; his story was as follows:

Custer kept down the river on the north bank four miles, after Reno had crossed to the south side above. He thought Reno would drive down the valley, to attack the village at the upper end, while he (Custer) would go in at the lower end. Custer had to go further down the river and further away from Reno than he wished on account of the steep bank along the north side; but at last he found a ford and dashed for it. The Indians met him and poured in a heavy fire from across the narrow river. Custer dismounted to fight on foot, but could not get his skirmishers over the stream.

Meantime hundreds of Indians, on foot and on ponies, poured over the river, which was only about three feet deep, and filled the ravine on each side of Custer's men. Custer then fell back to some high ground behind him and seized the ravines in his immediate vicinity. The Indians completely surrounded Custer and poured in a terrible fire on all sides. They charged Custer on foot in vast numbers, but were again and again driven back.

The fight began about 2 o'clock, and lasted almost until the sun went down over the hills. The men fought desperately, and after the ammunition in their belts was exhausted went to their saddlebags, got more and continued the fight. Custer lived until nearly all of his men had been killed or wounded, and went about encouraging his soldiers to fight on. He got a shot in the left side and sat down, with his pistol in his hand. Another shot struck Custer in the breast, and he fell over. The last officer killed was a man who rode a white horse—believed to be Lieut. Cooke, as Cooke and Calhoun were the only officers who rode white horses.

When he saw Custer hopelessly surrounded he watched his opportunity, got a Sioux blanket, put it on, and worked up a ravine, and when the Sioux charged, he got among them and they did not know him from one of their own men. There were some mounted Sioux, and seeing one fall, he ran to him, mounted his pony, and galloped down as if going towards the white men, but went up a ravine and got away.

As he rode off he saw, when nearly a mile from the battle field, a dozen or more soldiers in a ravine, fighting with Sioux all around them. He thinks all were killed, as they were outnumbered five to one, and apparently dismounted. The battle was desperate in the extreme, and more Indians than white men must have been killed.

The following extract is from a letter written to Gen. Sheridan by Gen. Terry at his camp on the Big Horn, July 2d:

We calculated it would take Gibbon's command until the 26th to reach the mouth of the Little Big Horn, and that the wide sweep I had proposed Custer should make would require so much time that Gibbon would be able to co-operate with him in attacking any Indians that might be found on the stream. I asked Custer how long his marches would be. He said they would be at the rate of about 30 miles a day.

Measurements were made and calculations based on that rate of progress. I talked with him about his strength, and at one time suggested that perhaps it would be well for me to take Gibbon's cavalry and go with him. To the latter suggestion he replied: that, without reference to the command, he would prefer his own regiment alone. As a homogeneous body, as much could be done with it as with the two combined. He expressed the utmost confidence that he had all the force that he could need, and I shared his confidence.

The plan adopted was the only one which promised to bring the infantry into action, and I desired to make sure of things by getting up every available man. I offered Custer the battery of Gatling guns, but he declined it, saying that it might embarrass him, and that he was strong enough without it. The movements proposed by General Gibbon's column were carried out to the letter, and had the attack been deferred until it was up, I cannot doubt that we should have been successful.

A gentleman who accompanied Gen. Custer on the Yellowstone and Black Hills expeditions, contributed to the *New York Tribune* the following:

Gen. Custer was a born cavalryman. He was never more in his element than when mounted on Dandy, his favorite horse, and riding at the head of his regiment. He once said to me, "I would rather be a private in the cavalry than a line officer in the infantry." He was the personification of bravery and dash. If he had only added discretion to his valor he would have been a perfect soldier. His impetuosity very often ran away with his judgment. He was impatient of control. He liked to act independently of others, and take all the risk and all the glory to himself. He frequently got himself into trouble by assuming more authority than really belonged to his rank.

It was on the Yellowstone expedition where he came into collision with Gen. Stanley, his superior officer, and was placed under arrest and compelled to ride at the rear of his column for two or three days, until Gen. Rosser, who fought against Custer in the Shenandoah Valley during the war but was then acting as engineer of the Northern Pacific Railroad, succeeded in effecting a reconciliation.

Custer and Stanley afterward got on very well, and perhaps the quarrel would never have occurred if the two generals had been left alone to themselves without the intervention of camp gossips, who sought to foster the traditional jealousy between infantry and cavalry. For Stanley was the soul of generosity, and Custer did not really mean to be arrogant; but from the time when he entered West Point to the day when he fell on the Big Horn, he was accustomed to take just as much liberty as he was entitled to.

For this reason, Custer worked most easily and effectively when under general orders, when not hampered by special instructions, or his success made dependent on anybody else. Gen. Terry understood his man when, in the order directing him to march up the Rosebud, he very liberally said: "The Department Commander places too much confidence in your zeal, energy, and ability to wish to impose upon you precise orders which might hamper your action when nearly in contact with the enemy." But Gen. Terry did not understand Custer if he thought he would wait for Gibbon's support before attacking an Indian camp. Undoubtedly he ought to have done this; but with his native impetuosity, his reckless daring, his confidence in his own regiment, which had never failed him, and his love of public approval, Custer could no more help charging this Indian camp, than he could help charging just so many buffaloes.

He had never learned to spell the word "defeat"; he knew nothing but success, and if he had met the Indians on the open plains, success would undoubtedly have been his; for no body of Indians could stand the charge of the 7th Cavalry when it swept over the Plains like a whirlwind. But in the Mauvaises Terres and the narrow valley of the Big Horn he did it at a fearful risk.

With all his bravery and self-reliance, his love of independent action, Custer was more dependent than most men on the kind approval of his fellow. He was even vain; he loved display in dress and in action. He would pay $40 for a pair of troop boots to wear on parade, and have everything else in keeping.

On the Yellowstone expedition he wore a bright red shirt, which made him the best mark for a rifle of any man in the regiment. I remonstrated with him for this reckless exposure, but found an appeal to his wife more effectual, and on the next campaign he wore a buckskin suit. He formerly wore his hair very long, letting it fall in a heavy mass upon his shoulders, but cut it off before going out on the Black Hills, producing quite a change in his appearance. But if vain and ambitious, Custer had none of those great vices which are so common and so distressing in the army. He never touched liquor in any form; he did not smoke, or chew, or gamble.

He could outride almost any man in his regiment, I believe, if it were put to a test. When he set out to reach a certain point at a certain time, you could be sure that he would be there if he killed every horse in the command. He was sometimes too severe in forcing marches, but he never seemed to get tired himself, and he never expected his men to be so.

In cutting our way through the forest of the Black Hills, I have often seen him take an ax and work as hard as any of the pioneers. He was never idle when he had a pretext for doing anything, whatever he did he did thoroughly. He would overshoot the mark, but never fall short. He fretted in garrison sometimes, because it was too inactive; but he found an outlet here for his energies in writing articles for the press.

He had a remarkable memory. He could recall in its proper order every detail of any action, no matter how remote, of which he was participant. He was rather verbose in writing, and had no gifts as a speaker; but his writings interested the masses from their close attention to details, and from his facility with the pen as with the sword in bringing a thing to a climax. As he was apt to overdo in action, so he was apt to exaggerate in statement, not from any willful disregard of the truth, but because he saw things bigger than they really were. He did not distort the truth; he magnified it.

He was a natural optimist. He took rose-colored views of everything, even of the miserable lands of the Northern Pacific Railroad. He had a historical memory, but not a historical mind. He was no philosopher; he could reel off facts from his mind better than he could analyze or mass them. He was not a student, or a deep thinker. He loved to take part in events rather than to brood over them. He was fond of fun, genial and pleasant in his manner; a loving and devoted husband. It was my privilege to spend two weeks in his family at one time, and I know how happy he was in his social relations.

The following rambling remarks are accredited to a general, who name is not given:

The truth about Custer is, that he was a pet soldier, who had risen not above his merit, but higher than men of equal merit. He fought with Phil Sheridan, and through the patronage of Sheridan he rose; but while Sheridan liked his valor and dash he never trusted his judgment. He was to Sheridan what Murat was to Napoleon. While Sheridan is always cool, Custer was always aflame. Rising to high command early in life, he lost the repose necessary to success in high command. . . .

Then Custer must rush into politics, and went swinging around the circle with Johnson. He wanted to be a statesman, and but for Sheridan's influence with Grant, the republicans would have thrown him; but you see we all liked Custer, and did not mind his little freaks in that way any more than we would have minded temper in a woman. Sheridan, to keep Custer in his place, kept him out on the Plains at work. He gave him a fine command—one of the best cavalry regiments in the service. The colonel, Sturgis, was allowed to bask in the sunshine in a large city, while Custer was the real commander. In this service Custer did well, and vindicated the partiality of Sheridan as well as the kind feelings of his friends. . . .

The old spirit which sent Custer swinging around the circle revived in him. He came East and took a prominent part in reforming the army. This made feeling, and drew upon Custer the anger of the inside forces of the administration.

Then he must write his war memoirs. Well, in these memoirs he began to write recklessly about the army. He took to praising McClellan as the greatest man of the war, and, coming as it did when the democrats began to look lively, it annoyed the administration. Grant grew so much annoyed that even Sheridan could do no good, and Custer was disgraced. Technically it was not a disgrace. All that Grant did was to put Terry, a general, over Custer, a lieutenant-colonel, who had his regiment all the same; but all things considered, it was a disgrace.

The following is from an article by Gen. A. B. Nettleton, published in the *Philadelphia Times*:

It must be remembered that in fighting with cavalry, which was Custer's forte, instantaneous quickness of eye—that is the lightning-like formation and execution of successive correct judgments on a rapidly-shifting situation—is the first thing, and the second is the power of inspiring the troopers with that impetuous yet intelligent ardor with which a mounted brigade becomes a thunderbolt, and without which it remains a useless mass of horses and riders.

These qualities Gen. Custer seemed to me to manifest, throughout the hard fighting of the last year of the war, to a degree that was simply astounding, and in a manner that marked him as one of the few really great cavalry commanders developed by the wars of the present century. Of fear, in the sense of dread of death or of bodily harm, he was absolutely destitute, yet his love of life and family and home was keen and constant, leaving no room in his nature for desperation, recklessness, or conscious rashness.

In handling his division under Sheridan's general oversight, he seemed to act always on the belief that in campaigning with cavalry, when a certain work must be done, audacity is the truest caution. In action, when all was going well and success was only a question of time or of steady "pounding," Gen. Custer did not unnecessarily expose himself, but until the tide of battle had been turned in the right direction, and especially when disaster threatened, the foremost point in our division's line was almost invariably marked by the presence of Custer, his waving division tri-color and his plucky staff.

A major-general of wide and splendid fame at twenty-five, and now slain at thirty-six, the gallant Custer had already lived long if life be measured by illustrious deeds.

The following is from a sketch of Gen. Custer published in the *Army and Navy Journal*:

Custer was passionately addicted to active and exciting sports as the turf and hunting. He was a splendid horseman and a lover of the horse; he attended many American race-meetings and ran his own horses several times in the West. His greyhounds and staghounds went with him at the head of his regiment, to be let slip at antelope or buffalo. With rifle or shotgun he was equally expert, and had killed his grizzly bear in the most approved fashion. . . .

Bold to rashness; feverish in camp, but cool in action; with the personal vanity of a carpet knight, and the endurance and insensibility to fatigue of the hardiest and boldest rough rider; a prince of scouts; a chief of guides, threading a trackless prairie with unerring eye of a native and the precision of the needle to the star; by no means a martinet, his men were led by the golden chain of love, admiration and confidence.

He had the proverbial assurance of a hussar, but his personal appearance varied with occasion. During the war he was "Custer of the golden locks, his broad sombrero turned up from his hard-bronzed face, the ends of his crimson cravat floating over his shoulder, gold galore spangling his jacket sleeves, a pistol in his boot, jangling spurs on his heels, and a ponderous claymore swinging at his side."

And long after, when he roamed a great Indian fighter on the Plains, the portrait was only slightly changed. The cavalry jacket was exchanged for the full suit of buckskin, beautifully embroidered by Indian maidens; across his saddle rested a modern sporting rifle, and at his horse's feet demurely walked hounds of unmixed breed. Again, within a few months, he appears in private society as an honored guest; scrupulously avoiding anything like display, but in a quiet conventional suit of blue, with the "golden locks" closely shorn, and the bronzed face pale from recent indisposition, he moves almost unnoticed in the throng.

The faithful correspondent who perished with Gen. Custer on the Little Big Horn portrayed him thus:

A man of strong impulses, of great hearted friendships and bitter enmities; of quick, nervous temperament, undaunted courage, will, and determination; a man possessing electric mental capacity, and of iron frame and constitution; a brave, faithful, gallant soldier, who has warm friends and bitter enemies; the hardest rider, the greatest pusher; with the most untiring vigilance overcoming seeming impossibilities, and with an ambition to succeed in all things he undertakes; a man to do right, as he construes right, in every case; one respected and beloved by his followers, who would freely follow him into the "jaws of hell."

Gen. Custer's last battle "will stand in history as one of the most heroic engagements ever fought, and his name will be respected so long as chivalry is applauded and civilization battles against barbarism."

9

THE BATTLE OF LAS GUASIMAS WITH THE ROUGH RIDERS

THEODORE ROOSEVELT

On landing we spent some active hours in marching our men a quarter of a mile or so inland, as boat-load by boat-load they disembarked. Meanwhile one of the men, Knoblauch, a New Yorker, who was a great athlete and a champion swimmer, by diving in the surf off the dock, recovered most of the rifles which had been lost when the boat-load of cavalry capsized. The country would have offered very great difficulties to an attacking force had there been resistance. It was little but a mass of rugged and precipitous hills, covered for the most part by dense jungle. Five hundred resolute men could have prevented the disembarkation at very little cost to themselves.

There had been about that number of Spaniards at Daiquiri that morning, but they had fled even before the ships began shelling. In their place we found hundreds of Cuban insurgents, a crew of as utter tatterdemalions as human eyes ever looked on, armed with every kind of rifle in all stages of dilapidation. It was evident, at a glance, that they would be no use in serious fighting, but it was hoped that they might be of service in scouting. From a variety of causes, however, they turned out to be nearly useless, even for this purpose, so far as the Santiago campaign was concerned.

We were camped on a dusty, brush-covered flat, with jungle on one side, and on the other a shallow, fetid pool fringed with palm-trees. Huge land-crabs scuttled noisily through the underbrush, exciting much interest among the men. Camping was a simple matter, as each man carried all he had, and the officers had nothing. I took a light mackintosh and a tooth-brush. Fortunately, that night it did not rain; and from the palm-leaves we built shelters from the sun.

General Lawton, a tall, fine-looking man, had taken the advance. A thorough soldier, he at once established outposts and pushed reconnoitering parties ahead on the trails. He had as little baggage as the rest of us. Our own Brigade-Commander, General Young, had exactly the same impedimenta that I had, namely, a mackintosh and a tooth-brush.

Next morning we were hard at work trying to get the stuff unloaded from the ship, and succeeded in getting most of it ashore, but were utterly unable to get transportation for anything but a very small quantity. The great shortcoming throughout the campaign was the utterly inadequate transportation. If we had been allowed to take our mule-train, we could have kept the whole cavalry division supplied.

In the afternoon, word came to us to march. General Wheeler, a regular game-cock, was as anxious as Lawton to get first blood, and he was bent upon putting the cavalry division to the front as quickly as possible. Lawton's advance guard was in touch with the Spaniards, and there had been a skirmish between the latter and some Cubans, who were repulsed. General Wheeler made a reconnaissance in person, found out where the enemy was, and directed General Young to take our brigade and move forward so as to strike him next morning. He had the power to do this, as when General Shafter was afloat he had command ashore.

I had succeeded in finding Texas, my surviving horse, much the worse for his fortnight on the transport and his experience in getting off, but still able to carry me.

It was mid-afternoon and the tropic sun was beating fiercely down when Colonel Wood started our regiment—the First and Tenth Cavalry and some of the infantry regiments having already marched. Colonel Wood himself rode in advance, while I led my squadron, and Major Brodie followed with his. It was a hard march, the hilly jungle trail being so narrow that often we had to go in single file. We marched fast, for Wood was bound to get us ahead of the other regiments, so as to be sure of our place in the body that struck the enemy next morning. If it had not been for his energy in pushing forward, we should certainly have missed the fight. As it was, we did not halt until we were at the extreme front.

The men were not in very good shape for marching, and moreover they were really horsemen, the majority being cowboys who had never done much walking. The heat was intense and their burdens very heavy. Yet there was very little straggling. Whenever we halted they instantly took off their packs and threw themselves on their backs. Then at the word to start they would spring into place again. The captains and lieutenants tramped along, encouraging the men by example and word.

A good part of the time I was by Captain Llewellen, and was greatly pleased to see the way in which he kept his men up to their work. He never pitied or coddled his troopers, but he always looked after them. He helped them whenever he could, and took rather more than his full share of hardship and danger, so that his men naturally followed him with entire devotion. Jack Greenway was under him as lieutenant, and to him the entire march was nothing but an enjoyable outing, the chance of fight on the morrow simply adding the needed spice of excitement.

It was long after nightfall when we tramped through the darkness into the squalid coast hamlet of Siboney. As usual when we made a night camp, we simply drew the men up in column of troops, and then let each man lie down where he was. Black thunder-clouds were gathering. Before they broke the fires were made and the men cooked their coffee and pork, some frying the hardtack with the pork. The officers, of course, fared just as the men did. Hardly had we finished eating when the rain came, a regular tropic downpour. We sat about, sheltering ourselves as best we could, for the hour or two it lasted; then the fires were relighted and we closed around them, the men taking off their wet things to dry them, so far as possible, by the blaze.

Wood had gone off to see General Young, as General Wheeler had instructed General Young to hit the Spaniards, who were about four miles away, as soon after daybreak as possible. Meanwhile, I strolled over to Captain Capron's troop. He and I, with his two lieutenants, Day and Thomas, stood around the fire, together with two or three non-commissioned officers and privates; among the latter were Sergeant Hamilton Fish and Trooper Elliot Cowdin, both of New York. Cowdin, together with two other troopers, Harry Thorpe and Munro Ferguson, had been on my Oyster Bay Polo Team some years before.

Hamilton Fish had already shown himself one of the best non-commissioned officers we had. A huge fellow, of enormous strength and endurance and dauntless courage, he took naturally to a soldier's life. He never complained and never shirked any duty of any kind, while his power over his men was great. So good a sergeant had he made that Captain Capron, keen to get the best men under him, took him when he left Tampa—for Fish's troop remained behind.

As we stood around the flickering blaze that night I caught myself admiring the splendid bodily vigor of Capron and Fish—the captain and the sergeant. Their frames seemed of steel, to withstand all fatigue; they were flushed with health; in their eyes shone high resolve and fiery desire. Two finer types of the fighting man, two better representatives of the American soldier, there were not in the whole army. Capron was going over his plans for the fight when we should meet the Spaniards on the morrow, Fish occasionally asking a question. They were both filled with eager longing to show their mettle, and both were rightly confident that if they lived they would win honorable renown and would rise high in their chosen profession. Within twelve hours they both were dead.

I had lain down when toward midnight Wood returned. He had gone over the whole plan with General Young. We were to start by sunrise toward Santiago, General Young taking four troops of the Tenth and four troops of the First up the road which led through the valley; while Colonel Wood was to lead our eight troops along a hill-trail to the left, which joined the valley road about four miles on, at a point where the road went over a spur of the mountain chain and from thence went downhill toward Santiago. The Spaniards had their lines at the junction of the road and the trail.

Before describing our part in the fight, it is necessary to say a word about General Young's share, for, of course, the whole fight was under his direction, and the fight on the right wing under his immediate supervision. General Young had obtained from General Castillo, the commander of the Cuban forces, a full description of the country in front. General Castillo promised Young the aid of eight hundred Cubans, if he made a reconnaissance in force to find out exactly what the Spanish strength was. This promised Cuban aid did not, however, materialize, the Cubans, who had been beaten back by the Spaniards the day before, not appearing on the firing-line until the fight was over.

General Young had in his immediate command a squadron of the First Regular Cavalry, two hundred and forty-four strong, under the command of Major Bell, and a squadron of the Tenth Regular Cavalry, two hundred and twenty strong, under the command of Major Norvell. He also had two Hotchkiss mountain guns, under Captain Watson of the Tenth.

He started at a quarter before six in the morning, accompanied by Captain A. L. Mills, as aide. It was at half-past seven that Captain Mills, with a patrol of two men in advance, discovered the Spaniards as they lay across where the two roads came together, some of them in pits, others simply lying in the heavy jungle, while on their extreme right they occupied a big ranch.

Where General Young struck them they held a high ridge a little to the left of his front, this ridge being separated by a deep ravine from the hill-trail still farther to the left, down which the Rough Riders were advancing. That is, their forces occupied a range of high hills in the form of an obtuse angle, the salient being toward the space between the American forces, while there were advance parties along both roads. There were stone breastworks flanked by blockhouses on that part of the ridge where the two trails came together. The place was called Las Guasimas, from trees of that name in the neighborhood.

General Young, who was riding a mule, carefully examined the Spanish position in person. He ordered the canteens of the troops to be filled, placed the Hotchkiss battery in concealment about nine hundred yards from the Spanish lines, and then deployed the regulars in support, having sent a Cuban guide to try to find Colonel Wood and warn him. He did not attack immediately, because he knew that Colonel Wood, having a more difficult route, would require a longer time to reach the position. During the delay General Wheeler arrived; he had been up since long before dawn, to see that everything went well. Young informed him of the dispositions and plan of attack he made. General Wheeler approved of them, and with excellent judgment left General Young a free hand to fight his battle.

So, about eight o'clock Young began the fight with his Hotchkiss guns, he himself being up on the firing-line. No sooner had the Hotchkiss one-pounders opened than the Spaniards opened fire in return, most of the time firing by volleys executed in perfect time, almost as on parade. They had a couple of light guns, which our people thought were quick firers. The denseness of the jungle, and the fact that they used absolutely smokeless powder, made it exceedingly difficult to place exactly where they were, and almost immediately Young, who always liked to get as close as possible to his enemy, began to push his troops forward. They were deployed on both sides of the road in such thick jungle that it was only here and there that they could possibly see ahead, and some confusion, of course, ensued, the support gradually getting mixed with the advance.

Captain Beck took A Troop of the Tenth in on the left, next Captain Galbraith's troop of the First; two other troops of the Tenth were on the extreme right. Through the jungle ran wire fences here and there, and as the troops got to the ridge they encountered precipitous heights. They were led most gallantly, as American regular officers always lead their men; and the men followed their leaders with the splendid courage always shown by the American regular soldier. There was not a single straggler among them, and in not one instance was an attempt made by any trooper to fall out in order to assist the wounded or carry back the dead, while so cool were they and so perfect their fire discipline, that in the entire engagement the expenditure of ammunition was not over ten rounds per man.

Major Bell, who commanded the squadron, had his leg broken by a shot as he was leading his men. Captain Wainwright succeeded to the command of the squadron. Captain Knox was shot in the abdomen. He continued for some time giving orders to his troops, and refused to allow a man in the firing-line to assist him to the rear. His First Lieutenant, Byram, was himself shot, but continued to lead his men until the wound and the heat overcame him and he fell in a faint.

The advance was pushed forward under General Young's eye with the utmost energy, until the enemy's voices could be heard in the entrenchments. The Spaniards kept up a very heavy firing, but the regulars would not be denied, and as they climbed the ridges the Spaniards broke and fled.

Meanwhile, at six o'clock, the Rough Riders began their advance. We first had to climb a very steep hill. Many of the men, foot-sore and weary from their march of the preceding day, found the pace up this hill too hard, and either dropped their bundles or fell out of line, with the result that we went into action with less than five hundred men—as, in addition to the stragglers, a detachment had been left to guard the baggage on shore. At the time I was rather inclined to grumble to myself about Wood setting so fast a pace, but when the fight began I realized that it had been absolutely necessary, as otherwise we should have arrived late and the regulars would have had very hard work indeed.

Tiffany, by great exertions, had corralled a couple of mules and was using them to transport the Colt automatic guns in the rear of the regiment. The dynamite gun was not with us, as mules for it could not be obtained in time.

Captain Capron's troop was in the lead, it being chosen for the most responsible and dangerous position because of Capron's capacity. Four men, headed by Sergeant Hamilton Fish, went first; a support of twenty men followed some distance behind; and then came Capron and the rest of his troop, followed by Wood, with whom General Young had sent Lieutenants Smedburg and Rivers as aides. I rode close behind, at the head of the other three troops of my squadron, and then came Brodie at the head of his squadron.

The trail was so narrow that for the most part the men marched in single file, and it was bordered by dense, tangled jungle, through which a man could with difficulty force his way; so that to put out flankers was impossible, for they could not possibly have kept up with the march of the column. Every man had his canteen full. There was a Cuban guide at the head of the column, but he ran away as soon as the fighting began. There were also with us, at the head of the column, two men who did not run away, who, though non-combatants—newspaper correspondents—showed as much gallantry as any soldier in the field. They were Edward Marshall and Richard Harding Davis.

After reaching the top of the hill the walk was very pleasant. Now and then we came to glades or rounded hill-shoulders, whence we could look off for some distance. The tropical forest was very beautiful, and it was a delight to see the strange trees, the splendid royal palms and a tree which looked like a flat-topped acacia, and which was covered with a mass of brilliant scarlet flowers.

We heard many bird-notes, too, the cooing of doves and the call of a great brush cuckoo. Afterward we found that the Spanish guerrillas imitated these bird-calls, but the sounds we heard that morning, as we advanced through the tropic forest, were from birds, not guerrillas, until we came right up to the Spanish lines. It was very beautiful and very peaceful, and it seemed more as if we were off on some hunting excursion than as if we were about to go into a sharp and bloody little fight.

Of course, we accommodated our movements to those of the men in front. After marching for somewhat over an hour, we suddenly came to a halt, and immediately afterward Colonel Wood sent word down the line that the advance guard had come upon a Spanish outpost. Then the order was passed to fill the magazines, which was done.

The men were totally unconcerned, and I do not think they realized that any fighting was at hand; at any rate, I could hear the group nearest me discussing in low murmurs, not the Spaniards, but the conduct of a certain cow-puncher in quitting work on a ranch and starting a saloon in some New Mexican town. In another minute, however, Wood sent me orders to deploy three troops to the right of the trail, and to advance when we became engaged; while, at the same time, the other troops, under Major Brodie, were deployed to the left of the trail where the ground was more open than elsewhere—one troop being held in reserve in the centre, besides the reserves on each wing. Later all the reserves were put into the firing-line.

To the right the jungle was quite thick, and we had barely begun to deploy when a crash in front announced that the fight was on. It was evidently very hot, and L Troop had its hands full; so I hurried my men up abreast of them. So thick was the jungle that it was very difficult to keep together, especially when there was no time for delay, and while I got up Llewellen's troops and Kane's platoon of K Troop, the rest of K Troop under Captain Jenkins, which, with Bucky O'Neill's troop, made up the right wing, were behind, and it was some time before they got into the fight at all.

Meanwhile, I had gone forward with Llewellen, Greenway, Kane, and their troopers until we came out on a kind of shoulder, jutting over a ravine, which separated us from a great ridge on our right. It was on this ridge that the Spaniards had some of their entrenchments, and it was just beyond this ridge that the Valley Road led, up which the regulars were at that very time pushing their attack; but, of course, at the moment we knew nothing of this.

The effect of the smokeless powder was remarkable. The air seemed full of the rustling sound of the Mauser bullets, for the Spaniards knew the trails by which we were advancing, and opened heavily on our position. Moreover, as we advanced we were, of course, exposed, and they could see us and fire. But they themselves were entirely invisible. The jungle covered everything, and not the faintest trace of smoke was to be seen in any direction to indicate from whence the bullets came. It was some time before the men fired; Llewellen, Kane, and I anxiously studying the ground to see where our opponents were, and utterly unable to find out.

We could hear the faint reports of the Hotchkiss guns and the reply of two Spanish guns, and the Mauser bullets were singing through the trees over our heads, making a noise like the humming of telephone wires; but exactly where they came from we could not tell. The Spaniards were firing high and for the most part by volleys, and their shooting was not very good, which perhaps was not to be wondered at, as they were a long way off. Gradually, however, they began to get the range and occasionally one of our men would crumple up. In no case did the man make any outcry when hit, seeming to take it as a matter of course; at the outside, making only such a remark as: "Well, I got it that time."

With hardly an exception, there was no sign of flinching. I say with hardly an exception, for though I personally did not see an instance, and though all the men at the front behaved excellently, yet there were a very few men who lagged behind and drifted back to the trail over which we had come. The character of the fight put a premium upon such conduct, and afforded a very severe test for raw troops, because the jungle was so dense that as we advanced in open order, every man was, from time to time, left almost alone and away from the eyes of his officers. There was unlimited opportunity for dropping out without attracting notice, while it was peculiarly hard to be exposed to the fire of an unseen foe, and to see men dropping under it, and yet to be, for some time, unable to return it, and also to be entirely ignorant of what was going on in any other part of the field.

It was Richard Harding Davis who gave us our first opportunity to shoot back with effect. He was behaving precisely like my officers, being on the extreme front of the line, and taking every opportunity to study with his glasses the ground where we thought the Spaniards were. I had tried some volley firing at points where I rather doubtfully believed the Spaniards to be, but had stopped firing and was myself studying the jungle-covered mountain ahead with my glasses, when Davis suddenly said: "There they are, Colonel; look over there; I can see their hats near that glade," pointing across the valley to our right.

In a minute I, too, made out the hats, and then pointed them out to three or four of our best shots, giving them my estimate of the range. For a minute or two no result followed, and I kept raising the range, at the same time getting more men on the firing-line. Then, evidently, the shots told, for the Spaniards suddenly sprang out of the cover through which we had seen their hats and ran to another spot; and we could now make out a large number of them.

I accordingly got all of my men up in line and began quick firing. In a very few minutes our bullets began to do damage, for the Spaniards retreated to the left into the jungle, and we lost sight of them. At the same moment a big body of men who, it afterward turned out, were Spaniards, came in sight along the glade, following the retreat of those whom we had just driven from the trenches. We supposed that there was a large force of Cubans with General Young, not being aware that these Cubans had failed to make their appearance, and as it was impossible to tell the Cubans from the Spaniards, and as we could not decide whether these were Cubans following the Spaniards we had put to flight, or merely another troop of Spaniards retreating after the first (which was really the case), we dared not fire, and in a minute they had passed the glade and were out of sight.

At every halt we took advantage of the cover, sinking down behind any mound, bush, or tree trunk in the neighborhood. The trees, of course, furnished no protection from the Mauser bullets. Once I was standing behind a large palm with my head out to one side, very fortunately; for a bullet passed through the palm, filling my left eye and ear with the dust and splinters.

No man was allowed to drop out to help the wounded. It was hard to leave them there in the jungle, where they might not be found again until the vultures and the land-crabs came, but war is a grim game and there was no choice. One of the men shot was Harry Heffner of G Troop, who was mortally wounded through the hips. He fell without uttering a sound, and two of his companions dragged him behind a tree. Here he propped himself up and asked to be given his canteen and his rifle, which I handed to him. He then again began shooting, and continued loading and firing until the line moved forward and we left him alone, dying in the gloomy shade. When we found him again, after the fight, he was dead.

At one time, as I was out of touch with that part of my wing commanded by Jenkins and O'Neill, I sent Greenway, with Sergeant Russell, a New Yorker, and trooper Rowland, a New Mexican cow-puncher, down in the valley to find out where they were. To do this the three had to expose themselves to a very severe fire, but they were not men to whom this mattered. Russell was killed; the other two returned and reported to me the position of Jenkins and O'Neill. They then resumed their places on the firing-line.

After a while I noticed blood coming out of Rowland's side and discovered that he had been shot, although he did not seem to be taking any notice of it. He said the wound was only slight, but as I saw he had broken a rib, I told him to go to the rear to the hospital. After some grumbling he went, but fifteen minutes later he was back on the firing-line again and said he could not find the hospital—which I doubted. However, I then let him stay until the end of the fight.

After we had driven the Spaniards off from their position to our right, the firing seemed to die away so far as we were concerned, for the bullets no longer struck around us in such a storm as before, though along the rest of the line the battle was as brisk as ever. Soon we saw troops appearing across the ravine, not very far from where we had seen the Spaniards whom we had thought might be Cubans.

Again we dared not fire, and carefully studied the new-comers with our glasses; and this time we were right, for we recognized our own cavalry-men. We were by no means sure that they recognized us, however, and were anxious that they should, but it was very difficult to find a clear spot in the jungle from which to signal; so Sergeant Lee of Troop K climbed a tree and from its summit waved the troop guidon. They waved their guidon back, and as our right wing was now in touch with the regulars, I left Jenkins and O'Neill to keep the connection, and led Llewellen's troop back to the path to join the rest of the regiment, which was evidently still in the thick of the fight.

I was still very much in the dark as to where the main body of the Spanish forces were, or exactly what lines the battle was following, and was very uncertain what I ought to do; but I knew it could not be wrong to go forward, and I thought I would find Wood and then see what he wished me to do. I was in a mood to cordially welcome guidance, for it was most bewildering to fight an enemy whom one so rarely saw.

I had not seen Wood since the beginning of the skirmish, when he hurried forward. When the firing opened some of the men began to curse. "Don't swear—shoot!" growled Wood, as he strode along the path leading his horse, and everyone laughed and became cool again. The Spanish outposts were very near our advance guard, and some minutes of the hottest kind of firing followed before they were driven back and slipped off through the jungle to their main lines in the rear.

Here, at the very outset of our active service, we suffered the loss of two as gallant men as ever wore uniform. Sergeant Hamilton Fish at the extreme front, while holding the point up to its work and firing back where the Spanish advance guards lay, was shot and instantly killed; three of the men with him were likewise hit. Captain Capron, leading the advance guard in person, and displaying equal courage and coolness in the way that he handled them, was also struck, and died a few minutes afterward.

The command of the troop then devolved upon the First Lieutenant, young Thomas. Like Capron, Thomas was the fifth in line from father to son who had served in the American army, though in his case it was in the volunteer and not the regular service; the four preceding generations had furnished soldiers respectively to the Revolutionary War, the War of 1812, the Mexican War, and the Civil War. In a few minutes Thomas was shot through the leg, and the command devolved upon the Second Lieutenant, Day (a nephew of "Albemarle" Cushing, he who sunk the great Confederate ram). Day, who proved himself to be one of our most efficient officers, continued to handle the men to the best possible advantage, and brought them steadily forward. L Troop was from the Indian Territory. Captain McClintock was hurried forward to its relief with his Troop B of Arizona men. In a few minutes he was shot through the leg and his place was taken by his First Lieutenant, Wilcox, who handled his men in the same soldierly manner that Day did.

Among the men who showed marked courage and coolness was the tall color-sergeant, Wright; the colors were shot through three times.

When I had led G Troop back to the trail I ran ahead of them, passing the dead and wounded men of L Troop, passing young Fish as he lay with glazed eyes under the rank tropic growth to one side of the trail. When I came to the front I found the men spread out in a very thin skirmish line, advancing through comparatively open ground, each man taking advantage of what cover he could, while Wood strolled about leading his horse, Brodie being close at hand.

How Wood escaped being hit, I do not see, and still less how his horse escaped. I had left mine at the beginning of the action and was only regretting that I had not left my sword with it, as it kept getting between my legs when I was tearing my way through the jungle. I never wore it again in action. Lieutenant Rivers was with Wood, also leading his horse. Smedburg had been sent off on the by no means pleasant task of establishing communications with Young.

Very soon after I reached the front, Brodie was hit, the bullet shattering one arm and whirling him around as he stood. He had kept on the extreme front all through, his presence and example keeping his men entirely steady, and he at first refused to go to the rear; but the wound was very painful, and he became so faint that he had to be sent. Thereupon, Wood directed me to take charge of the left wing in Brodie's place, and to bring it forward; so over I went.

I now had under me Captains Luna, Muller, and Houston, and I began to take them forward, well spread out, through the high grass of a rather open forest. I noticed Goodrich, of Houston's troop, tramping along behind his men, absorbed in making them keep at good intervals from one another and fire slowly with careful aim. As I came close up to the edge of the troop, he caught a glimpse of me, mistook me for one of his own skirmishers who was crowding in too closely, and called out, "Keep your interval, sir; keep your interval, and go forward."

A perfect hail of bullets was sweeping over us as we advanced. Once I got a glimpse of some Spaniards, apparently retreating, far in the front, and to our right, and we fired a couple of rounds after them. Then I became convinced, after much anxious study, that we were being fired at from some large red-tiled buildings, part of a ranch on our front. Smokeless powder, and the thick cover in our front, continued to puzzle us, and I more than once consulted anxiously the officers as to the exact whereabouts of our opponents. I took a rifle from a wounded man and began to try shots with it myself. It was very hot and the men were getting exhausted, though at this particular time we were not suffering heavily from bullets, the Spanish fire going high.

As we advanced, the cover became a little thicker and I lost touch of the main body under Wood; so I halted and we fired industriously at the ranch buildings ahead of us, some five hundred yards off. Then we heard cheering on the right, and I supposed that this meant a charge on the part of Wood's men, so I sprang up and ordered the men to rush the buildings ahead of us. They came forward with a will. There was a moment's heavy firing from the Spaniards, which all went over our heads, and then it ceased entirely. When we arrived at the buildings, panting and out of breath, they contained nothing but heaps of empty cartridge-shells and two dead Spaniards, shot through the head.

The country all around us was thickly forested, so that it was very difficult to see any distance in any direction. The firing had now died out, but I was still entirely uncertain as to exactly what had happened. I did not know whether the enemy had been driven back or whether it was merely a lull in the fight, and we might be attacked again; nor did I know what had happened in any other part of the line, while as I occupied the extreme left, I was not sure whether or not my flank was in danger.

At this moment one of our men who had dropped out arrived with the information (fortunately false) that Wood was dead. Of course, this meant that the command devolved upon me, and I hastily set about taking charge of the regiment. I had been particularly struck by the coolness and courage shown by Sergeants Dame and McIlhenny, and sent them out with small pickets to keep watch in front and to the left of the left wing. I sent other men to fill the canteens with water, and threw the rest out in a long line in a disused sunken road, which gave them cover, putting two or three wounded men, who had hitherto kept up with the fighting-line, and a dozen men who were suffering from heat exhaustion—for the fighting and running under that blazing sun through the thick dry jungle was heart-breaking—into the ranch buildings.

Then I started over toward the main body, but to my delight encountered Wood himself, who told me the fight was over and the Spaniards had retreated. He also informed me that other troops were just coming up. The first to appear was a squadron of the Ninth Cavalry, under Major Dimick, which had hurried up to get into the fight, and was greatly disappointed to find it over. They took post in front of our lines, so that our tired men were able to get a rest, Captain McBlain, of the Ninth, good-naturedly giving us some points as to the best way to station our outposts. Then General Chaffee, rather glum at not having been in the fight himself, rode up at the head of some of his infantry, and I marched my squadron back to where the rest of the regiment was going into camp, just where the two trails came together, and beyond—that is, on the Santiago side of—the original Spanish lines.

The Rough Riders had lost 8 men killed and 34 wounded, aside from two or three who were merely scratched and whose wounds were not reported. The First Cavalry lost 7 men killed and 8 wounded; the Tenth Cavalry, 1 man killed and 10 wounded; so, out of 964 men engaged on our side, 16 were killed and 52 wounded.

The Spaniards were under General Rubin, with, as second in command, Colonel Alcarez. They had two guns, and eleven companies of about 100 men each: three belonging to the Porto Rico regiment, three to the San Fernandino, two to the Talavero, two being so-called mobilized companies from the mineral districts, and one a company of engineers; over 1,200 men in all, together with two guns.

General Rubin reported that he had repulsed the American attack, and Lieutenant Tejeiro states in his book that General Rubin forced the Americans to retreat, and enumerates the attacking force as consisting of three regular regiments of infantry, the Second Massachusetts and the Seventy-first New York (not one of which fired a gun or were anywhere near the battle), in addition to the sixteen dismounted troops of cavalry. In other words, as the five infantry regiments each included twelve companies, he makes the attacking force consist of just five times the actual amount. As for the "repulse," our line never went back ten yards in any place, and the advance was practically steady; while an hour and a half after the fight began we were in complete possession of the entire Spanish position, and their troops were fleeing in masses down the road, our men being too exhausted to follow them.

General Rubin also reports that he lost but seven men killed. This is certainly incorrect, for Captain O'Neill and I went over the ground very carefully and counted eleven dead Spaniards, all of whom were actually buried by our burying squads. There were probably two or three men whom we missed, but I think that our official reports are incorrect in stating that forty-two dead Spaniards were found; this being based upon reports in which I think some of the Spanish dead were counted two or three times.

Indeed, I should doubt whether their loss was as heavy as ours, for they were under cover, while we advanced, often in the open, and their main lines fled long before we could get to close quarters. It was a very difficult country, and a force of good soldiers resolutely handled could have held the pass with ease against two or three times their number. As it was, with a force half of regulars and half of volunteers, we drove out a superior number of Spanish regular troops, strongly posted, without suffering a very heavy loss. Although the Spanish fire was very heavy, it does not seem to me it was very well directed; and though they fired with great spirit while we merely stood at a distance and fired at them, they did not show much resolution, and when we advanced, always went back long before there was any chance of our coming into contact with them.

Our men behaved very well indeed. The newspaper press failed to do full justice to the regulars, in my opinion, from the simple reason that everybody knew that they would fight, whereas there had been a good deal of question as to how the Rough Riders, who were volunteer troops, and the Tenth Cavalry would behave; so there was a tendency to exalt our deeds at the expense of those of the First Regulars, whose courage and good conduct were taken for granted.

It was a trying fight beyond what the losses show, for it is hard upon raw soldiers to be pitted against an unseen foe, and to advance steadily when their comrades are falling around them, and when they can only occasionally see a chance to retaliate. Wood's experience in fighting Apaches stood him in good stead. An entirely raw man at the head of the regiment, conducting, as Wood was, what was practically an independent fight, would have been in a very trying position. The fight cleared the way toward Santiago, and we experienced no further resistance.

That afternoon we made camp and dined, subsisting chiefly on a load of beans which we found on one of the Spanish mules which had been shot. We also looked after the wounded. Dr. Church had himself gone out to the firing-line during the fight, and carried to the rear some of the worst wounded on his back or in his arms. Those who could walk had walked in to where the little field-hospital of the regiment was established on the trail.

We found all our dead and all the badly wounded. Around one of the latter the big, hideous land-crabs had gathered in a gruesome ring, waiting for life to be extinct. One of our own men and most of the Spanish dead had been found by the vultures before we got to them; and their bodies were mangled, the eyes and wounds being torn.

The Rough Rider who had been thus treated was in Bucky O'Neill's troop; and as we looked at the body, O'Neill turned to me and asked, "Colonel, isn't it Whitman who says of the vultures that 'they pluck the eyes of princes and tear the flesh of kings'?" I answered that I could not place the quotation. Just a week afterward we were shielding his own body from the birds of prey.

One of the men who fired first, and who displayed conspicuous gallantry, was a Cherokee, who was hit seven times, and of course had to go back to the States. Before he rejoined us at Montauk Point he had gone through a little private war of his own; for on his return he found that a cowboy had gone off with his sweetheart, and in the fight that ensued he shot his rival. Another man of L Troop who also showed marked gallantry was Elliot Cowdin. The men of the plains and mountains were trained by life-long habit to look on life and death with iron philosophy. As I passed by a couple of tall, lank, Oklahoma cow-punchers, I heard one say, "Well, some of the boys got it in the neck!" to which the other answered with the grim plains proverb of the South: "Many a good horse dies."

Thomas Isbell, a Cherokee in the squad under Hamilton Fish, was among the first to shoot and be shot at. He was wounded no less than seven times. The first wound was received by him two minutes after he had fired his first shot, the bullet going through his neck. The second hit him in the left thumb. The third struck near his right hip, passing entirely through the body. The fourth bullet (which was apparently from a Remington and not from a Mauser) went into his neck and lodged against the bone, being afterward cut out. The fifth bullet again hit his left hand. The sixth scraped his head and the seventh his neck. He did not receive all the wounds at the same time, over half an hour elapsing between the first and the last. Up to receiving the last wound he had declined to leave the firing-line, but by that time he had lost so much blood that he had to be sent to the rear. The man's wiry toughness was as notable as his courage.

We improvised litters and carried the more sorely wounded back to Siboney that afternoon and the next morning; the others walked. One of the men who had been most severely wounded was Edward Marshall, the correspondent, and he showed as much heroism as any soldier in the whole army. He was shot through the spine, a terrible and very painful wound, which we supposed meant that he would surely die; but he made no complaint of any kind, and while he retained consciousness persisted in dictating the story of the fight.

A very touching incident happened in the improvised open-air hospital after the fight, where the wounded were lying. They did not groan, and made no complaint, trying to help one another. One of them suddenly began to hum, "My Country, 'Tis of Thee," and one by one the others joined in the chorus, which swelled out through the tropic woods, where the victors lay in camp beside their dead.

I did not see any sign among the fighting men, whether wounded or unwounded, of the very complicated emotions assigned to their kind by some of the realistic modern novelists who have written about battles. At the front everyone behaved quite simply and took things as they came, in a matter-of-course way; but there was doubtless, as is always the case, a good deal of panic and confusion in the rear where the wounded, the stragglers, a few of the packers, and two or three newspaper correspondents were, and in consequence the first reports sent back to the coast were of a most alarming character, describing, with minute inaccuracy, how we had run into ambush.

The packers with the mules which carried the rapid-fire guns were among those who ran, and they let the mules go in the jungle; in consequence the guns were never even brought to the firing-line, and only Fred Herrig's skill as a trailer enabled us to recover them. By patient work he followed up the mules' tracks in the forest until he found the animals.

Among the wounded who walked to the temporary hospital at Siboney was the trooper, Rowland, of whom I spoke before. There the doctors examined him, and decreed that his wound was so serious that he must go back to the States. This was enough for Rowland, who waited until nightfall and then escaped, slipping out of the window and making his way back to camp with his rifle and pack, though his wound must have made all movement very painful to him. After this, we felt that he was entitled to stay, and he never left us for a day, distinguishing himself again in the fight at San Juan.

Next morning we buried seven dead Rough Riders in a grave on the summit of the trail, Chaplain Brown reading the solemn burial service of the Episcopalians, while the men stood around with bared heads and joined in singing, "Rock of Ages." Vast numbers of vultures were wheeling round and round in great circles through the blue sky overhead. There could be no more honorable burial than that of these men in a common grave—Indian and cowboy, miner, packer, and college athlete—the man of unknown ancestry from the lonely Western plains, and the man who carried on his watch the crests of the Stuyvesants and the Fishes, one in the way they had met death, just as during life they had been one in their daring and their loyalty.

The army was camped along the valley, ahead of and behind us, our outposts being established on either side. From the generals to the privates all were eager to march against Santiago. At daybreak, when the tall palms began to show dimly through the rising mist, the scream of the cavalry trumpets tore the tropic dawn; and in the evening, as the bands of regiment after regiment played "The Star-Spangled Banner," all, officers and men alike, stood with heads uncovered, wherever they were, until the last strains of the anthem died away in the hot sunset air.

10

TAKING MOUNT SURIBACHI

COLONEL JOSEPH H. ALEXANDER

D-DAY

Weather conditions around Iwo Jima on D-day morning, February 19, 1945, were almost ideal. At 0645 Admiral Turner signaled: "Land the landing force!"

Shore bombardment ships did not hesitate to engage the enemy island at near-point-blank range. Battleships and cruisers steamed as close as two thousand yards to level their guns against island targets. Many of the "Old Battleships" had performed this dangerous mission in all theaters of the war. Marines came to recognize and appreciate their contributions. It seemed fitting that the old *Nevada*, raised from the muck and ruin of Pearl Harbor, should lead the bombardment force close ashore. Marines also admired the battleship *Arkansas*, built in 1912, and recently returned from the Atlantic where she had battered German positions at Pointe du Hoc at Normandy during the epic Allied landing on June 6, 1944.

Lieutenant Colonels Donald M. Weller and William W. "Bucky" Buchanan, both artillery officers, had devised a modified form of the "rolling barrage" for use by the bombarding gunships against beachfront targets just before H-hour. This concentration of naval gunfire would advance progressively as the troops landed, always remaining four hundred yards to their front. Air spotters would help regulate the pace. Such an innovation appealed to the three division commanders, each having served in France during World War I. In those days, a good rolling barrage was often the only way to break a stalemate.

The shelling was terrific. Admiral Hill would later boast that "there were no proper targets for shore bombardment remaining on Dog-Day morning." This proved to be an overstatement, yet no one could deny the unprecedented intensity of firepower Hill delivered against the areas surrounding the landing beaches. As General Kuribayashi would ruefully admit in an assessment report to Imperial General Headquarters, "we need to reconsider the power of bombardment from ships; the violence of the enemy's bombardments is far beyond description."

The amphibious task force appeared from over the horizon, the rails of the troopships crowded with combat-equipped marines watching the spectacular fireworks. The Guadalcanal veterans among them realized a grim satisfaction watching American battleships leisurely pounding the island from just offshore. The war had come full cycle from the dark days of October 1942 when the 1st Marine Division and the Cactus Air Force endured similar shelling from Japanese battleships.

The marines and sailors were anxious to get their first glimpse of the objective. Correspondent John P. Marquand, the Pulitzer Prize–winning writer, recorded his own first impressions of Iwo: "Its silhouette was like a sea monster, with the little dead volcano for the head, and the beach area for the neck, and all the rest of it, with its scrubby brown cliffs for the body." Lieutenant David N. Susskind, USNR, wrote down his initial thoughts from the bridge of the troopship *Mellette*: "Iwo Jima was a rude, ugly sight. . . . Only a geologist could look at it and not be repelled." As described in a subsequent letter home by US Navy Lieutenant Michael F. Keleher, a surgeon in the 25th Marines:

> The naval bombardment had already begun, and I could see the orange-yellow flashes as the battleships, cruisers, and destroyers blasted away at the island broadside. Yes, there was Iwo— surprisingly close, just like the pictures and models we had been studying for six weeks. The volcano was to our left, then the long, flat black beaches where we were going to land, and the rough rocky plateau to our right.

The commanders of the 4th and 5th Marine Divisions, Major Generals Clifton B. Cates and Keller E. Rockey, respectively, studied the island through binoculars from their respective ships. Each division would land two reinforced regiments abreast. From left to right, the beaches were designated Green, Red, Yellow, and Blue. The 5th Division would land the 28th Marines on the left flank, over Green Beach, the 27th Marines over Red. The 4th Division would land the 23rd Marines over Yellow Beach and the 25th Marines over Blue Beach on the right flank. General Schmidt reviewed the latest intelligence reports with growing uneasiness and requested a reassignment of reserve forces with General Smith. The 3rd Marine Division's 21st Marines would replace the 26th Marines as corps reserve, thus releasing the latter regiment to the 5th Division.

Schmidt's landing plan envisioned the 28th Marines cutting the island in half, then returning to capture Suribachi, while the 25th Marines would scale the Rock Quarry and then serve as the hinge for the entire corps to swing around to the north. The 23rd Marines and 27th Marines would capture the first airfield and pivot north within their assigned zones.

General Cates was already concerned about the right flank. Blue Beach Two lay directly under the observation and fire of suspected Japanese positions in the Rock Quarry, whose steep cliffs overshadowed the right flank like Suribachi dominated the left. The 4th Marine Division figured that the 25th Marines would have the hardest objective to take on D-day. Said Cates, "If I knew the name of the man on the extreme right of the right-hand squad, I'd recommend him for a medal before we go in."

The choreography of the landing continued to develop. Iwo Jima would represent the pinnacle of forcible amphibious assault against a heavily fortified shore, a complex art mastered painstakingly by the Fifth Fleet over many campaigns. Seventh Air Force Martin B-24 Liberator bombers flew in from the Marianas to strike the smoking island. Rocket ships moved in to saturate nearshore targets.

Then it was time for the fighter and attack squadrons from Mitscher's Task Force 58 to contribute. The navy pilots showed their skills at bombing and strafing, but the troops naturally cheered the most at the appearance of F4U Corsairs flown by Marine Fighter Squadrons 124 and 213, led by Lieutenant Colonel William A. Millington from the fleet carrier *Essex*. Colonel Vernon E. Megee, in his shipboard capacity as air officer for General Smith's Expeditionary Troops staff, had urged Millington to put on a special show for the troops in the assault waves. "Drag your bellies on the beach," he told Millington.

The marine fighters made an impressive approach parallel to the island, then virtually did Megee's bidding, streaking low over the beaches, strafing furiously. The geography of the Pacific War since Bougainville had kept many of the ground marines separated from their own air support, which had been operating in areas other than where they had been fighting, most notably the Central Pacific. "It was the first time a lot of them had ever seen a marine fighter plane," said Megee. The troops were not disappointed.

The planes had barely disappeared when naval gunfire resumed, carpeting the beach areas with a building crescendo of high-explosive shells. The ship-to-shore movement was well under way, an easy thirty-minute run for the tracked landing vehicles (LVTs). This time there were enough LVTs to do the job: 68 LVT(A)4 armored amtracs mounting snub-nosed 75mm cannon leading the way, followed by 380 troop-laden LVT 4s and LVT 2s.

The waves crossed the line of departure on time and chugged confidently toward the smoking beaches, all the while under the climactic bombardment from the ships. Here there was no coral reef, no killer neap tides to be concerned with. The navy and marine frogmen had reported the approaches free of mines or tetrahedrons. There was no premature cessation of fire. The "rolling barrage" plan took effect. Hardly a vehicle was lost to the desultory enemy fire.

The massive assault waves hit the beach within two minutes of H-hour. A Japanese observer watching the drama unfold from a cave on the slopes of Suribachi reported, "At nine o'clock in the morning several hundred landing craft with amphibious tanks in the lead rushed ashore like an enormous tidal wave." Lieutenant Colonel Robert H.

Williams, executive officer of the 28th Marines, recalled that "the landing was a magnificent sight to see—two divisions landing abreast; you could see the whole show from the deck of a ship." Up to this point, so far, so good.

The first obstacle came not from the Japanese but from the beach and the parallel terraces. Iwo Jima was an emerging volcano; its steep beaches dropped off sharply, producing a narrow but violent surf zone. The soft black sand immobilized all wheeled vehicles and caused some of the tracked amphibians to belly down. The boat waves that closely followed the LVTs had more trouble. Ramps would drop, a truck or jeep would attempt to drive out, only to get stuck. In short order a succession of plunging waves hit the stalled craft before they could completely unload, filling their sterns with water and sand, broaching them broadside. The beach quickly resembled a salvage yard.

The infantry, heavily laden, found its own "foot-mobility" severely restricted. In the words of Corporal Edward Hartman, a rifleman with the 4th Marine Division: "The sand was so soft it was like trying to run in loose coffee grounds." From the 28th Marines came this early, laconic report: "Resistance moderate, terrain awful."

The rolling barrage and carefully executed landing produced the desired effect, suppressing direct enemy fire, providing enough shock and distraction to enable the first assault waves to clear the beach and begin advancing inward. Within minutes, six thousand marines were ashore. Many became thwarted by increasing fire over the terraces or down from the highlands, but hundreds leapt forward to maintain assault momentum.

The 28th Marines on the left flank had rehearsed on similar volcanic terrain on the island of Hawaii. Now, despite increasing casualties among their company commanders and the usual disorganization of landing, elements of the regiment used their initiative to strike across the narrow neck of the peninsula. The going became progressively costly as more and more Japanese strongpoints along the base of Suribachi seemed to spring to life. Within ninety minutes of the landing, however, elements of the 1st Battalion, 28th Marines, had reached the western shore, seven hundred yards across from Green Beach. Iwo Jima had been severed—"like cutting off a snake's head," in the words of one marine. It would represent the deepest penetration of what was becoming a very long and costly day.

The other three regiments experienced difficulty leaving the black sand terraces and wheeling across toward the first airfield. The terrain was an open bowl, a shooting gallery in full view from Suribachi on the left and the rising tableland to the right. Any thoughts of a "cakewalk" quickly vanished as well-directed machine-gun fire whistled across the open ground and mortar rounds began dropping along the terraces. Despite these difficulties, the 27th Marines made good initial gains, reaching the southern and western edges of the first airfield before noon.

The 23rd Marines landed over Yellow Beach and sustained the brunt of the first round of Japanese combined arms fire. These troops crossed the second terrace only to be confronted by two huge concrete pillboxes, still lethal despite all the pounding. Overcoming these positions proved costly in casualties and time. More fortified positions appeared in the broken ground beyond. Colonel Walter W. Wensinger's call for tank support could not be immediately honored because of congestion problems on the beach. The regiment clawed its way several hundred yards toward the eastern edge of the airstrip.

No assault units found it easy going to move inland, but the 25th Marines almost immediately ran into a buzz saw trying to move across Blue Beach. General Cates had been right in his appraisal. "That right flank was a bitch if there ever was one," he would later say. Lieutenant

Colonel Hollis W. Mustain's 1st Battalion, 25th Marines, managed to scratch forward three hundred yards under heavy fire in the first half-hour, but Lieutenant Colonel Chambers's 3rd Battalion, 25th Marines, took the heaviest beating of the day on the extreme right, trying to scale the cliffs leading to the Rock Quarry. Chambers landed fifteen minutes after H-hour. "Crossing that second terrace," he recalled, "the fire from automatic weapons was coming from all over. You could've held up a cigarette and lit it on the stuff going by. I knew immediately we were in for one hell of a time."

This was simply the beginning. While the assault forces tried to overcome the infantry weapons of the local defenders, they were naturally blind to an almost imperceptible stirring taking place among the rocks and crevices of the interior highlands. With grim anticipation, General Kuribayashi's gunners began unmasking the big guns—the heavy artillery, giant mortars, rockets, and antitank weapons held under tightest discipline for this precise moment. Kuribayashi had patiently waited until the beaches were clogged with troops and material. Gun crews knew the range and deflection to each landing beach by heart; all weapons had been preregistered on these targets long ago. At Kuribayashi's signal, these hundreds of weapons began to open fire. It was shortly after 1000.

The ensuing bombardment was as deadly and terrifying as any the marines had ever experienced. There was hardly any cover. Japanese artillery and mortar rounds blanketed every corner of the 3,000-yard-wide beach. Large-caliber coast defense guns and dual-purpose antiaircraft guns firing horizontally added a deadly scissors of direct fire from the high ground on both flanks. Marines stumbling over the terraces to escape the rain of projectiles encountered the same disciplined machine-gun fire and minefields which had slowed the initial advance. Casualties mounted appallingly.

Two marine combat veterans observing this expressed a grudging admiration for the Japanese gunners. "It was one of the worst bloodlettings of the war," said Major Karch of the 14th Marines. "They rolled those artillery barrages up and down the beach—I just didn't see how anybody could live through such heavy fire barrages." Said Lieutenant Colonel Joseph L. Stewart, "The Japanese were superb artillerymen. . . . Somebody was getting hit every time they fired."

At sea, Lieutenant Colonel Weller tried desperately to deliver naval gunfire against the Japanese gun positions shooting down at 3rd Battalion, 25th Marines, from the Rock Quarry. It would take longer to coordinate this fire: The first Japanese barrages had wiped out the 3rd Battalion, 25th Marines' entire Shore Fire Control Party.

As the Japanese firing reached a general crescendo, the four assault regiments issued dire reports to the flagship. Within a ten-minute period, these messages crackled over the command net:

1036: (From 25th Marines) "Catching all hell from the quarry. Heavy mortar and machine-gun fire!"

1039: (From 23d Marines) "Taking heavy casualties and can't move for the moment. Mortars killing us."

1042: (From 27th Marines) "All units pinned down by artillery and mortars. Casualties heavy. Need tank support fast to move anywhere."

1046: (From 28th Marines) "Taking heavy fire and forward movement stopped. Machine-gun and artillery fire heaviest ever seen."

The landing force suffered and bled but did not panic. The profusion of combat veterans throughout the rank and file of each regiment helped the rookies focus on the objective. Communications remained effective. Keen-eyed aerial observers spotted some of the now-exposed gun positions and directed naval gunfire effectively. Carrier planes screeched in low to drop napalm canisters. The heavy Japanese fire would continue to take an awful toll throughout the first day and night, but it would never again be so murderous as that first unholy hour.

Marine Sherman tanks played hell getting into action on D-day. Later in the battle these combat vehicles would be the most valuable weapons on the battlefield for the marines; this day was a nightmare. The assault divisions embarked many of their tanks on board medium landing ships (LSMs), sturdy little craft that could deliver five Shermans at a time. But it was tough disembarking them on Iwo's steep beaches. The stern anchors could not hold in the loose sand; bow cables run forward to "deadmen" LVTs parted under the strain. On one occasion the lead tank stalled at the top of the ramp, blocking the other vehicles and leaving the LSM at the mercy of the rising surf. Other tanks bogged down or threw tracks in the loose sand.

Many of those that made it over the terraces were destroyed by huge horned mines or disabled by deadly accurate 47mm antitank fire from Suribachi. Other tankers kept coming. Their relative mobility, armored protection, and 75mm gunfire were most welcome to the infantry scattered among Iwo's lunar-looking, shell-pocked landscape.

Both division commanders committed their reserves early. General Rockey called in the 26th Marines shortly after noon. General Cates ordered two battalions of the 24th Marines to land at 1400; the 3rd Battalion, 24th Marines, followed several hours later. Many of the reserve battalions suffered heavier casualties crossing the beach than the assault units, a result of Kuribayashi's punishing bombardment from all points on the island.

Mindful of the likely Japanese counterattack in the night to come—and despite the fire and confusion along the beaches—both divisions also ordered their artillery regiments ashore. This process, frustrating and costly, took much of the afternoon. The wind and surf began to pick up as the day wore on, causing more than one low-riding DUKW to swamp with its precious 105mm howitzer cargo. Getting the guns ashore was one thing; getting them up off the sand was quite another. The 75mm pack howitzers fared better than the heavier 105s. Enough marines could readily hustle them up over the terraces, albeit at great risk. The 105s seemed to have a mind of their own in the black sand. The effort to get each single weapon off the beach was a saga in its own right.

Somehow, despite the fire and unforgiving terrain, both Colonel Louis G. DeHaven, commanding the 14th Marines, and Colonel James D. Waller, commanding the 13th Marines, managed to get batteries in place, registered, and rendering close fire support well before dark, a singular accomplishment.

Japanese fire and the plunging surf continued to make a shambles out of the beachhead. Late in the afternoon, Lieutenant Michael F. Keleher, USNR, the battalion surgeon, was ordered ashore to take over the 3rd Battalion, 25th Marines, aid station from its gravely wounded surgeon. Keleher, a veteran of three previous assault landings, was appalled by the carnage on Blue Beach as he approached: "Such a sight on that beach! Wrecked boats, bogged-down jeeps, tractors and tanks; burning vehicles; casualties scattered all over."

On the left center of the action, leading his machine-gun platoon in the 1st Battalion, 27th Marines' attack against the southern portion of the airfield, the legendary "Manila John" Basilone fell mortally wounded by a Japanese mortar shell, a loss keenly felt by all marines on the island. Farther east, Lieutenant Colonel Robert Galer, the other Guadalcanal Medal of Honor marine (and one of the Pacific War's earliest fighter aces), survived the afternoon's fusillade along the beaches and began reassembling his scattered radar unit in a deep shell hole near the base of Suribachi.

Late in the afternoon, Lieutenant Colonel Donn J. Robertson led his 3rd Battalion, 27th Marines, ashore over Blue Beach, disturbed at the intensity of fire still being directed on the reserve forces this late on D-day. "They were really ready for us," he recalled. He watched with pride and wonderment as his marines landed under fire, took casualties, and stumbled forward to clear the beach. "What impels a young guy landing on a beach in the face of fire?" he asked himself. Then it was Robertson's turn. His boat hit the beach too hard; the ramp wouldn't drop. Robertson and his command group had to roll over the gunwales into the churning surf and crawl ashore, an inauspicious start.

The bitter battle to capture the Rock Quarry cliffs on the right flank raged all day. The beachhead remained completely vulnerable to enemy direct-fire weapons from these heights; the marines had to storm them before many more troops or supplies could be landed. In the end, it was the strength of character of Captain James Headley and Lieutenant Colonel "Jumping Joe" Chambers who led the survivors of the 3rd Battalion, 25th Marines, onto the top of the cliffs. The battalion paid an exorbitant price for this achievement, losing twenty-two officers and five hundred troops by nightfall.

The two assistant division commanders, Brigadier Generals Franklin A. Hart and Leo D. Hermle, of the 4th and 5th Marine Divisions, respectively, spent much of D-day on board the control vessels, marking both ends of the Line of Departure, four thousand yards offshore.

This reflected yet another lesson in amphibious techniques learned from Tarawa: Having senior officers that close to the ship-to-shore movement provided landing force decision-making from the most forward vantage point.

By dusk General Leo D. Hermle opted to come ashore. At Tarawa he had spent the night of D-day essentially out of contact at the fire-swept pier-head. This time he intended to be on the ground. Hermle had the larger operational picture in mind, knowing the corps commander's desire to force the reserves and artillery units onshore despite the carnage in order to build credible combat power. Hermle knew that whatever the night might bring, the Americans now had more troops on the island than Kuribayashi could ever muster. His presence helped his division to forget about the day's disasters and focus on preparations for the expected counterattacks.

Japanese artillery and mortar fire continued to rake the beachhead. The enormous spigot mortar shells (called "flying ashcans" by the troops) and rocket-boosted aerial bombs were particularly scary—loud, whistling projectiles, tumbling end over end. Many sailed completely over the island; those that hit along the beaches or the south runways invariably caused dozens of casualties with each impact. Few marines could dig a proper foxhole in the granular sand ("like trying to dig a hole in a barrel of wheat"). Among urgent calls to the control ship for plasma, stretchers, and mortar shells came repeated cries for sandbags.

Veteran marine combat correspondent Lieutenant Cyril P. Zurlinden, soon to become a casualty himself, described that first night ashore:

At Tarawa, Saipan, and Tinian, I saw Marines killed and wounded in a shocking manner, but I saw nothing like the ghastliness that hung over the Iwo beachhead. Nothing any of us had ever known could compare with the utter anguish, frustration, and constant inner battle to maintain some semblance of sanity.

Personnel accounting was a nightmare under those conditions, but the assault divisions eventually reported the combined loss of 2,420 men to General Schmidt (501 killed, 1,755 wounded, 47 dead of wounds, 18 missing, and 99 combat fatigue). These were sobering statistics, but Schmidt now had 30,000 marines ashore. The casualty rate of 8 percent left the landing force in relatively better condition than at the first days at Tarawa or Saipan. The miracle was that the casualties had not been twice as high. General Kuribayashi had possibly waited a little too long to open up with his big guns.

The first night on Iwo was ghostly. Sulfuric mists spiraled out of the earth. The marines, used to the tropics, shivered in the cold, waiting for Kuribayashi's warriors to come screaming down from the hills. They would learn that this Japanese commander was different. There would be no wasteful, vainglorious *banzai* attacks, this night or any other. Instead, small teams of infiltrators, which Kuribayashi termed "Prowling Wolves," probed the lines, gathering intelligence. A barge full of Japanese special landing forces tried a small counter landing on the western beaches and died to the man under the alert guns of the 28th Marines and its supporting LVT crews.

Otherwise, the night was one of continuing waves of indirect fire from the highlands. One high velocity round landed directly in the hole occupied by the 1st Battalion, 23rd Marines' commander, Lieutenant Colonel Ralph Haas, killing him instantly. The marines took casualties throughout the night. But with the first streaks of dawn, the veteran landing force stirred. Five infantry regiments looked north; a sixth turned to the business at hand in the south: Mount Suribachi.

SURIBACHI

The Japanese called the dormant volcano Suribachi-yama; the marines dubbed it "Hotrocks." From the start the marines knew their drive north would never succeed without first seizing that hulking rock dominating the southern plain. "Suribachi seemed to take on a life of its own, to be watching these men, looming over them," recalled one observer, adding, "the mountain represented to these Marines a thing more evil than the Japanese."

Colonel Kanehiko Atsuchi commanded the two thousand soldiers and sailors of the Suribachi garrison. The Japanese had honeycombed the mountain with gun positions, machine-gun nests, observation sites, and tunnels, but Atsuchi had lost many of his large-caliber guns in the direct naval bombardment of the preceding three days. General Kuribayashi considered Atsuchi's command to be semiautonomous, realizing the invaders would soon cut communications across the island's narrow southern tip. Kuribayashi nevertheless hoped Suribachi could hold out for ten days, maybe two weeks.

Some of Suribachi's stoutest defenses existed down low, around the rubble-strewn base. Here nearly seventy camouflaged concrete blockhouses protected the approaches to the mountain; another fifty bulged from the slopes within the first hundred feet of elevation. Then came the caves, the first of hundreds the marines would face on Iwo Jima.

The 28th Marines had suffered nearly four hundred casualties in cutting across the neck of the island on D-day. On D+1, in a cold rain, they prepared to assault the mountain. Lieutenant Colonel Chandler Johnson, commanding the 2nd Battalion, 28th Marines, set the tone for the morning as he deployed his tired troops forward: "It's going to be a hell of a day in a hell of a place to fight the damned war!" Some of the 105mm batteries of the 13th Marines opened up in support, firing directly overhead. Gun crews fired from positions hastily dug in the black sand directly next to the 28th Marines command post. Regimental executive officer Lieutenant Colonel Robert H. Williams watched the cannoneers fire at Suribachi "eight hundred yards away over open sights."

As the marines would learn during their drive north, even 105mm howitzers would hardly shiver the concrete pillboxes of the enemy. As the prep fire lifted, the infantry leapt forward, only to run immediately into very heavy machine-gun and mortar fire. Colonel Harry B. "Harry the Horse" Liversedge bellowed for his tanks. But the 5th Tank Battalion was already having a frustrating morning. The tankers sought a defilade spot in which to rearm and refuel for the day's assault. Such a location did not exist on Iwo Jima those first days. Every time the tanks congregated to service their vehicles they were hit hard by Japanese mortar and artillery fire from virtually the entire island. Getting sufficient vehicles serviced to join the assault took most of the morning. Hereafter the tankers would maintain and reequip their vehicles at night.

This day's slow start led to more setbacks for the tankers; Japanese antitank gunners hiding in the jumbled boulders knocked out the first approaching Shermans. Assault momentum slowed further. The 28th Marines overran forty strongpoints and gained roughly two hundred yards all day. They lost a marine for every yard gained. The tankers unknowingly redeemed themselves when one of their final 75mm rounds caught Colonel Atsuchi as he peered out of a cave entrance, killing him instantly.

Elsewhere, the morning light on D+1 revealed the discouraging sights of the chaos created along the beaches by the combination of Iwo Jima's wicked surf and Kuribayashi's unrelenting barrages. In the words of one dismayed observer:

The wreckage was indescribable. For two miles the debris was so thick that there were only a few places where landing craft could still get in. The wrecked hulls of scores of landing boats testified to one price we had to pay to put our troops ashore. Tanks and half-tracks lay crippled where they had bogged down in the coarse sand. Amphibian tractors, victims of mines and well-aimed shells, lay flopped on their backs. Cranes, brought ashore to unload cargo, tilted at insane angles, and bulldozers were smashed in their own roadways.

Bad weather set in, further compounding the problems of general unloading. Strong winds whipped sea swells into a nasty chop; the surf turned uglier. These were the conditions faced by Lieutenant Colonel Carl A. Youngdale in trying to land the 105mm-howitzer batteries of his 4th Battalion, 14th Marines. All twelve of these guns were pre-loaded in DUKWs, one to a vehicle. Added to the amphibious trucks' problems of marginal seaworthiness with that payload was contaminated fuel. As Youngdale watched in horror, eight DUKWs suffered engine failures, swamped, and sank, with great loss of life. Two more DUKWs broached in the surf zone, spilling their invaluable guns into deep water. At length Youngdale managed to get his remaining two guns ashore and into firing position.

General Schmidt also committed one battery of 155mm howitzers of the corps artillery to the narrow beachhead on D+1. Somehow these weapons managed to reach the beach intact, but it then took hours to get tractors to drag the heavy guns up over the terraces. These, too, commenced firing before dark, their deep bark a welcome sound to the infantry.

Concern with the heavy casualties in the first twenty-four hours led Schmidt to commit the 21st Marines from corps reserve. The seas

proved to be too rough. The troops had harrowing experiences trying to debark down cargo nets into the small boats bobbing violently
alongside the transports; several fell into the water. The boating process took hours. Once afloat, the troops circled endlessly in their small
Higgins boats, waiting for the call to land. Wiser heads prevailed. After
six hours of awful seasickness, the 21st Marines returned to its ships
for the night.

Even the larger landing craft, the LCTs and LSMs, had great difficulty beaching. Sea anchors needed to maintain the craft perpendicular to the breakers rarely held fast in the steep, soft bottom. "Dropping
those stern anchors was like dropping a spoon in a bowl of mush," said
Admiral Hill.

Hill contributed significantly to the development of amphibious
expertise in the Pacific War. For Iwo Jima, he and his staff developed
armored bulldozers to land in the assault waves. They also experi-
mented with hinged Marston matting, used for expeditionary airfields,
as a temporary roadway to get wheeled vehicles over soft sand. On the
beach at Iwo, the bulldozers proved to be worth their weight in gold.
The Marston matting was only partially successful—LVTs kept chew-
ing it up in passage—but all hands could see its potential.

Admiral Hill also worked with the Naval Construction Battalion
(NCB) personnel—Seabees, as they were called—in an attempt to
bring supply-laden causeways and pontoon barges ashore. Again, the
surf prevailed, broaching the craft, spilling the cargo. In desperation,
Hill's beach masters turned to round-the-clock use of DUKWs and
LVTs to keep combat cargo flowing.

Once the DUKWs got free of the crippling load of 105mm howitzers, they did fine. LVTs were probably better, because they could
cross the soft beach without assistance and conduct resupply or
medevac missions directly along the front lines. Both vehicles suffered

from inexperienced LST crews in the transport area who too often would not lower their bow ramps to accommodate LVTs or DUKWs approaching after dark. In too many cases, vehicles loaded with wounded marines thus rejected became lost in the darkness, ran out of gas, and sank. The amphibian tractor battalions lost 148 LVTs at Iwo Jima. Unlike Tarawa, Japanese gunfire and mines accounted for less than 20 percent of this total. Thirty-four LVTs fell victim to Iwo's crushing surf; eighty-eight sank in deep water, mostly at night.

Once ashore and clear of the loose sand along the beaches, the tanks, half-tracks, and armored bulldozers of the landing force ran into the strongest minefield defenses yet encountered in the Pacific War. Under General Kuribayashi's direction, Japanese engineers had planted irregular rows of antitank mines and the now-familiar horned antiboat mines along all possible exits from both beaches. The Japanese supplemented these weapons by rigging enormous makeshift explosives from five-hundred-pound aerial bombs, depth charges, and torpedo heads, each triggered by an accompanying pressure mine. Worse, Iwo's loose soil retained enough metallic characteristics to render the standard mine detectors unreliable. The marines were reduced to using their own engineers on their hands and knees out in front of the tanks, probing for mines with bayonets and wooden sticks.

While the 28th Marines fought to encircle Suribachi and the beach masters and shore party attempted to clear the wreckage from the beaches, the remaining assault units of the VAC resumed their collective assault against Airfield No. 1. In the 5th Marine Division's zone, the relatively fresh troops of the 1st Battalion, 26th Marines, and the 3rd Battalion, 27th Marines, quickly became bloodied in forcing their way across the western runways, taking heavy casualties from time-fuzed air bursts fired by Japanese dual-purpose antiaircraft guns zeroed along the exposed ground. In the adjacent 4th Division zone, the 23rd

Marines completed the capture of the airstrip, advancing eight hundred yards, but sustaining high losses.

Some of the bitterest fighting in the initial phase of the landing continued to occur along the high ground above the Rock Quarry on the right flank. Here the 25th Marines, reinforced by the 1st Battalion, 24th Marines, engaged in literally the fight of its life. The marines found the landscape, and the Japanese embedded in it, unreal.

The second day of the battle had proven unsatisfactory on virtually every front. To cap off the frustration, when the 1st Battalion, 24th Marines, finally managed a breakthrough along the cliffs late in the day, their only reward was two back-to-back cases of "friendly fire." An American air strike inflicted eleven casualties; misguided salvos from an unidentified gunfire support ship took down ninety more. Nothing seemed to be going right.

The morning of the third day, D+2, seemed to promise more of the same frustrations. Marines shivered in the cold wind and rain; Admiral Hill twice had to close the beach due to high surf and dangerous undertows. But during one of the grace periods, the 3rd Division's 21st Marines managed to come ashore, all of it extremely glad to be free of the heaving small boats. General Schmidt assigned it to the 4th Marine Division at first.

The 28th Marines resumed its assault on the base of Suribachi—more slow, bloody fighting, seemingly boulder by boulder. On the west coast, the 1st Battalion, 28th Marines, made the most of field artillery and naval gunfire support to reach the shoulder of the mountain. Elsewhere, murderous Japanese fire restricted any progress to a matter of yards. Enemy mortar fire from all over the volcano rained down on the 2nd Battalion, 28th Marines, trying to advance along the eastern shore. Recalled rifleman Richard Wheeler of the experience, "It was terrible, the worst I can remember us taking."

That night the amphibious task force experienced the only significant air attack of the battle. Fifty kamikaze pilots from the 22nd Mitate special attack unit left Katori Airbase near Yokosuka and flung themselves against the ships on the outer perimeter of Iwo Jima. In desperate action that would serve as a prelude to Okinawa's fiery engagements, the kamikazes sank the escort carrier *Bismarck Sea* with heavy loss of life and damaged several other ships, including the veteran *Saratoga*, finally knocked out of the war. All fifty Japanese planes were expended.

It rained even harder on the fourth morning, D+3. Marines scampering forward under fire would hit the deck, roll, attempt to return fire—only to discover that the loose volcanic grit had combined with the rain to jam their weapons. The 21st Marines, as the vanguard of the 3rd Marine Division, hoped for good fortune in its initial commitment after relieving the 23rd Marines. The regiment instead ran headlong into an intricate series of Japanese emplacements which marked the southeastern end of the main Japanese defenses. The newcomers fought hard all day to scratch and claw an advance of two hundred net yards. Casualties were disproportionate.

On the right flank, Lieutenant Colonel Chambers continued to rally the 3rd Battalion, 25th Marines, through the rough pinnacles above the Rock Quarry. As he strode about directing the advance of his decimated companies that afternoon, a Japanese gunner shot him through the chest. Chambers went down hard, thinking it was all over: "I started fading in and out. I don't remember too much about it except the frothy blood gushing out of my mouth. . . . Then somebody started kicking the hell out of my feet. It was [Captain James] Headley, saying, "Get up; you were hurt worse on Tulagi!"

Captain Headley knew Chambers's sucking chest wound portended a grave injury. He sought to reduce his commander's shock until they could get him out of the line of fire. This took doing. Lieutenant Michael F. Keleher, USNR, now the battalion surgeon, crawled forward with one of his corpsmen. Willing hands lifted Chambers on a stretcher. Keleher and several others, bent double against the fire, carried him down the cliffs to the aid station, and eventually on board a DUKW, making the evening's last run out to the hospital ships.

All three battalion commanders in the 25th Marines had now become casualties. Chambers would survive to receive the Medal of Honor; Captain Headley would command the shot-up 3rd Battalion, 25th Marines, for the duration of the battle.

By contrast, the 28th Marines on D+3 made commendable progress against Suribachi, reaching the shoulder at all points. Late in the day, combat patrols from the 1st Battalion, 28th Marines, and the 2nd Battalion, 28th Marines, linked up at Tobiishi Point at the southern tip of the island. Recon patrols returned to tell Lieutenant Colonel Johnson that they found few signs of live Japanese along the mountain's upper slopes on the north side.

At sundown Admiral Spruance authorized Task Force 58 to strike Honshu and Okinawa, then retire to Ulithi to prepare for the Ryukyuan campaign. All eight Marine Corps fighter squadrons thus left the Iwo Jima area for good. Navy pilots flying off the ten remaining escort carriers would pick up the slack. Without slighting the skill and valor of these pilots, the quality of close air support to the troops fighting ashore dropped off after this date. The escort carriers, for one thing, had too many competing missions, namely combat air patrols, antisubmarine sweeps, searches for downed aviators, and harassing strikes against neighboring Chichi Jima. Marines on Iwo Jima complained of slow response time to air-support requests, light payloads (rarely greater than one-hundred-pound bombs), and high delivery altitudes (rarely below 1,500 feet).

The navy pilots did deliver a number of napalm bombs. Many of these failed to detonate, although this was not the fault of the aviators; the early napalm "bombs" were simply old wing-tanks filled with the mixture, activated by unreliable detonators. The marines also grew concerned about these notoriously inaccurate area weapons being dropped from high altitudes.

By Friday, February 23 (D+4), the 28th Marines stood poised to complete the capture of Mount Suribachi. The honor went to the 3rd Platoon (reinforced), Company E, 2nd Battalion, 28th Marines, under the command of First Lieutenant Harold G. Schrier, the company executive officer. Lieutenant Colonel Johnson ordered Schrier to scale the summit, secure the crater, and raise a fifty-four-by-twenty-eight-inch American flag for all to see. Schrier led his forty-man patrol forward at 0800.

The regiment had done its job, blasting the dozens of pillboxes with flame and demolitions, rooting out snipers, knocking out the masked batteries. The combined-arms pounding by planes, field pieces, and naval guns the past week had likewise taken its toll on the defenders. Those who remained popped out of holes and caves to resist Schrier's advance, only to be cut down. The marines worked warily up the steep northern slope, sometimes resorting to crawling on hands and knees.

Part of the enduring drama of the Suribachi flag-raising was the fact that it was observed by so many people. Marines all over the island could track the progress of the tiny column of troops during its ascent ("Those guys oughta be getting flight pay," said one wag). Likewise, hundreds of binoculars from the ships offshore watched Schrier's marines climbing ever upward. Finally, they reached the top and momentarily disappeared from view. Those closest to the volcano could hear distant gunfire. Then, at 1020, there was movement on the summit; suddenly the Stars and Stripes fluttered bravely.

Lusty cheers rang out from all over the southern end of the island. The ships sounded their sirens and whistles. Wounded men propped themselves up on their litters to glimpse the sight. Strong men wept unashamedly. Navy Secretary Forrestal, thrilled by the sight, turned to Holland Smith and said, "The raising of that flag means a Marine Corps for another five hundred years."

Three hours later an even larger flag went up to more cheers. Few would know that Associated Press photographer Joe Rosenthal had just captured the embodiment of the American warfighting spirit on film. *Leatherneck* magazine photographer Staff Sergeant Lou Lowery had taken a picture of the first flag-raising and almost immediately got in a firefight with a couple of enraged Japanese. His photograph would become a valued collector's item. But Rosenthal's would enthrall the free world.

Captain Thomas M. Fields, commanding officer of Company D, 2nd Battalion, 26th Marines, heard his men yell "Look up there!" and turned in time to see the first flag go up. His first thought dealt with the battle still at hand: "Thank God [they] won't be shooting us down from behind anymore."

The 28th Marines took Suribachi in three days at the cost of more than five hundred troops (added to its D-day losses of four hundred men). Colonel Liversedge began to reorient his regiment for operations in the opposite direction, northward. Unknown to all, the battle still had another month to run its bloody course.

11

THE LOSS OF THE
INDIANAPOLIS

RAYMOND B. LECH

Five minutes past midnight on July 30, 1945, the first torpedo smashed into the starboard bow of the United States heavy cruiser *Indianapolis*, and an ear-shattering explosion rocked the ship. Three seconds later, the second torpedo found its mark directly under the bridge and blew up. The vessel lifted slightly out of the water, quivered, then promptly settled back down. At the same time, from the bridge to the bow on the starboard side, water was sent soaring into the midnight sky; flame, steam, and smoke belched out of her forward stack, and an enormous ball of fire swept through the entire forward half of the ship. Within seconds, the fire died away. Once again the *Indianapolis* was level and riding high, but now with the bow gone and two huge gaping holes in her right side.

From midships forward, the cruiser was a complete disaster; no light, no power, no communication, no pressure. Although the rear half of the vessel was untouched, the tons of water that gushed into the forward part of the cruiser sealed the fate of the *Indianapolis.*

IN THE WATER THE FIRST DAY: MONDAY, JULY 30, 1945

Quartermaster 3rd Class Vincent Allard found himself with six or seven other men, all desperately hanging onto a coiled floater net. One of them had a bared knife and was busy cutting the tangles in the net so that it would uncoil and spread out. While this was going on, Allard heard a cry for help. He quickly swam toward the sound and in a few seconds found a sailor floating on a pontoon from one of the ship's planes. He guided the man back to the group clustered around the net, but no sooner did he return when again he heard cries for help. Off he went once more and soon spotted two men holding onto a potato crate. One of the boys could swim, but the other could not and was very scared. Telling the swimmer to stick close, Allard began helping the nonswimmer to the safety of the net. On the way toward the group, he heard someone yell that he had a raft. Since it seemed that the raft was closer than the net, Allard changed course and headed for the sound. The voice called again, and Allard thought he recognized it as the *Indianapolis*'s skipper, Captain Charles Butler McVay III. Allard called out to ask if it were the captain calling, and Captain McVay replied that it was and to come aboard. They swam a short distance and reached the rafts.

The man who could swim climbed unassisted into the empty second raft, McVay and Allard helped the other sailor in, and then Allard joined McVay in his raft. The two men in the second raft had swallowed an enormous amount of water, and at first Captain McVay thought they were both dying. But after a while, they came around. Just before sunrise, they met up with five men on another raft that had a floater net tied to it. They lashed this raft to theirs, and, at first light Monday morning, the group consisted of three rafts, one net, and nine men. Captain McVay was the only officer.

An inspection of the rafts turned up two canoe paddles, a box of cigarettes, fishing gear, signaling mirrors, and a tin container that held twelve Very (star) shells and a pistol. They also found a canvas bag holding a first-aid kit and matches, but it was soaked and everything inside was useless except for some sealed tubes of ointment. During the day, a water breaker holding three gallons of water floated by. This was given to McVay to be tasted, but salt water had leaked into the archaic wooden container and the water was undrinkable. So as not to create unnecessary fear, the captain didn't pass on the bad news but told everyone it would be rationed out when he thought it was "absolutely necessary that they have a drink."

No food was found on any of the rafts, but fortunately, sometime during the day, an emergency ration can drifted by. Upon opening, they found it was dry inside, and they pulled out a number of cans of Spam and small tins of malted milk tablets and biscuits. The skipper told the other eight men that one twelve-ounce tin of Spam would be opened daily and divided equally. In addition, everyone would daily receive two biscuits and two malted-milk tablets. Under this quota, he figured they had rations to last ten days.

When the rafts crashed into the sea, their gratings had broken. Nevertheless the men made themselves as comfortable as possible and hung on while they were tossed about by the heavy swells of the unending ocean. At one moment they would be deep in a valley of waves and the next moment on top, looking down into that same valley. While on this unwanted roller-coaster ride, resting momentarily on the crest of a wave, they spotted two other rafts also on the crest of their waves. One raft was about 1,500 yards away and appeared to have one man on it who was calling for help. The other raft was much farther away and looked like it held a group of men who seemed to be in good condition. At this time though, McVay's group was too exhausted to paddle over to the near raft, and any investigation had to be held off until the next day.

During this first day, a monstrous shark decided to investigate the raft and its edible cargo. The shark kept swimming under the raft. The dorsal fin was "almost as white as a sheet of paper," while the body was a darker color. The shark could therefore always be spotted because of the visibility of its white fin in the water. The frightened men attempted to catch the pilot fish by knocking them off with canoe paddles, but this was an exercise in futility. They also tried hitting the shark with paddles, but when they occasionally did manage to do so he swam away and returned a few minutes later. In the days to follow, this unwanted nuisance was to become a real menace.

After spotting the two distant rafts, McVay and the others assumed that they were the only survivors of the ship and, all in all, figured no more than twenty-five or thirty men, including themselves, made it off. What they didn't know at the time was that they had drifted seven to ten miles north of the main groups.

Stranded in the middle of the deep and seemingly never-ending Philippine Sea, the captain understandably became very depressed. He daydreamed about taking a bath, drinking a cocktail, and relaxing in comfort, and in the midst of such thoughts he wished to live, but soon reality broke in upon his fantasies.

He dreaded the idea of seeing again the wives of his now dead officers. While at Mare Island, he and Mrs. McVay had gotten to know these women, and now "I knew there was nothing I could say to them . . ." His mind drifted back to Guam. He remembered the moment when he was told no escort was needed, and he cursed the people there for not having one available; if there had been an escort, it could have radioed for help and picked up survivors. His final, and unfortunately most nagging thought, was of his personal responsibility: he was the captain, like it or not.

Two hours prior to the close of their first day, a plane flew overhead, its red-and-green running lights clearly visible. McVay fired one of the star shells skyward, but it went unnoticed. The container holding the shells had sixteen fillers but only twelve shells, which was the standard issue for this type of raft. It irked McVay to see four empty slots. Why couldn't they just fill the entire thing up and be done with it?

As the day drew to an end, however, spirits were high in anticipation of the morrow's rescue. The *Indianapolis* was due in Leyte Gulf in the morning, and when the heavy cruiser didn't show up, questions would be asked, a search made, and rescue would be on the way.

After narrowly escaping from his after engine room, Lieutenant Richard Redmayne swam from the starboard side of the *Indianapolis*. Within five minutes, he found a kapok life preserver, which he put on, and for about a half hour he rested in the water alone. Then he spotted a life raft with men on it and joined them. During the remaining dark morning hours, two more rafts and two floater nets joined the group. The three rafts and two nets were lashed together, and they continued to drift, picking up water breakers, floating food containers, and other men.

Surveying the area at first light, they found the hostile sea covered with a heavy oil slick, five-inch powder cans, and an assortment of junk. Many of the men were terribly sick from swallowing sea water and oil, and the ones who had passed out in the water were being held up by their shipmates. A head count was attempted, and they discovered that their group consisted of approximately 150 men, including four officers and five chiefs. Lieutenant Redmayne, as the senior officer, took charge.

In addition to the three rafts and two nets, about 90 percent of the people in the water in this group were wearing life jackets; the ones who didn't have any held onto the side of the rafts or onto men who had jackets, or they hugged empty ammo cans. The rafts themselves were very overcrowded, each one averaging fifteen to twenty men, and the sailors who had been put on the rafts were the ones the officers and others in charge thought to be in the worst condition.

On Monday, nothing much happened. The large group floated, drifted, survived. They spotted the same two afternoon planes McVay had seen and also fired flares at the one plane that evening, with no success.

Certain early signs of insubordination surfaced. One of the men on the floater net was Petty Officer F. Giulio. Because of his particular job aboard ship, he was well known among the crew. On this first day, he kept complaining that he should be put on a raft since the life jacket kept slipping around his legs and he had a hard time keeping afloat. Giulio was the senior ranking man on that net and therefore their natural leader.

Distributed among the rafts and nets were four water casks and about nine or ten emergency tins of food, which contained malted-milk tablets, biscuits, and Spam. During the late afternoon, Giulio and some of his followers broke into the rations and began to eat. A short distance away, Chief Petty Officer Clarence Benton spotted them and immediately ordered them to stop, since all rations were to be divided equally. For the time being, Giulio and his small group obeyed the order.

During the evening Lieutenant Redmayne allowed a small amount of food to be rationed equally to all the men in the group.

At approximately 1:30 A.M., Quartermaster 1st Class Robert Gause spotted a fin. By estimating the distance between the dorsal and tail, he guessed the shark to be about twelve feet long.

Quite a few sailors in his group were critically wounded. There were a large number of severe flash burns of the face, arms, and body, and some men had compound fractures of one sort or another. There were no medical supplies of any kind for the frustrated Doctor Lewis Haynes, and many of the men with fractures and burns died from shock during the first few hours. After removing their life jackets, the dead were allowed to slip away. Before the boiling sun rose over the distant horizon on Monday morning, about fifty of the original 400 were dead.

By daybreak, this mass of floating humanity had split into three subgroups. The largest group contained about 200 men, the second 100, and the smallest about 50. These subgroups were separated from each other by a distance of only several hundred yards, at most. Leader of the group of 200 men was Captain Edward Parke, Commanding Officer of the Marine Detachment and holder of the Bronze Star for bravery on Guadalcanal. Strong and athletic, he was superb in his energy, leadership, and self-sacrifice. Dr. Haynes remembered him as the typical Marine, one who was very strict with the group and had the situation well in hand.

The main objective was for everyone to stay together. Captain Parke found a cork life ring with about 100 feet of attached line. To prevent drifting, he strung the line out and each man grabbed a piece of it and took up the slack. In this way, they formed a long line of men which began to curl on itself, as a wagon train would circle against attack. The wounded were brought into the middle and tied to the life ring itself by the strings on their jackets. There was no confusion, and the men stayed well grouped together. If someone did drift off the line, Parke swam over to the man and herded him back in. On several occasions, he gave his jacket to a man without one and swam unsupported until he could find another preserver.

Bravery in this enormous group of "swimmers" was everywhere. Commander Lipski, the ship's gunnery officer, who had been very badly burned, was cheerfully supported all day Monday by Airman 1st Class Anthony Maday. Lieutenant Commander Coleman, who came aboard in Guam, was the leader of a group, and he worked unceasingly to keep them together. Time after time, he swam out to bring in stragglers. Ultimately, Commander Coleman became so weak that he died from exhaustion. And there was Ensign Moynelo, who organized a large group of men. For three days, he kept the group together, rounded up drifters, and took off his own jacket many times and gave it to those without until he could find another. Finally he, too, collapsed and died.

Shortly after dawn on Monday, Lieutenant Commander Moss W. Flannery, commanding officer of VPB-133 based on Tinian, climbed into his Ventura bomber and headed out over the Philippine Sea on routine antisubmarine patrol. Visibility was unlimited and in order to obtain better horizon shots for navigation, instead of flying at his normal 5,000 feet, he dropped down and flew between 1,500 and 2,000 feet. At 9:20 A.M., he flew directly over Dr. Haynes and his group of 350 men. In the water, the men saw this plane coming directly at them, the sun reflecting off its front window, and they began splashing the water with their hands and feet to draw attention. Ensign Park, one of the ship's aviators, had some green marker dye in his jacket and spread it in the water. They all firmly believed that they had been seen and estimated that within five hours seaplanes from Guam would be landing in their midst.

Flannery, however, couldn't see a thing. The best way to spot something as small as a head in the ocean is not to look out at an angle but straight down, and at a height of 500 to 800 feet, not 1,500 feet. Flannery was looking out his side window, and his biggest problem was the glassy sea.

By 10:00 A.M., the sun was reflecting so sharply off the sea that everyone began to suffer from intense photophobia, an intolerance to light. Dr. Haynes was very concerned, since he considered this far worse than snow blindness. It caused severe pain, which was relieved only when the sun went down. Closing the eyelids did not help since the sun burnt right through. In order to somewhat ease the discomfort, the men ripped their clothing and blindfolded themselves. Fortunately, their bodies did not burn; they were all covered by fuel oil, which the searing rays of the sun could not penetrate.

For the remainder of the first day, there was constant change among the three subgroups. They would merge for a short time then break apart again. The wounded stayed in fairly good shape, and only a few men died. In order to determine death, Dr. Haynes would place his finger on the pupil of an eye and if there was no reflex it was assumed the man was dead. The jacket would be removed and the body allowed to drift away. In the background, some of the men would recite the Lord's Prayer.

By noontime, the sea became choppy again, with large swells. Practically everyone by this time had swallowed some of the oil-soaked water, and they were all throwing up. Thirst was beginning to get to the men, and Haynes, while trying unsuccessfully to find some first-aid supplies, visited all three groups and cautioned them against drinking salt water. For the moment, all the men agreed not to drink from the sea.

The survivors were beginning to see sharks in the area, but, so far, there were no major attacks. Giles McCoy, of the Marine detachment, saw a shark attack a dead man. He believed that because of the dead men in the water so much food was available that the sharks were not inclined to bother with those still alive.

That, however, had been in the morning and afternoon. By the time that the merciless sun began to set, large numbers of sharks had arrived on the scene, and the men were scared. Cuts were bleeding. When a shark approached a group, everyone would kick, punch, and create a general racket. This often worked, and the predator would leave. At other times, however, the shark "would have singled out his victim and no amount of shouts or pounding of the water would turn him away. There would be a piercing scream and the water would be churned red as the shark cut his victim to ribbons."

IN THE WATER THE SECOND DAY: TUESDAY, JULY 31, 1945

Yesterday they had been too exhausted to paddle over to the raft holding the one lone man, and this morning he was still calling to them. Thinking him hurt, the McVay group began the tremendous task of pulling nine men on three lashed rafts and a floater net to this isolated and scared soul. Changing the two men paddling once every half hour, it took them four and a half hours to traverse the 1,600 yards separating them and their objective. Upon finally reaching the young man, they saw that, besides being lonely, there was nothing wrong with the new member, and McVay said, "As misery loves company, he wanted somebody to talk to."

There still remained the other group farther away that had been spotted the day before, but the men were now too exhausted to try to reach them. Besides, most of the men had blisters on their hands, and these were creating saltwater ulcers. The new man told the skipper he had seen no one else in the water, and the captain was convinced that his group, plus the small pack of men in the distance, were the sole survivors, even though it seemed incredible that no one else had escaped.

In the morning there was no wind, but the sea could still be described as rough. As the day wore on, the endless water calmed down. There were very long, sweeping swells, but they didn't break and no whitecaps could be seen. Considering the circumstances, the group was comfortable and in fairly good shape.

During the day, Vincent Allard took the large canvas bag that had held the matches, first-aid kits, etc., and fashioned out of the fabric a "cornucopia" cap for everyone. The men pulled the hats over their ears, and this, together with the fuel oil that covered them, saved them from the scorching rays of the sun. To further protect their hands from sunburn, they placed them under the oil-covered water sloshing around in the grating of the rafts.

The fishing kit they found on one of the rafts was a delight to any fisherman's eye, and both McVay and Allard were excellent fishermen. But it didn't help much since there were a number of sharks in the area, and the one big monster of the first day was still performing his merry-go-round act. They did manage to catch some black fish which McVay thought to be in the parrot family; although the meat was very white, he was afraid to let the men eat it. Instead, he used this flesh as bait, hoping to catch nearby schools of bonito and mackerel. However, every time they dropped the line, the shark took what they offered, and, after a while, they gave up the idea of fishing.

During this second twenty-four hour period, two planes had been spotted; one at 1:00 A.M. and the second at 9:00 P.M. A pair of star shells were fired at both planes, but they weren't seen. The men griped about the shells, for once they reached their maximum height they burst like fireworks and then immediately died. The group wished parachutes were attached, which would float the light back and give the aviator more time to recognize the distress signal.

At dawn on the second day, the isolated Redmayne group had about sixty men on rafts and another sixty to eighty in the water. Meanwhile, during the dark morning hours, some of the more seriously injured men had died.

The water breakers turned out to be a disappointment. Some of the casks were empty while the others contained either salt or cruddy black water. Lieutenant Redmayne said, "It was dirty and tasted as though the salt content was about equal to the salt content of the seawater." These casks were made of wood, and when the rafts crashed into the sea the seams on the casks split, thereby allowing fresh water to escape and salt water to seep in. The casks were large, heavy, and difficult to handle, and in the standard life raft the water would probably become salty after the first use. Once the seal was broken to pour water, it couldn't properly be resealed, thus allowing salt water to seep in. Should the cup become lost, serving fresh water from the cask resulted in great wastage.

First-aid equipment was generally useless, since the containers were not watertight. Anything in tubes remained sealed, but there weren't enough remedies to go around for burns and eye troubles caused by salt water and fuel oil. The food stayed in good condition but, here again, there was a problem since the primary staple was Spam. Not only did this increase thirst because it was salty, but Spam draws sharks. The men discovered this when they opened a can of Spam and sharks gathered all around them.

The policy of the group was to put all men on rafts who were sick, injured, or didn't have life jackets or belts. The problem with this, however, was that men with belts or jackets began taking them off and allowing them to drift away in order to qualify for the relative safety of a raft. This necessitated keeping a close watch on the men. Giulio and his small band were now beginning to start trouble. Giulio, who was still on a floater net, kept insisting that he deserved some time on a raft. This request was not granted, and he continued to complain.

During the early part of this second day, some of the men swam over to Ensign Donald Blum and reported that the food had been broken into. Blum swam back with them to take a look and saw men eating and drinking. This was immediately reported to Redmayne, who then ordered that all food and water be placed on one raft and guarded at all times by the officers and chiefs. Later in the day there were reports that Giulio was again stealing food, but it was not clear whether food was being taken from the guarded raft or all the food had not been handed in. Ensign Harlan Twible, who was on a floater net about forty feet from Giulio, yelled out in a loud, clear voice, "The first man I see eating food not rationed I will report if we ever get in." He further told them that they were acting like a bunch of recruits and not seamen. As far as can be ascertained, there were no deaths in this group during the second day, and everyone appeared to be in fairly good shape. The only problem was Giulio and his gang. The next day would be a different story.

Even though total blackness surrounded them, because of the choppy sea the men were having a very difficult time sleeping. In this inky isolation, some of the weaker members of the crew, who could not face what they thought must be ahead of them, gave up all hope; they silently slipped out of their life jackets and committed suicide by drowning. Numerous deadly fights broke out over life jackets, and about twenty-five men were killed by their shipmates. At dawn, Dr. Haynes saw that the general condition of the men was not good, and the group appeared to be smaller. Haynes later recalled that basically two factors, other than lack of water, contributed greatly to the high mortality: the heat from the tropical sun and the ingestion of salt water. The drinking of salt water in his group was generally not deliberate but occurred during bouts of delirium or from the accidental swallowing of water in the choppy sea.

The constant breaking of waves over the men's heads the first two days, particularly when they tried to rest, caused most of them to develop a mechanical sinusitis. The swallowing of small amounts of seawater and fuel oil could not be avoided, and the sun caused intense headache and photophobia. The combination of these factors resulted in many deaths.

During the latter part of the day, the sea grew calmer. The men's thirst, however, had become overpowering as the placid water became very clear. As the day wore on, the men became more and more exhausted and complained of their thirst. Dr. Haynes noticed that the younger men, largely those without families, started to drink salt water first. As the hot sun continued to beat down on them, an increasing number of survivors were becoming delirious, talking incoherently, and drinking tremendous amounts of salt water.

They started becoming maniacal, thrashing around in the water and exhibiting considerable strength and energy compared to those who were exhausted but still sane. These spells would continue until the man either drowned or went into a coma. Several brave men, wearing rubber life belts, tried to support maniacal men and also drowned, for during the struggles the belts developed punctures or rips and deflated. Haynes kept swimming from one huge huddle of sailors to another, desperately trying to help. All during this time, people were getting discouraged and calling out for help, and he would be there to reassure and calm them down.

There were sharks in the area again. The clear water allowed the men to look down and see them. It seems that during this second day, however, the sharks were going after dead men, especially the bodies that were sinking down into the deeper ocean. They didn't seem to bother the men on the surface.

Things became progressively worse from sundown on the second day. The men's stories become mixed up, and some accounts are totally incoherent, making it difficult to piece together what actually happened. Haynes remembered that shortly after sundown they all experienced severe chills, which lasted for at least an hour. These were followed by high fever, as most of the group became delirious and got out of control. The men fought with one another, thinking there were Japanese in the group, and disorganization and disintegration occurred rapidly. Captain Parke worked until he collapsed. Haynes was so exhausted that he drifted away from the group.

Some of the men attempted to help their shipmates. They swam outside the group, rounding up stragglers and towing them back in. The kapok jackets had a brass ring and also a snap on the back. At night, people who had these jackets on would form a circle and hook them all together. The rest of the men would get in the middle. The corrallers themselves were worried, however, since the jackets had lost so much buoyancy that the feeling of security they provided was rapidly ebbing.

By nightfall, more and more people were removing their preservers and throwing them away. Most of these men died. Haynes swam from one batch of crazed men to another, trying to calm them down. He would locate the groups by the screaming of the delirious men. From this night on, what happened in the water can only be described as a nightmare.

IN THE WATER THE THIRD DAY: WEDNESDAY, AUGUST 1, 1945

The captain and the men with him were continuing to fare relatively well. McVay still believed that his ship went down with all hands and that, at most, there could only be thirty survivors.

From the opening of this day, the central thought on the minds of the men was to kill the shark; it was big, it kept circling closer and closer, and they were frightened. This monster could easily rip the raft apart with one swift motion of his enormous jaws. But the only weapon they had was a knife from the fishing kit, with a one-inch blade, and there was no way they could tackle this massive creature with a blade that small. So the day passed with the men sitting and staring at the shark, annoyed that a larger weapon was not in the kit and further chafed that not one man had a sheath knife, an implement customarily carried by many of the sailors aboard ship.

Just before first light, a plane flew over, and two star shells were fired. Again at 1:00 P.M., a bomber, heading toward Leyte, passed above. They tried to attract this second plane with mirrors, yellow signal flags, and splashing, but to no avail.

Although the order had been given the day before to bring all food to the command raft, there was still a certain amount of hoarding going on. This morning, however, several more rafts handed their cached rations over to Redmayne. During the day, one cracker, a malted-milk tablet, and a few drops of precious water were allocated to each man. Some survivors tried their luck at fishing but, as with the McVay group, the numerous sharks in the area kept stealing the bait. Not everyone realized there was safety in numbers. Some men swam away. Attempts to stop them failed, and soon after leaving the security of the group these sailors were usually dragged beneath the surface by the sharks.

Toward late afternoon, some of the sailors started becoming delirious again. More and more men were drinking salt water. Chief Benton (Redmayne's assistant) attempted to talk to these half-crazed men in a calm, reassuring voice, but it wasn't much use. Fights broke out, men started swimming away, and people committed suicide by drowning themselves. A sailor yelled to Redmayne that things were getting very bad on his raft, and Ensign Eames was sent over to investigate. Upon returning, Eames reported that some of the men were making homosexual advances toward one of the other men. Upon hearing these reports, the chief engineer's reaction was to have the people around him recite the Lord's Prayer.

Giulio had been on a net for the previous two days, but this morning the pharmacist's mate decided to transfer him to a raft because Giulio complained that his eyes were bothering him. Shortly thereafter, it was noticed that Giulio and the people with him were eating and drinking. Upon checking the stored rations on the command raft, it was discovered that two of the four water breakers were missing, plus several cans of rations. The officers and chiefs ordered Giulio to return everything immediately, but he ignored them. Some of the senior people then swam over to the mutineers and tried to grab the food and water away, but they were unsuccessful since Giulio and his small band were much stronger than the tired officers. Throughout the day, he and his gang had themselves a veritable Roman feast while others suffered and died.

The early morning hours found Doctor Haynes with a large pack of swimmers headed by Captain Parke of the Marines who, through willpower, strength, and sheer determination, kept the group under control. Before dawn Haynes twice became delirious. At one point, he remembered, "The waves kept hitting me in the face, and I got the impression that people were splashing water in my face as a joke, and I pleaded with them that it wasn't funny and that I was sick. I begged them to stop and kept swimming furiously to make them stop, and then my head cleared."

Most of the men had become hysterical, and some were quickly going mad. A few of the sailors got the idea that people were trying to drown them and that there were Japanese in the group. The cry would circulate, "Kill him!" Fights broke out, knives were drawn, and several men were brutally stabbed. Mass hysteria reigned.

The doctor did his best to calm them down but was unsuccessful and at one point he himself was held underwater by an insane crewman and had to fight his way back up. Captain Parke desperately tried to regain control but finally became delirious himself and eventually died. Once Parke was gone, the mass madness forced the subgroup to further dissolve, and the men scattered. They wanted to be alone, for no one trusted anyone else.

Under a cloudless sky and full moon, Haynes drifted, isolated but totally alert. A man floated by, and they instinctively backed away from each other. Everyone was crazy. Haynes hated being alone, however, and not very far away he heard the noises that the irrational members of another group were making and began swimming toward the sound. Only a few yards short of this band of men, his strength gave out, and he screamed for help. Breaking off from the pack, his chief pharmacist's mate, John Schmueck, grabbed him and towed him to the safety of their numbers.

Supported by Schmueck, who put his arm through the back of Haynes's jacket and lifted the doctor's body so that it rested on his own hip, Doctor Haynes fell asleep for a few hours. Schmueck himself was not in good shape and was having a difficult time with his rubber life ring. It was defective, and for two days—until he finally got a kapok jacket—he had had to hold his finger over the valve. When the ring would deflate too much, he would have to blow it up again and then hold his finger on it some more.

The new group was well organized and ably led by Ensign Moynelo. Someone in the group suggested using the leg straps on the kapok jackets to snap the men together. This worked very well and prevented them from drifting apart. By daybreak the sea was mirror calm, but the condition of the men was becoming critical. They had difficulty thinking clearly, and most of them talked incoherently and had hallucinations.

By this time, the kapok jackets just kept the men's heads out of the water. There was a great deal of anxiety within Moynelo's group concerning the buoyancy of the preservers since the Navy Manual stated that jackets would remain buoyant for only two days, and they were now well into their third. However, the kapok preservers maintained fair buoyancy, even after one hundred hours, and the mental distress that the men felt on this account turned out to have been uncalled for.

Preservers were, unfortunately, fairly easy to obtain. When a man died (and they were now dying en masse), Haynes would remove his jacket and add it to a pile in the middle of the group. This became their reserve when somebody's jacket went on the "fritz."

Sanity, as we know it, virtually disappeared on this third day. The few men who retained some semblance of sense tried to help their weaker shipmates, but it was a losing battle. Chief Gunner Harrison recalled that "Doctor Haynes's conduct throughout the time he was in the water was, in my opinion, above his normal call of duty. The comfort the men got from just talking to him seemed to quiet them down and relieve some of their worry."

Haynes felt that what kept him going was taking care of the men. They constantly asked him questions about whether the water was salty all the way down and when he thought the planes were coming.

Gunner Harrison remembered, "Early one morning somebody woke me up and wanted to know why we did not stop at an island that we passed. That story caused a great deal of trouble. Several of them believed that those islands were there—three islands. Lieutenant McKissick even dreamed he went to the island and there was a hotel there and they would not let him on the island. The first time I heard the story was, this kid woke me up and wanted to know why we did not stop there." All day long, small numbers of men broke off from the gathering and swam for the "island," never to be seen again.

Noticing a line of men stretching for some distance, Commander Haynes curiously swam to it and asked what was going on. He was told to be quiet for there was a hotel up ahead but it only had one room, and when it was your turn to get in you could sleep for fifteen minutes. Haynes turned and swam away from this procession of patient survivors.

Stragglers were continually being rounded up and herded back to the group. Sometimes the job would take up to an hour but Haynes knew that they had to stay together in order to be found.

On this Wednesday afternoon, Ensign Moynelo disappeared with the group who were going to swim to Leyte. It all started out when some quartermaster claimed to have figured out the current and the wind, and how long it would take to swim to Leyte. Approximately twenty-five men joined him. They anticipated that it would take them a day and a half to reach the Philippines, based upon a two-knot current and swimming at one knot per hour. Once this large party disappeared from sight, it was never seen again. This was the largest single group of men lost during the days in the water.

All of the strong leaders were now dead, except for Gunner Harrison and Commander Haynes. The doctor recalled that "Gunner Harrison and I were about the only ones left who were well enough to think, and he was just like the Rock of Gibraltar. He always had a smile and kept the group together. He used to say to the fellows, 'If that old broken-down Rickenbacker can stay out on the ocean for a week, we can stay for a month.'" Because of Harrison's leadership, "we managed to keep together. His morale was high, and his cheerful exhortations kept everyone united."

The doctor continued to pronounce men dead. He would remove their jackets, recite the Lord's Prayer, and release the bodies. The water was very clear, and Doctor Haynes remembered the bodies looking like small dolls sinking in the deep sea. He watched them until they faded from sight. A cloud of death hung over everyone, and rescue was no longer discussed. By early evening, all was calm—it was no longer a question of who would die, but when.

IN THE WATER THE FOURTH DAY: THURSDAY, AUGUST 2, 1945

With Lieutenant Redmayne delirious, Ensign Twible tried to command the group until he became totally exhausted and his effectiveness limited. Chief Benton was in a little better shape, however, and issued many orders on his own. During the morning, a man swam over to Twible's raft with cans of crackers and said Giulio sent them. No reason was given, and it is not known whether this was in response to a direct order or a limited act of charity.

More and more people were losing touch with their rational selves. For example, there were plenty of good kapok jackets available, but an insane sailor went up to a man wearing one of the rubber rings, ripped it off his body, and swam away. Unnecessary and foolish acts of this type were taking place throughout the groups. As Freud said, "The primitive stages can always be reestablished; the primitive mind is, in the fullest meaning of the word, imperishable."

The pharmacist's mate in this group, Harold Anthony, worked as hard as humanly possible to aid men in the water and became extremely fatigued. During the night he mentioned to one of his friends that he couldn't keep this pace up much longer and would probably be dead shortly. Twelve hours later, with the relentless Pacific sun beating down on this lonely spot of ocean, the lifeless body of the corpsman was permitted to drift away.

Doctor Haynes's group disbanded again. Small groups were continually forming and breaking up. The night had been particularly difficult, and most of the men suffered from chills, fever, and delirium. These lonely people were now dying in droves, and the helpless physician could only float and watch. By Thursday morning, August 2, the condition of most of the men was critical. Many were in comas and could be aroused only with exceptional effort. The group no longer existed, with the men drifting off and dying one by one. This isolation from the companionship of another human was cataclysmic.

At 9:00 A.M., on Thursday, August 2, securely strapped in the pilot's seat, Lieutenant (jg) Wilbur C. Gwinn pushed the throttles forward, brought the motors of his twin-engine Ventura bomber to an ear-splitting roar, and raced down the Peleliu runway. His mission was a regular day reconnaissance patrol of Sector 19V258. He was to report and attempt to sink any Japanese submarine in his area. The route for the outward leg of his journey just happened to have him flying directly over the heads of the dying men of the *Indianapolis*.

At the very rear of a Ventura is an antenna that trails behind the aircraft. It is used primarily for navigation. In order to keep the antenna from whipping around in the wind, which would make it useless, a weight (known as a "sock") is secured to the end. Once Gwinn gained enough speed to get airborne, he pulled back and the nose of the bomber pointed up toward the blue sky. At the same time, he lost the weight from his navigational antenna. With this "trailing antenna sock" gone, he had two choices: turn around and get it fixed, or continue on patrol and navigate by dead reckoning. Because the weather was excellent, Lieutenant Gwinn decided to go on, took the plane up to 3,000 feet, and over a glassy sea began looking for enemy submarines.

Dead reckoning navigation is not very accurate, and over the Pacific Ocean it is neither a very comfortable nor enviable position to be in. At 11:00 A.M., about an hour and forty-five minutes out of Peleliu, Gwinn figured that since caution is the better part of valor, the whipping antenna being pulled behind the plane should somehow be anchored down. Because the radioman was busy with something else and his co-pilot was concentrating on filling out a weather report, Gwinn resolved to repair it himself. Crawling through the after tunnel of the Ventura, he reached the narrow end and stared at the long, slender, thrashing piece of metal, wondering how to fix it. While attempting to come up with some creative solution to his problem, Gwinn happened to look down from his 3,000-foot perch into the Philippine Sea. At that precise moment, he saw it. The thin line of oil could only have come from a leaking submarine, and the startled pilot rushed back to his left-hand seat and began flying the airplane.

At 11:18 A.M., he changed his course so as to follow the snake-like slick. Not being able to see very well, he brought the bomber down to 900 feet. Mile after mile the slick continued, never seeming to reach an end. Five miles later, he suddenly saw them—thirty heads wrapped in a twenty-five-mile orbit of oil. Many were clinging to the sides of a raft, while others floated and feebly made motions to the plane. Who in the world could these people be? At 11:20 A.M., about two minutes after sighting what had looked like black balls on the water, the pilot dropped down to a wave-skimming 300 feet.

He ordered his radioman to get a message off, and at 11:25 A.M., the following transmission was sent:

SIGHTED 30 SURVIVORS
011-30 NORTH 133-30 EAST
DROPPED TRANSMITTER AND LIFEBOAT EMERGENCY
IFF ON 133-30

Now that he had positioned the thirty survivors, there was nothing more Gwinn could do so he decided to spread out his search. Following the slick on a northerly course, six miles farther on he found forty more men. Continuing on, four miles more had him pass over another fifty-five to seventy-five people—and still further north, he found scattered groups of twos and threes. After an hour of flying and looking, Lieutenant Gwinn estimated that there were 150 men in the water.

The survivors were dispersed along a line about twenty miles long. He noticed a group so crowded on rafts that he was unable to tell the exact number of rafts they had. He could barely spot a lone oil-covered man, even at his low altitude, unless he was splashing the water.

Gwinn's antenna problem now had to be solved—quickly. The position he sent out in his first message was calculated by dead reckoning and couldn't possibly be accurate. He had to fix the whipping antenna, and once again he crawled through the dark tunnel to reach the end of the bomber. Once there, he put his hand out the tail, grabbed the long rod, and pulled it inside. Taking a rubber hose, he tied it around the tip of the antenna and pushed the length back out, hoping, while crawling back to the pilot's seat, that there would be enough weight to stop the shaking and get a decent fix. They tried, and it worked.

One hour and twenty minutes after sending his first message of thirty survivors, a second dispatch from the bomber was transmitted:

SEND RESCUE SHIP
11-15N 133-47E 150 SURVIVORS
IN LIFE BOAT AND JACKETS
DROPPED RED RAMROD

Gwinn received orders to stick around.

Doctor Haynes saw the thing and prayed it was real. Flying very low, the bomber zoomed over his head and as quickly as it came, it passed and soon was a dot on the opposite horizon. At that moment, Haynes knew he and his fellow survivors were dead men. Their last ounce of strength was giving out, and this plane was like all the others—blind to the living hell beneath it.

After scouting the area, there was no doubt in Gwinn's mind that these were American sailors below him. Turning the plane, he looked for a group which appeared to be alone and without rafts, and began dropping everything in the plane that floated.

When Doctor Haynes saw the distant dot suddenly reverse course and come back toward them, low over the water, he then knew that they had been sighted. Like a sudden tropical squall, things began falling from the sky. Two life rafts were dropped, together with cans of

fresh water. The water cans ruptured on landing but the most important thing was that Gwinn saw them, and those fortunate enough to be
still alive knew rescue was near.

Once there was nothing left to drop to the splashing, oil-covered
men, Gwinn released dye markers and smoke bombs so as not to lose
the position.

It would not be until the next day that the Navy finally discovered that these were survivors from the *Indianapolis*. By this time, the
entire Pacific was curious as to who these people were. Ashore, many
people thought that they had Japanese in the water and weren't in
too big a rush to get things moving. A short time before, in this same
area, escorts from a convoy had reported they had attacked a Japanese
submarine.

However, after the second report citing "150 survivors" came in,
all hell broke loose. Because submarines don't carry 150 men, Pacific
Fleet knew they had a surface vessel to contend with, and if a Japanese warship had been sunk they would have known about it. It finally
dawned on CinCPac that they might have an American ship down,
and panic started to set in. Shortly after Gwinn's second message was
received, CinCPac (now in a state of agitation) began radioing ships to
report their positions.

For an hour after his second dispatch, Gwinn was all alone, attempting to comfort the dying men beneath him as best he could. Then
another plane, on transport duty to the Philippines, appeared. It stayed
with the Ventura for about an hour and dropped three of its rafts.

Back at Gwinn's base, the communications officer decoded the first
message concerning the thirty survivors and quickly passed it on to his
(and Gwinn's) boss, Lieutenant Commander George Atteberry, commanding officer of VPB-152. This was the Peleliu unit of the Search
and Reconnaissance Command of Vice Admiral Murray, Commander,

Marianas. The unit was under the command of Rear Admiral W. R. Greer.

Atteberry calculated the fuel supply of the lone, circling bomber and estimated that Gwinn would have to leave the scene by 3:30 P.M. in order to land with a small amount of reserve fuel. Not wanting to leave the survivors alone, Commander Atteberry started making some fast decisions.

Not far from the Ventura squadron was a squadron of seaplanes (Dumbos), and Atteberry picked up the phone and told the duty officer of VPB-23 to get a seaplane out to the area by 3:30 P.M. Not having intercepted Gwinn's message, "23" was skeptical about the whole thing and not eager to cooperate. Not liking this attitude, Atteberry drove over to their unit to ascertain the ready status personally. Once there, he decided they couldn't get a plane up in time to relieve Gwinn, so he quickly drove back to his own unit and ordered his plane and crew to get ready for takeoff. At exactly the same moment Gwinn's second message came in, Atteberry, whose call sign was "Gambler Leader," was lifting his bomber off the Peleliu runway.

During the hour and a half flight out, "Leader" was in constant contact with his squadron office and was happy to hear that "23" finally had gotten airborne and on the way. At 2:15 P.M., Atteberry spotted Gwinn, together with the PBM, the large seaplane on transport duty, and immediately established voice contact with both. The commander was given a quick tour of the groups in order to size up the situation. Finally, so that the men in the water wouldn't think they were being deserted, the pilot of the PBM was ordered to circle the southwest half of the huge slick while "Gambler Leader" ranged the northeast portion.

Gwinn's fuel supply was running low, and twenty minutes after Atteberry arrived, he sent Gwinn on his way. Lieutenant Gwinn's third and final message read:

RELIEF BY 70V [Atteberry]
RETURNING TO BASE

The PBM also had to go, and for forty-five minutes Commander Atteberry was all alone, circling and comforting those below by his presence. Then out of his cockpit window, he saw the big, lumbering Dumbo waddling toward him from the distant southern horizon.

Patrol Bombing Squadron 23 was told that Atteberry and his planes were going to remain on the scene until "23" got one of their Catalinas out there. Lieutenant R. Adrian Marks happened to be the duty pilot at the time, and 1,400 gallons of gas were loaded into his seaplane. While this was taking place, Marks, together with his air combat intelligence officer, went to group operations to see if they could gather any more information than what Commander Atteberry had given them. Operations had nothing to offer and, unable to believe that there were so many men (i.e., thirty men as per Gwinn's first transmission) in the water, Marks assumed he was going out to pick up a ditched pilot. With a full tank of gas and extra air-sea rescue gear, Lieutenant Marks shoved his mammoth down the Peleliu runway and, once airborne, turned north. The time was 12:45 P.M.

On the way out, "Playmate 2" (Marks's call sign) received word that instead of thirty men in the sea there were now about 150. This was absolutely incomprehensible to Marks, and he assumed that the message must have been garbled in transmission. However, he "thought it would be a good idea to get to the scene as quickly as possible." At 3:03 P.M., he began picking up radio signals from Atteberry, and a little over three hours from take off, at 3:50 P.M., "Playmate 2" made visual contact and established communications with the commander.

Marks was dumbfounded—how did all these people get here? "Gambler Leader" instructed "Playmate 2" not to drop a single thing—there was much more than met the eye. For a half hour, Atteberry gave Marks the tour. Then the Dumbo dropped everything it had (saving only one small raft for itself), concentrating on those floaters who had only jackets.

With everything out of the plane, Marks wondered what he could do next. Looking down at the bobbing mass of humanity, he knew they were in horrible shape but also just as important—and maybe more so—he saw the sharks. Therefore, at "about 16:30 I decided a landing would be necessary to gather in the single ones. This decision was based partly on the number of single survivors, and the fact that they were bothered by sharks. We did observe bodies being eaten by sharks." Marks told "Gambler Leader" he was going in, and Atteberry notified his base that the Dumbo was landing and that he himself needed relief.

Preparations were made inside the Catalina for landing, while Marks looked for a spot where he thought the floating plane would do the most good. Never having made a landing at sea before, he was a little nervous. However, "At 17:15 a power stall was made into the wind. The wind was due North, swells about twelve feet high. The plane landed in three bounces, the first bounce being about fifteen feet high." "Playmate 2" was down safe—but not very sound.

The hull was intact, but rivets had sprung loose and seams ripped opened from impact. While rivet holes were plugged with pencils and cotton shoved into the seams, the radio compartment was taking on water and was being bailed out at the rate of ten to twelve buckets per hour. In the meantime, the co-pilot went aft and began organizing the rescue effort.

Because of the high swells, Marks couldn't see anything from his cockpit seat. Atteberry stayed in direct communication with him, however, and guided the Dumbo toward the survivors. Both pilots made the decision to stay away from men on rafts, since they appeared to be in better shape than those floating alone. There were problems, however, for although every effort was made to pick up the single ones it was necessary to avoid passing near the men on life rafts because they would jump onto the plane.

The side hatch had been opened, and the plane's ladder was hung out. Standing on the rungs was a crewman and, when they passed a swimmer, he would grab him and pull him aboard. This was very unsatisfactory though, because the people in the water were too weak to hang on. Furthermore, when a burned survivor, or one whose arm or leg was broken, was snatched, the pain was excruciating. They tried throwing out their remaining raft with a rope attached for a swimmer to grab (they were too frail to jump in). Then they would reel the raft back in. This proved to be impractical, because Marks continually kept the plane taxiing and anyone hanging on was dragged through the water. Finally, they settled on going up to a man, cutting the engines, bringing him aboard, and then starting up again and going to another swimmer. Once the engines were cut, silence enveloped the area except for the terrifying cries for help heard by the crew of "Playmate 2."

Before night fell, Marks had picked up thirty people and crammed them into the body of his leaking seaplane. All were in bad shape, and they were immediately given water and first aid. Naturally, as soon as the first man was plucked from the sea, Lieutenant Marks learned the *Indianapolis* had gone down. There was no way, however, that he was going to transmit this word in the clear and "I was too busy to code a message of this nature." So it would not be until Friday, August 3, that the U.S. Navy finally learned that one of their heavy cruisers had been sunk just after midnight on July 30.

In the sky above the drifting Dumbo, Atteberry was busy directing Marks and telling other planes coming into the area where to
drop their gear in order "to obtain the best possible distribution
among them." Between the first sighting and midnight, planes continually flew in, and, at one point, there were eleven aircraft on the
scene.

With night upon him, it was impossible for Marks to pick up any
more individual swimmers, and he therefore taxied toward a large
assembly of men who had had rafts dropped to them earlier in the
day. This was Commander Haynes's group. Survivors were packed like
sardines inside the hull of the Dumbo, so Marks ordered these men to
be laid on top of the wings, covered with parachutes, and given water.
This damaged the wing fabric, and it became doubtful whether the
Catalina would ever fly again.

In the black of this Pacific night, things began to settle down; the
stillness was interrupted only by the occasional pained moans of the
Indianapolis crew. Marks couldn't move the plane for fear of running
people down, so they drifted and waited for rescue. Just before midnight, a searchlight on the far horizon pierced the onyx sky, and at the
same time a circling plane dropped a parachute flare over "Playmate
2." The ship changed course and steered toward the beat-up PBY and
her precious cargo of fifty-six former Indianapolis crewmen.

It was 4:55 P.M. when 1st Lieutenant Richard Alcorn, U.S. Army Air
Corps, 4th Emergency Rescue Squadron, forced his Catalina into the
air over Palau. Two hours and twenty minutes later, he arrived, and
after quickly surveying the situation tossed three of his eleven rafts
out the door. He also saw Marks's plane already on the water picking
up survivors. Noticing that the swimmers didn't have enough strength
to pull themselves into the rubber boats, Alcorn decided not to throw

*

anymore out. Instead he landed at 7:30 P.M., bringing his plane down two miles north of Marks.

Within minutes his crew saw the first survivor and pulled him into the aircraft. Then they taxied a few feet, stopped; taxied again, stopped—and kept this up until darkness without seeing another living soul. When Alcorn stopped and searched, they found a tremendous amount of debris in the area, most of it having fallen from the sky during the day.

They also saw bodies, dead bodies everywhere. In the dark, they floated silently with their lone passenger. Soon they heard cries for help from a group of men and sergeants Needham and Higbee volunteered to take one of the rafts, pick them up, and bring them back. Alcorn agreed, but with one provision—they could only go as far as the rope attached to raft and plane would take them. Unfortunately, the umbilical cord was not long enough, and the men returned disappointed.

Overhead, planes circled all night. Marks's Dumbo was totally out of commission, but Alcorn continued to signal to the flyers and they reassuringly flashed back to the two. By the end of the day, still no one on shore knew for certain who the people in the water were.

After Gwinn's second frightful message was received, one of the largest rescue operations in U.S. Naval history began. The *Cecil J. Doyle* (DE 368) was heading home after an unsuccessful submarine hunt, when she suddenly received orders from the Western Carolines Sub Area to reverse course and steam north to pick up survivors. This was immediately after Gwinn's first transmission. Once the second message came in, the destroyer escort increased speed to 22.5 knots.

At 2:35 P.M., *Doyle*'s radio room made voice contact with Commander Atteberry, and they were kept informed of what was going on. The ship was asked to rush but replied that there was no way they could make it to the area until after midnight.

The destroyers *Ralph Talbot* and *Madison*, both on separate patrol off Ulithi, at 4:00 P.M. turned their sleek bows northward and hastened to the scene at 32 knots. It was 6:56 P.M. when the *Madison* made contact with the *Doyle* and pointed out that she wouldn't be able to help until 3:00 the next morning, and the *Talbot* announced that her ETA wasn't until 4:00 A.M.

At 9:49 P.M., *Doyle*'s lookouts spotted their first star shell, and from that moment on flares were always visible. An hour later, the ship's giant 24-inch searchlight was switched on and pointed skyward to give the guarding planes an idea of where she was. Instead of seeking individual people in the water, the destroyer escort headed straight for Marks's Dumbo and, shortly after midnight, the first survivor from the incredibly luckless *Indianapolis* was pulled aboard a rescue ship.

It was noon when they noticed the circling plane far to the south of them. An hour later, there was another, and as the day wore on the planes swarmed over the line separating sky from sea. Frantically the men signaled, but they were too small to be seen. They ripped the kapok out of jackets, threw the silky fiber into an empty 40-mm ammo can, and set it afire, hoping the rising smoke would draw attention to their plight. It didn't work.

Captain McVay was confused and couldn't imagine what was going on. If the men in his group were the only survivors of the ill-fated cruiser, what was going on ten miles to the south of them? They began to feel discouraged, for as darkness blanketed their isolated spot of ocean the search seemed to be moving further away. McVay was almost certain they were not going to be found and ordered all rations cut in half.

Midnight saw them staring at the tiny pinprick of Doyle's light piercing the black sky, and now they were certain of other survivors. They were also certain, though, that the search area didn't extend north to their position and that it would be a long time, if ever, before they were found. No one slept, and, as the night wore on, this lonely group was very frightened.

The planes had no problem spotting the large Redmayne group and in the afternoon rafts, rations, and other emergency gear showered downward. With the security of sentinels circling above them, the men calmed down and patiently waited for rescue.

After Gwinn dropped the two rafts, they were quickly inflated, and, while the men held onto the side, Haynes was pushed in to investigate. The doctor ordered the sickest men put on the raft. He found an 11-ounce can of water and doled it out in a plastic cup at the rate of one ounce per man. An enormous amount of equipment was dropped to this "swimmer" group including a ten-man boat that soon had thirty people in it. But, during the day, it became so hot in the rafts that a great many men jumped back in the water to cool off.

Once the supplies were delivered, the group had almost everything they needed to keep them relatively comfortable until rescue ships arrived. Included in this bonanza were fresh water, rations, emergency medical supplies, and sun helmets. Dr. Haynes greatly appreciated the helmets for, when properly used, not only did they protect the wearer from the roasting sun but they also had a screen which dropped down in front of the face and prevented water from getting in the eyes and up the nose. As for the food, they found it impossible to eat the meat and crackers, but the malted-milk tablets and citrus candies went down easily.

Even though so much was dropped to them, the men's deteriorating physical condition made it essential that they be taken out of the water and given rudimentary first aid and medication; otherwise they wouldn't be alive when the ships came. Commander Haynes decided to swim for the plane. He told the group to stay where they were and explained what he was going to do. Then he swam toward Marks's plane and, after what seemed like two hours, finally reached it. His group still didn't have enough water, and he asked the crew of the plane to swing closer and give them some. They did so, and an emergency kit containing K-rations and a quart of water.

When nightfall came, they were in much better shape and had enough rafts so that all but four or five were out of the water. Fresh water was still a problem, but at sundown Haynes found a saltwater converter in one of the rafts. He spent all night trying to make fresh water out of salt water. Because he was so exhausted, the directions didn't help and the effort was a failure. He eventually made two batches of water which tasted horrible, but which the men drank. They even asked for more, but it had taken almost four hours to make the first batch and Haynes had had it. The doctor, who had worked so hard over the last four days, finally surrendered. He took the converter, flung it into the hated sea, and began to cry.

IN THE WATER THE FIFTH DAY: FRIDAY, AUGUST 3, 1945

Ten minutes after midnight, in a rough sea with a north-northwest wind blowing between 8 and 10 mph, the *Cecil J. Doyle* lowered her heavy motor whaleboat. It headed directly for the closer of the two Dumbos. Twenty minutes later, it returned with eighteen former crewmen of the *Indianapolis*, taken from Marks's plane. As soon as the first man was lifted aboard, he was asked, "Who are you?" Minutes later, an urgent secret dispatch was sent to the Commander of the Western Carolines:

HAVE ARRIVED AREA X
AM PICKING UP SURVIVORS
FROM U.S.S. INDIANAPOLIS
(CA 35) TORPEODED [*sic*]
AND SUNK LAST SUNDAY NIGHT

Between 12:30 and 4:45 A.M., *Doyle* raised from the brutal sea ninety-three men, which included all survivors aboard Marks's plane and the lone man on Alcorn's. In addition about forty men were retrieved from the water and the rafts. While the whaleboat shuttled back and forth, the mother ship slowly cruised the area, sweeping the watery expanse with her huge searchlight and following the flares dropped from the circling planes. The crew of the whaleboat, meanwhile, had a tough time removing men from the plane and bringing them aboard ship. Transfer was difficult because of the condition of the survivors, some of whom were badly burned from the fires on board the ship, one of whom had a broken leg, and they all were terribly weak from thirst and exposure.

At 1:10 A.M., the *Doyle* saw a searchlight to the north and soon discovered it to be the high-speed transport U.S.S. *Bassett*. Two hours later, the destroyer escort U.S.S. *Dufilho* also appeared. Until dawn, the *Doyle*, *Bassett*, and *Dufilho* worked independently, hoisting men to the safety of their steel decks. Sunup brought the two destroyers *Madison* and *Ralph Talbot* on the scene.

First light allowed Marks to inspect his Catalina, and he quickly determined that it would never fly again. At 6:00 A.M., *Doyle* sent her boat over to the Dumbo and transferred the crew and all salvageable gear to the ship.

Lieutenant Alcorn was relieved of his lone survivor by *Doyle* at 4:00 A.M. and, with the sun rising over the eastern horizon, he had to decide whether or not to take off. The sea was very rough and a heavy wind was blowing, but, fortunately, his Catalina was not nearly as beat up as Marks's. He resolved to try it, and at 7:30 A.M., with no trouble at all, he powered his way down the endless runway and lifted off. At almost the same time, *Doyle* poured eighty rounds of 40-mm gunfire into Marks's abandoned plane, and she sunk in the same area as the ship whose men she had so valiantly rescued.

After sinking the seaplane, *Doyle* secured from general quarters, and all of her survivors were logged in, treated, and put to bed. The crew of the *Doyle* were extremely helpful to their fellow sailors who had so recently suffered through a living hell. Men moved out of their bunks to make room for the former crewmen of the *Indianapolis* and constantly hovered around them, waiting for the slightest request that they could fill. The men were all given baths, and the oil was removed from their tired bodies. Every thirty minutes, a half glass of water, hot soup, hot coffee, and fruit were served to them, and this continued throughout the night and into the next day. The *Doyle*'s doctor examined everyone and listed them all in medical condition ranging from serious to acute.

As it searched for the living, *Doyle* passed by the bodies of twenty-five to fifty dead sailors floating in life jackets. At 12:20 P.M., *Madison* ordered *Doyle* to take off for Peleliu, and this, the first ship on the scene, was now the first to leave, heading south at 22.5 knots.

All McVay and his isolated band could do was watch the distant searchlights, the falling flares, the circling planes. When the sun rose over the horizon, they were in despair. The entire morning was spent staring at the activity very far away. It did not seem to be coming closer.

At 11:30 A.M., they spotted a plane making a box search. It was a very wide pattern, and on each leg it came closer. They found it extremely depressing, for the plane gave no recognition sign. Captain McVay contended that they were never spotted from the air. But they were, for this plane, flown by Marks's squadron leader, Lieutenant Commander M. V. Ricketts, saw them and reported that he sighted two rafts, with five survivors in one and four in the other. By voice radio, he directed the U.S.S. *Ringness* (APD 100) to pick them up.

Like *Bassett*, *Ringness* was a high-speed transport sent by Philippine Sea Frontier, and it had just arrived. After receiving Ricketts's message, *Ringness* headed for the spot, and at 4,046 yards she picked McVay up on radar. On the rafts, the spell of isolation and despair was suddenly broken when somebody cried, "My God, look at this! There are two destroyers bearing down on us. Why, they're almost on top of us." The two destroyers were both transports, *Ringness* and the newly arrived *Register*. *Register* turned north to pick up another small group while *Ringness* headed for McVay.

Everyone made it aboard under his own power, and all were immediately given first aid. They had lost about 14 percent of their body weight, and during the afternoon they were given ice cream, coffee, and as much water as they could drink. During the entire four and one-half days on the rafts, no one in the group asked for a drink. This was surprising to McVay, since he had assumed people couldn't go that long without water—but they did.

While *Doyle* was taking care of the "Haynes group," *Bassett* took care of Lieutenant Redmayne and his men. Lowering her four landing craft at 2:30 A.M., *Bassett*'s boats picked up most of Redmayne's people. A head count was taken, and a little over eighty sailors were collected from the original group of 150. *Bassett* next sent a message to Frontier Headquarters:

SURVIVORS ARE FROM USS
INDIANAPOLIS (CA 35) WHICH
WAS TORPEDOED 29 JULY [*sic*] X
CONTINUING TO PICK UP
SURVIVORS X MANY BADLY
INJURED

Ralph Talbot picked up twenty-four survivors and then spent most of the afternoon sinking eight rafts and a small boat with her 20-mm guns. Later she transferred her survivors to *Register*.

As soon as *Madison* arrived in the area, *Bassett* reported that she had 150 survivors aboard and desperately needed a doctor. Shortly thereafter, at 5:15 A.M., *Madison's* physician, Lieutenant (jg) H. A. Stiles, was transferred to the transport. It was at the time the landing craft from *Bassett* came over to pick up Doctor Stiles that *Madison* first learned the survivors were from the *Indianapolis*.

During the day scouting lines were formed with the planes birddogging, but nothing was seen except for the dead, and they were generally left where they were. The unpleasant task of recovery and identification was postponed until the next day. The last living man plucked from the Philippine Sea was Captain McVay, who was the last man to enter it.

By the time the blazing Pacific sun reached its zenith on this day, not another living person from *Indianapolis* was to be found in that enormous ocean. She had sailed from San Francisco with 1,196 young men, was torpedoed, and about 800 of her crew escaped from the sinking ship. Of these 800, 320 were rescued; two later died in the Philippines, and two on Peleliu. Because of complacency and carelessness, approximately 500 U.S. sailors (no one will ever know the exact number) died in the waters of the Philippine Sea.

12

SUPPLYING THE EMBATTLED MARINES AT KHE SANH

CAPTAIN MOYERS S. SHORE II, USMC

"Attention to Colors."

The order having been given, Captain William H. Dabney, a product of the Virginia Military Institute, snapped to attention, faced the jerry-rigged flag-pole, and saluted, as did every other man in Company I, 3d Battalion, 26th Marines. The ceremony might well have been at any one of a hundred military installations around the world except for a few glaring irregularities. The parade ground was a battle-scarred hill-top to the west of Khe Sanh and the men in the formation stood half submerged in trenches or foxholes. Instead of crisply starched utilities, razor sharp creases, and gleaming brass, these Marines sported scraggly beards, ragged trousers, and rotted helmet liner straps.

The only man in the company who could play a bugle, Second Lieutenant Owen S. Matthews, lifted the pock-marked instrument to his lips and spat out a choppy version of "To the Colors" while two enlisted men raced to the RC-292 radio antenna which served as the flag-pole and gingerly attached the Stars and Stripes. As the mast with its shredded banner came upright, the Marines could hear the ominous "thunk," "thunk," "thunk," to the southwest of their position, which meant that North Vietnamese 120mm mortar rounds had left their tubes. They also knew that in 21 seconds those "thunks" would be replaced by much louder, closer sounds, but no one budged until Old Glory waved high over the hill.

When Lieutenant Matthews sharply cut off the last note of his piece, Company I disappeared; men dropped into trenches, dived headlong into foxholes, or scrambled into bunkers. The area which moments before had been bristling with humanity was suddenly a ghost town. Seconds later explosions walked across the hilltop spewing black smoke, dirt, and debris into the air. Rocks, splinters, and spent shell fragments rained on the flattened Marines but, as usual, no one was hurt. As quickly as the attack came, it was over.

While the smoke lazily drifted away, a much smaller banner rose from the Marines' positions. A pole adorned with a pair of red, silk panties—Maggie's Drawers—was waved back and forth above one trenchline to inform the enemy that he had missed again. A few men stood up and jeered or cursed at the distant gunners; others simply saluted with an appropriate obscene gesture. The daily flag-raising ceremony on Hill 881 South was over.

This episode was just one obscure incident that coupled with hundreds of others made up the battle for Khe Sanh. The ceremony carried with it no particular political overtones but was intended solely as an open show of defiance toward the Communists as well as a morale booster for the troops. The jaunty courage, quiet determination, and macabre humor of the men on Hill 881S exemplified the spirit of the U.S. and South Vietnamese defenders who not only defied the enemy but, in a classic 77-day struggle, destroyed him.

The Khe Sanh Combat Base (KSCB) sat atop a plateau in the shadow of Dong Tri Mountain and overlooked a tributary of the Quang Tri River. The base had a small dirt airstrip, which had been surfaced by a U.S. Navy Mobile Construction Battalion (Seabees) in the summer of 1966; the field could accommodate helicopters and fixed-wing transport aircraft. Artillery support was provided by Battery F. The Khe Sanh area of operations was also within range of the 175mm guns of the U.S. Army's 2d Battalion, 94th Artillery at Camp Carroll and the Rockpile. In addition, there was a Marine Combined Action Company (CAC) and a Regional Forces company located in the village of Khe Sanh, approximately 3,500 meters south of the base.

The enemy had much to gain by taking Khe Sanh. If the garrison fell, the defeat might well turn out to be the coup de grace to American participation in the war. At first, the Marines anticipated a major pitched battle, similar to the one in 1967, but the enemy continued to bide his time and the battle at Khe Sanh settled into one of supporting arms.

At Khe Sanh, the periodic showers of enemy artillery shells were, quite naturally, a major source of concern to commanding officer Colonel David E. Lownds, who placed a high priority on the construction of stout fortifications. Understandably, not every newcomer to Khe Sanh immediately moved into a thick bunker or a six-foot trench with overhead cover. The colonel had spent most of his tour with a one-battalion regiment and had prepared positions for that battalion; then, almost overnight, his command swelled to five battalions. The new units simply had to build their own bunkers as quickly as they could.

The average bunker usually started as an 8×8 foot dugout with one 6×6 inch timber inserted in each corner and the center for support. The overhead consisted of planks, a strip of runway matting, sandbags, loose dirt, and more sandbags. Some enterprising Marines piled on more loose dirt, then took discarded 105mm casings and drove them into the top of the bunker like nails. These casings often caused pre-detonation of the heavier-caliber rounds. The combat engineers attached to the 26th Marines could build one of these bunkers in three or four days; the average infantrymen took longer.

The Marines were also faced with another question concerning their defenses: "How large an artillery round could you defend against and still remain within the realm of practicality?" Since the 26th Marines was supplied solely by air, building material was a prime consideration. Matting and sandbags were easy enough to come by, but lumber was at a premium. Fortifications which could withstand a hit from an 82mm mortar were a must because the North Vietnamese had an ample supply of these weapons but the base was also being pounded, to a lesser degree, by heavier-caliber guns. With the material available to the 26th Marines, it was virtually impossible to construct a shelter that was thick enough or deep enough to stop the heavy stuff.

Colonel Lownds decided to build a new regimental CP bunker. The engineers supplied the specifications for an overhead that would withstand a 122mm rocket; to be on the safe side, the colonel doubled the thickness of the roof. The day before the CP was to be occupied, a 152mm round landed squarely on top of the bunker and penetrated both layers.

The massing of enemy artillery made the hill outposts that much more important. Had they been able to knock the Marines from those summits, the North Vietnamese would have been able to fire right down the throats of the base defenders and make their position untenable. As it was, the companies on Hills 881S, 861, 861A, and 558 not only denied the enemy an unobstructed firing platform from which to pound the installation, they also served as the eyes for the rest of the regiment in the valley which was relatively blind to enemy movement.

While the 60mm and 82mm mortars were scattered around in proximity of the combat base, the North Vietnamese Army (NVA) rocket sites and artillery pieces were located well to the west, southwest, and northwest, outside of friendly counterbattery range. One particularly awesome and effective weapon was the Soviet-built 122mm rocket. When fired, the projectile was fairly accurate in deflection but, because it was powered by a propellant, the biggest margin of error was in range. The North Vietnamese preferred to position their launching sites so its gunners could track along the long axis of a given target; longs and shorts would land "in the ballpark."

The KSCB hugged the airstrip and was roughly in the shape of a rectangle with the long axis running east and west. This made the optimum firing positions for the 122mm rocket either to the east or west of the base in line with the runway. To the west, Hills 881S or 861 would have been ideal locations because in clear weather those vantage points provided an excellent view of Khe Sanh and were almost directly on line with the airstrip. Unfortunately for the NVA, the Marines had squatters' rights on those pieces of real estate and were rather hostile to claim jumpers. As an alternative, the North Vietnamese decided on 881N, but this choice had one drawback since the line of sight between that northern peak and the combat base was masked by the top of Hill 861.

Because of their greater range, the enemy's 130mm and 152mm artillery batteries were located even further to the west. These guns were cleverly concealed in two main firing positions. One was on Co

Roc Mountain which was southwest of where Route 9 crossed the Laotian border; the other area was 305, so called because it was on a bearing of 305 degrees (west-northwest) from Hill 881S at a range of about 10,000 meters. While the heavy caliber artillery rounds which periodically ripped into the base were usually referred to as originating from Co Roc, 305 was the source of about 60–70 percent of this fire, probably because it was adjacent to a main supply artery. Both sites were vulnerable only to air attack and were extremely difficult to pinpoint because of the enemy's masterful job of camouflage, his cautious employment, and the extreme distance from friendly observation posts. The NVA gunners fired only a few rounds every hour so that continuous muzzle flashes did not betray their positions and, after each round, quickly scurried out to cover the guns with protective nets and screens. Some pieces, mounted on tracks, were wheeled out of caves in Co Roc Mountain, fired, and returned immediately. Though never used in as great a quantity as the rockets and mortars, these shells wreaked havoc at Khe Sanh because there was very little that they could not penetrate; even duds went about four feet into the ground.

At the base the Marines had devised a crude but effective early warning system for such attacks. Motor transport personnel had mounted a horn from a two-and-a-half ton truck in the top of a tree and the lead wires were attached to two beer can lids. When a message was received from 881S, a Marine, who monitored the radio, pressed the two lids together and the blaring horn gave advanced warning of the incoming artillery rounds. The radio operator relayed the message over the regimental net and then dived into a hole. Men in the open usually had from five to eighteen seconds to find cover or just hit the deck before "all hell broke loose." When poor visibility obscured the view between 881S and the base, the radio operator usually picked himself up, dusted off, and jokingly passed a three-word message to Company I which indicated that the rounds had arrived on schedule—"Roger India . . . Splash."

The firing position which plagued the Marines the most was located to the southwest of the hill in a U-shaped draw known as "the Horseshoe." There were at least two NVA 120mm mortars in this area which, in spite of an avalanche of American bombs and artillery shells, were either never knocked out or were frequently replaced. These tubes were registered on the hill and harassed Company I constantly. Anyone caught above ground when one of the 120s crashed into the perimeter was almost certain to become a casualty because the explosion produced an extremely large fragmentation pattern. The only thing that the Marines had going for them was that they could frequently spot a tell-tale flash of an artillery piece or hear the "thunk" when a mortar round left the tube but the heavy shells took their toll. On Hill 881S alone, 40 Marines were killed throughout the siege and over 150 were wounded at least once.

Considering the sheer weight of the bombardment, enemy shells caused a relatively small number of fatalities at the base. Besides the solid fortifications, there were two factors which kept casualties to a minimum. The first was the flak jacket—a specially designed nylon vest reinforced with overlapping fiberglass plates. The jacket would not stop a high-velocity bullet but it did protect a man's torso and most vital organs against shell fragments. The bulky vest was not particularly popular in hot weather when the Marines were on patrol but in a static, defensive position the jacket was ideal. The second factor was the high quality of leadership at platoon and company level. Junior officers and staff noncommissioned officers (NCOs) constantly moved up and down the lines to supervise the younger, inexperienced Marines, many of whom had only recently arrived in Vietnam.

The veteran staff NCOs, long known as the "backbone of the Corps," knew from experience that troops had to be kept busy. A man who was left to ponder his problems often developed a fatalistic attitude that could increase his reaction time and decrease his lifetime. The crusty NCOs did not put much stock in the old cliché: "If a round has your name on it, there's nothing you can do." Consequently, the Marines worked; they dug trenches, filled sandbags, ran for cover, and returned to fill more sandbags. Morale remained high and casualties, under the circumstances, were surprisingly low.

Although the NVA encircled the KSCB and applied constant pressure, the defenders were never restricted entirely to the confines of the perimeter. The term "siege," in the strictest sense of the word, was somewhat of a misnomer because the Allies conducted a number of daily patrols, often as far as 500 meters from their own lines.

One vital area was the drop zone. When the weather turned bad in February, the KSCB was supplied primarily by parachute drops. Colonel Lownds set up his original zone inside the FOB-3 compound but later moved it several hundred meters west of Red Sector because he was afraid that the falling pallets might injure someone.

The Allies did more than prepare defenses and conduct patrols because the NVA launched three of its heaviest ground attacks during the first week in February. In the predawn hours of 5 February, the North Vietnamese lashed out at the Marine base and adjacent outposts with nearly 200 artillery rounds while a battalion from the 325C NVA Division assaulted Hill 861A. Colonel Lownds immediately placed all units on Red Alert and, within minutes, 1/13 was returning fire in support of E/2/26.

The fight on Hill 861A was extremely bitter. At 0305 the North Vietnamese opened up on American positions with a tremendous 82mm mortar barrage. This was followed by continuous volleys of

RPG rounds which knocked out several Marine crew-served weapons and shielded the advance of the NVA sappers and assault troops. The North Vietnamese blew lanes through the barbed wire along the northern perimeter and slammed into the Company E lines. Second Lieutenant Donald E. Shanley's 1st Platoon bore the brunt of the attack and reeled back to supplementary positions. Quickly the word filtered back to the company CP that the enemy was inside the wire, and Captain Earle G. Breeding ordered that all units employ tear gas in defense, but the North Vietnamese were obviously "hopped up" on some type of narcotic and the searing fumes had very little effect.

Following the initial assault there was a brief lull in the fighting. The NVA soldiers apparently felt that, having secured the northernmost trenchline, they owned the entire objective and stopped to sift through the Marine positions for souvenirs. Magazines and paperbacks were the most popular. Meanwhile, the temporary reversal only served to enrage the Marines. Following a shower of grenades, Lieutenant Shanley and his men charged back into their original positions and swarmed all over the surprised enemy troops.

The counterattack quickly deteriorated into a melee that resembled a bloody, waterfront barroom brawl—a style of fighting not completely alien to most Marines. Because the darkness and ground fog drastically reduced visibility, hand-to-hand combat was a necessity. Using their knives, bayonets, rifle butts, and fists, the men of the 1st Platoon ripped into the hapless North Vietnamese with a vengeance. Captain Breeding, a veteran of the Korean conflict who had worked his way up through the ranks, admitted that, at first, he was concerned over how his younger, inexperienced Marines would react in their first fight. As it turned out, they were magnificent.

The captain saw one of his men come face to face with a North Vietnamese in the inky darkness; the young American all but decapitated his adversary with a crushing, round-house right to the face, then leaped on the flattened soldier and finished the job with a knife. Another man was jumped from behind by a North Vietnamese who grabbed him around the neck and was just about to slit his throat, when one of the Marine's buddies jabbed the muzzle of his M-16 between the two combatants. With his selector on full automatic, he fired off a full magazine; the burst tore huge chunks from the back of the embattled Marine's flak jacket but it also cut the North Vietnamese in half.

Since the fighting was at such close quarters, both sides used hand grenades at extremely short-range. The Marines had the advantage because of their armored vests and they would throw a grenade, then turn away from the blast, hunch up, and absorb the fragments in their flak jackets and the backs of their legs. On several occasions, Captain Breeding's men used this technique and "blew away" enemy soldiers at less than 10 meters.

No one engaged in the donnybrook was exactly sure just how long it lasted—all were too busy fighting to check their watches. More than likely, the enemy was inside the wire less than a half hour. During the fighting, Captain Breeding fed fire team-sized elements from the 2d and 3d Platoons into the fray from both flanks of the penetration. The newcomers appeared to be afraid that they might miss all the action and tore into the enemy as if they were making up for lost time. Even though the E/2/26 company commander was no newcomer to blood and gore, he was awed by the ferocity of the attack. Captain Breeding later said: "It was like watching a World War II movie. Charlie didn't know how to cope with it . . . we walked all over them." Those dazed NVA soldiers who survived the vicious onslaught retreated into another meatgrinder; as they ran from the hill, they were blasted by recoilless rifle fire from 2/26 which was located on Hill 558.

At approximately 0610, the North Vietnamese officers rallied the battered remnants and tried again, but the second effort was also stopped cold. By this time, Captain Breeding, who was busier than the proverbial one-armed paper hanger, was assisting in the coordination of fire support from five separate sources.

The Marines of Captain Dabney's I/3/26, located on Hill 881S, provided extremely effective and enthusiastic support throughout the attack. In three hours, Captain Dabney's men pumped out close to 1,100 rounds from only three 81mm mortars, and the tubes became so hot that they actually glowed in the dark. Again, the bulk of the heavy artillery fire, along with radar controlled bombing missions, was placed on the northern avenues leading to the hill positions. The enemy units, held in reserve, were thus shredded by the bombardment as they moved up to continue the attack.

After the second assault fizzled out, the North Vietnamese withdrew, but enemy gunners shelled the base and outposts throughout the day. At 1430, replacements from 2/26 were helilifted to Hill 861A. Captain Breeding had lost seven men, most of whom were killed in the opening barrage, and another 35 were medevaced so the new arrivals brought E/2/26 back up to normal strength. On the other hand, the NVA suffered 109 known dead; many still remained in the 1st Platoon area where they had been shot, slashed, or bludgeoned to death.

As near as Captain Breeding could tell, he did not lose a single man during the fierce hand-to-hand struggle; all American deaths were apparently the result of the enemy's mortar barrage and supporting fire. The Marines never knew how many other members of the North Vietnamese had fallen as a result of the heavy artillery and air strikes but the number was undoubtedly high. All in all, it had been a bad day for the Communists.

The North Vietnamese took their revenge in the early morning hours of 7 February; their victims were the defenders of the Special Forces camp at Lang Vei. At 0042, an American advisor reported that the installation was under heavy attack by enemy tanks. This was the first time that the NVA had employed its armor in the south and, within 13 minutes, 9 PT-76 Soviet-built tanks churned through the defensive wire, rumbled over the anti-personnel minefields, and bulled their way into the heart of the compound. A North Vietnamese battalion, equipped with satchel charges, tear gas, and flame-throwers, followed with an aggressive infantry assault that was coordinated with heavy attacks by fire on the 26th Marines.

Colonel Lownds placed the base on Red Alert and called in immediate artillery and air in support. Although the Marines responded quickly, the defensive fires had little effect because, by that time, the enemy had overrun the camp. The defenders who survived buttoned themselves up in bunkers and, at 0243, called for artillery fire to dust off their own positions.

Part of Colonel Lownds' mission as coordinator of all friendly forces in the Khe Sanh area was to provide artillery support for Lang Vei and, if possible, to reinforce the camp in case of attack. Under the circumstances, a relief in strength was out of the question. Any column moving down the road, especially at night, would undoubtedly have been ambushed. If the Marines went directly over the mountains, they would have to hack through the dense growth and waste precious hours. A large-scale heliborne effort was ruled out because the North Vietnamese apparently anticipated such a move and withdrew their tanks to the only landing zones near the camp which were suitable for such an operation. Even with tactical aircraft providing suppressive fire, a helo assault into the teeth of enemy armor was ill-advised. The most important factor, however, was that NVA units in the area greatly outnumbered any force Colonel Lownds could commit.

Since a relief in force was undesirable, plans for a hit and run rescue attempt were quickly drawn up. Major General Norman J. Anderson, commanding the 1st MAW, and Colonel Jonathan F. Ladd of the U.S. Army Special Forces worked out the details. Two major points agreed upon were that the helicopters employed in the operation would be those which were not essential to the 26th Marines at the moment and that Marine fixed-wing support would be provided.

As soon as it was light, the survivors of the Lang Vei garrison managed to break out of their bunkers and work their way to the site of an older camp some 400–500 meters to the east. Later that same day, a raiding party boarded Quang Tri–based MAG-helicopters and took off for Lang Vei. A flight of Huey gunships, led by Lieutenant Colonel William J. White, Commanding Officer of Marine Observation Squadron 6, as well as jet aircraft escorted the transport choppers. While the jets and Hueys covered their approach, the helicopters swooped into a small strip at the old camp and took on survivors, including 15 Americans. In spite of the heavy suppressive fire provided by the escorts, three transport helos suffered battle damage during the evacuation. One overloaded chopper, flown by Captain Robert J. Richards of Marine Medium Helicopter Squadron 262, had to make the return trip to Khe Sanh at treetop level because the excess weight prevented the pilot from gaining altitude.

There was a large number of indigenous personnel—both military and civilian—who could not get out on the helicopters and had to move overland to Khe Sanh. A portion of these were members of the Laotian Volunteer Battalion 33 which on 23 January had been overrun at Ban Houei San, Laos (near the Laotian/South Vietnam border) by three NVA battalions. The remnants fled across the border and took refuge at Lang Vei and when the Special Forces camp fell, the Laotians continued their trek to the east with a host of other refugees. At 0800 on the 8th, about 3,000 approached the southern perimeter at Khe Sanh and requested admittance. Colonel Lownds, fearing that NVA infiltrators were in their midst, denied them entrance until each was searched and processed. This took place near the FOB-3 compound after which some of the refugees were evacuated. The Laotians were eventually returned to their own country.

Also on the morning of 8 February, the North Vietnamese launched the first daylight attack against the 26th Marines. At 0420, a reinforced battalion hit the 1st Platoon, A/1/9, which occupied Hill 64 some 500 meters west of the 1/9 perimeter. Following their usual pattern, the North Vietnamese tried to disrupt the Marines' artillery support with simultaneous bombardment of the base. To prevent friendly reinforcements from reaching the small hill the enemy also shelled the platoon's parent unit and, during the fight, some 350 mortar and artillery rounds fell on the 1/9 positions. North Vietnamese assault troops launched a two-pronged attack against the northwestern and southwestern corners of the A/1/9 outpost and either blew the barbed wire with bangalore torpedoes or threw canvas on top of the obstacles and rolled over them. The enemy soldiers poured into the trenchline and attacked the bunkers with RPGs and satchel charges. They also emplaced machine guns at the edge of the penetrations and pinned down those Marines in the eastern half of the perimeter who were trying to cross over the hill and reinforce their comrades.

The men in the northeastern sector, led by the platoon commander, Second Lieutenant Terence R. Roach Jr., counterattacked down the trenchline and became engaged in savage hand-to-hand fighting. While rallying his troops and directing fire from atop an exposed bunker, Lieutenant Roach was mortally wounded. From sheer weight of numbers, the North Vietnamese gradually pushed the Marines back until the enemy owned the western half of the outpost. At that point, neither side was able to press the advantage. Pre-registered mortar barrages from 1/9 and artillery fire from the KSCB had isolated the NVA assault units from any reinforcements but at the same time the depleted 1st Platoon was not strong enough to dislodge the enemy.

One Marine had an extremely close call during the fight but lived to tell about it. On the northern side of the perimeter, Private First Class Michael A. Barry of the 1st Squad was engaged in a furious hand grenade duel with the NVA soldiers when a ChiCom grenade hit him on top of the helmet and landed at the young Marine's feet. PFC Barry quickly picked it up and drew back to throw but the grenade went off in his hand. Had it been an American M-26 grenade, the private would undoubtedly have been blown to bits but ChiCom grenades frequently produced an uneven frag pattern. In this case, the bulk of the blast went down and away from the Marine's body; Barry had the back of his right arm, his back, and his right leg peppered with metal fragments but he did not lose any fingers and continued to function for the rest of the battle.

In another section of the trenchline, Lance Corporal Robert L. Wiley had an equally hair-raising experience. Wiley, a shell-shock victim, lay flat on his back in one of the bunkers which had been overrun by the enemy. His eardrums had burst, he was temporarily paralyzed and his glazed eyes were fixed in a corpse-like stare but the Marine was alive and fully aware of what was going on around him. Thinking that Wiley was dead, the North Vietnamese were only interested in rummaging through his personal effects for souvenirs. One NVA soldier found the Marine's wallet and took out several pictures, including a snapshot of his family gathered around a Christmas tree. After pocketing their booty, the North Vietnamese moved on; Lance Corporal Wiley was later rescued by the relief column.

At 0730, Lieutenant Colonel Mitchell committed a second platoon, headed by the Company A commander, Captain Henry J. M. Radcliffe, to the action. By 0900, the relief force had made its way to the eastern slope of the small hill and established contact with the trapped platoon. During the advance, Companies B and D, along with one section of tanks, delivered murderous direct fire to the flanks and front of Captain Radcliffe's column, breaking up any attempt by the enemy to interdict the linkup. After several flights of strike aircraft had pasted the reverse slope of the hill, the company commander led his combined forces in a frontal assault over the crest and, within 15 minutes, drove the North Vietnamese from the outpost.

Automatic weapons chopped down many North Vietnamese as they fled from the hill. The battered remnants of the enemy force retreated to the west and, once in the open, were also taken under fire by the rest of the Marine battalion. In addition, the artillery batteries at KSCB contributed to the slaughter and, when the smoke cleared, 150 North Vietnamese were dead. Although the platoon lines were restored, Colonel Lownds decided to abandon the position and, at 1200, the two units withdrew with their casualties. Marine losses that morning on the outpost were 21 killed and 26 wounded; at the base, 5 were killed and 6 wounded.

During the next two weeks, the NVA mounted no major ground attack but continued to apply pressure on the KSCB. There were daily clashes along the Marine lines but these were limited to small fire fights, sniping incidents, and probes against the wire. A decrease in activity along the various infiltration routes indicated that the enemy had completed his initial buildup and was busily consolidating positions from which to launch an all-out effort. The Allies continued to improve their defenses and by mid-February most units occupied positions with three or four layers of barbed wire, dense minefields, special detection devices, deep trenches, and mortar-proof bunkers. The battle reverted to a contest of supporting arms and the North Vietnamese stepped up their shelling of the base, especially with direct fire weapons. Attempts to silence the enemy guns were often frustrated because the Marines were fighting two battles during February—one with the NVA, the other with the weather.

The weather at Khe Sanh throughout February could be characterized in one word: miserable. The northeast monsoons had long since spilled over into the Khe Sanh Valley and every morning the base was shrouded with ground fog and low scud layers which dissipated around 1000 or 1100. When the sun finally managed to burn through, the cloud ceiling retreated slightly but still hovered low enough to prevent the unrestricted use of airborne artillery spotters and strike aircraft. It was during these periods, when the overcast was between 100 and 500 feet, that enemy artillery, rocket, and mortar fire was the heaviest. North Vietnamese forward observers, perched along the lower slopes of the surrounding hills, called in and adjusted barrages with little fear of retaliation against their own gun positions. Later in the afternoon, when the fog rolled in again and obscured the enemy's view, the incoming tapered off.

The Marines adjusted their schedule accordingly. They usually worked under the cover of the haze in the morning, went underground during the midday shelling, and returned to their duties later in the afternoon. While the extremely low cloud cover occasionally befriended the men at the base, it constantly plagued the pilots whose mission was to resupply the 26th Marines.

The job of transporting enough "bullets, beans, and bandages" to sustain the 6,680 Khe Sanh defenders fell to the C-130s of Marine

Aerial Refueler Transport Squadron 152 and the U.S. Air Force 834th Air Division; the C-123s of the 315th Air Commando Wing; the UH-34, CH-46, and UH-1E helicopters of Marine Aircraft Group 36 (MAG-36); and the CH-53 choppers of MAG-16.

Even under ideal circumstances, the airlift would have been a massive undertaking. The difficulties, however, were compounded by the poor visibility which was below minimum for airfield operations 40 percent of the time and the heavy volume of antiaircraft and artillery fire directed at the incoming transports. The North Vietnamese had moved several antiaircraft units into the hills east of the airstrip forcing the C-130 Hercules, the C-123 Providers, and the helicopters to run the gauntlet during their final approach. Under cover of the heavy fog, some audacious North Vietnamese gun crews positioned their antiaircraft weapons just off the eastern threshold of the runway and fired in the blind whenever they heard the drone of incoming planes. Several aircraft were hit while on GCA final and completely in the soup. Immediately after touchdown, the aircraft were subjected to intense mortar and rocket fire; in fact, the incoming was so closely synchronized with their arrival, the fixed-wing transports were nicknamed "mortar magnets" by the Marines.

The key to survival for the pilots was a steep approach through the eastern corridor, a short roll-out, and a speedy turnaround after landing. A small ramp paralleled the western end of the strip which the transport crews used as an unloading point. After roll-out, the pilot turned off the runway onto the easternmost taxiway, then wheeled onto the ramp while the loadmasters shoved the pallets of supplies out the back. All outgoing passengers were loaded on the double because the planes rarely stopped rolling. The pilot completed the loop by turning back onto the runway via the western taxiway and took off in the opposite direction from which he landed. It was not uncommon for the entire circuit to be completed within three minutes; even then, the planes were tracked by exploding mortar rounds.

On 10 February, a tragedy occurred which resulted in a drastic alteration of the unloading process. A Marine C-130, heavily laden with bladders of fuel for the 26th Marines, was making its approach to the field under intense fire. Just before the giant bird touched down, the cockpit and fuel bags were riddled by enemy bullets. With flames licking at one side, the stricken craft careened off the runway 3,100 feet from the approach end, spun around, and was rocked by several muffled explosions. The C-130 then began to burn furiously. Crash crews rushed to the plane and started spraying it with foam.

The pilot, Chief Warrant Officer Henry Wildfang, and his copilot suffered minor burns as they scrambled out the overhead hatch in the cockpit. Fire fighters in specially designed heat suits dashed into the flaming debris and pulled several injured crewmen and passengers to safety—rescue attempts came too late for six others. One of those killed in the crash, Lieutenant Colonel Carl E. Peterson, the 1st MAW Engineer Officer, was a reserve officer who only a few months before had volunteered for active duty. As a result of this accident and damage sustained by other transports while on the ground, C-130 landings at Khe Sanh were suspended.

With the field closed to C-130s, a U.S. Air Force innovation—the Low Altitude Parachute Extraction System or LAPES—was put into effect. This self-contained system, which had been used extensively during the renovation of the airstrip in the fall of 1967, enabled the aircraft to unload their cargo without landing. When making a LAPES run, the Hercules pilot made his approach from the east during which he opened the tail ramp and deployed a reefed cargo parachute. Prior to touchdown, he added just enough power to hold the aircraft about five feet above the ground. As the plane skimmed over the runway and approached the intended extraction point, the pilot electrically opened the streaming chute which was attached to the roller-mounted cargo pallets. The sudden jolt of the blossoming chute snatched the cargo from the rear hatch and the pallets came to a skidding halt on the runway. The pilot then jammed the throttles to the firewall, eased back on the yoke, and executed a high-angle, westerly pull-out to avoid ground fire while the Marines moved onto the runway with forklifts and quickly gathered in the supplies.

The system was quite ingenious and allowed the aircraft to pass through the V-ring in a matter of seconds. Even though the airmen could not control the skidding pallets after release, some pilots perfected their individual technique and were able to place the cargo on a 25-meter square with consistency. On one occasion, however, an extraction chute malfunctioned and the cargo rocketed off the western end of the runway; the eight-ton pallet of lumber smashed into a messhall located near the end of the strip and crushed three Marines to death.

Another technique—the Ground Proximity Extraction System or GPES—was also used but to a lesser degree than the LAPES. (15 GPES deliveries during the siege as compared to 52 LAPES.) Both utilized the low approach but with GPES the cargo was extracted by a hook extended from a boom at the rear of the aircraft. As the C-130 swooped low over the runway, the pilot tried to snag an arresting cable similar to the one used on aircraft carriers; only his hook was attached to the cargo bundles and not the plane. Upon engagement, the pallets were jerked from the rear hatch and came to a dead stop on the runway. With the GPES, the chance of a pallet skidding out of control or overturning was greatly reduced. The only problem that occurred was not with the system itself but with faulty installation.

The Marines who initially emplaced the GPES were frequently chased away from their work by incoming mortar rounds and, as a result of the periodic interruptions, the cable was not anchored properly. The first C-130 that snagged the wire ripped the arresting gear out by the roots. After the initial bugs were remedied, the system worked so successfully that, on one pass, a load containing 30 dozen eggs was extracted without a single eggshell being cracked.

Most of the time, however, the low overcast precluded the use of either extraction system and the preponderance of supplies was delivered by paradrops. This technique called for close air/ground coordination and the C-130 pilots relied on the Marine Air Traffic Control Unit (MATCU) at Khe Sanh to guide them into the drop zones. The Marine ground controller lined the aircraft up on the long axis of the runway for a normal instrument approach and when the Hercules passed a certain point over the eastern threshold of the field, the controller called "Ready, Ready, Mark." At "Mark," the pilot pushed a stop watch, activated his Doppler navigational system, turned to a predetermined heading and maintained an altitude of between 500 and 600 feet.

The Doppler device indicated any deviation from the desired track to the drop zone, which was west of Red Sector, and the release point was calculated by using the stop watch—20 to 26 seconds from "Mark," depending on the winds. At the computed release point, the pilot pulled the C-130 into an 8-degree nose-up attitude and 16 parachute bundles, containing 15 tons of supplies, slid from the rear of the aircraft and floated through the overcast into the 300-meter-square drop zone. Under Visual Flight Rules (VFR), the average computed error for the drops was only 95 meters. Even when these missions were executed completely under Instrument Flight Rules (IFR), the average distance that the bundles landed from the intended impact point was 133 meters—well inside the drop zone. On a few occasions, however, the parachute bundles missed the zone and drifted far enough away from the base to preclude a safe recovery. In these rare instances, friendly artillery and air strikes were brought to bear on the wayward containers to keep them from falling into the hands of the enemy. During the siege, Air Force C-130 crews conducted a total of 496 paradrops at Khe Sanh.

Although the paradrops were sufficient for bulk commodities such as rations and ammunition, there were certain items which had to be delivered or picked up personally. Medical supplies, special ammunition, and other delicate cargo would not withstand the jolt of a parachute landing. In addition, there were replacements to be shuttled into the base and casualties to be evacuated. With the cancellation of all C-130 landings, this job was left up to the sturdy C-123 Providers of the 315th Air Commando Wing as well as MAG-36 and MAG-16 helicopters.

The choppers could maneuver around areas of heavy ground fire, land, unload, take on medevacs, and depart very quickly but their payloads were limited. On the other hand, the C-123s had a larger cargo capacity but were restricted to a more rigid approach and provided better targets both in the pattern and on the ground. The Providers, however, required much less runway from which to operate than the C-130s and could land and take off using only 1,400 of the 3,900 foot strip. This saving feature enabled the pilots to make a steep approach, short roll-out, and rapid turnaround. The crews still had to undergo those frantic moments on the ground when the geysers of dirty-black smoke bracketed their aircraft. Nevertheless, the dauntless C-123 crews continued their perilous missions throughout the siege with great success.

No discussion of the airlift would be complete without mention of the MAG-36 and MAG-16 helicopter pilots who flew in and out of Khe Sanh daily delivering supplies, delicate cargo, reinforcements, and evacuating casualties. The chopper crews were faced with the same problems that plagued the fixed-wing transports—low ceilings and enemy ground fire—but to a greater degree because of their slow speed and vulnerability. MAG-36 operated primarily from Quang Tri and Dong Ha, and was reinforced from the group's main base at Phu Bai. These valiant pilots and crewmen in their Huey gunships, CH-46 transports, and UH-34s flew long hours, day and night, in all kinds of weather to sustain the Marines in and around Khe Sanh. The CH-53s of Da Nang–based MAG-16, with their heavier payload, also made a sizeable contribution to this effort.

The resupply of the hill outposts was a particularly hazardous aspect of the overall mission. Approximately 20 percent of Colonel Lownds' personnel occupied these redoubts and, for all practical purposes, were cut off from the rest of the garrison. The road north of the base was not secure and the perimeters atop the hills were too small and irregular for parachute drops; the only way that the isolated posts could be sustained was by helicopter. When the dense monsoon clouds rolled into the valley, the mountain tops were the first to become submerged and, as the overcast lifted, the last to reappear. During February, several of the outposts were completely obscured for more than a week and resupply was impossible. During these periods, the North Vietnamese took advantage of the reduced visibility and emplaced heavy automatic weapons along the neighboring peaks and waited for the ceiling to lift which invariably heralded the arrival of helicopters. As a result, the UH-1Es, UH-34s, and CH-46s were subjected to a hail of enemy bullets during each mission.

When the helicopters proceeded to the hills singly or in small groups, each mission was a hair-raising experience for both the chopper crews and the men on the ground. A good example of what often transpired during those frantic moments occurred early in the siege on Hill 881S when Captain Dabney called for a chopper to evacuate a badly wounded Marine.

One corporal was assigned as a stretcher bearer because he had a badly impacted wisdom tooth and, once aboard, he could ride out on the helicopter and have the tooth extracted at the main base. Because of the 120mm mortars located in the Horseshoe and the antiaircraft guns which ringed the hill, the men on 881S had to employ a variety of diversions to keep the enemy gunners from getting the range of the incoming choppers. In this instance, they threw a smoke grenade a good distance away from the actual landing zone in hopes that the gunners would register on the smoke and the helicopter would be in and out before the North Vietnamese could readjust. This meant that the helo had about 19 seconds to get off the ground.

The ruse did not come off as planned. The stretcher bearers had barely loaded the wounded man aboard the helicopter, a CH-46, when 120mm mortar rounds bracketed the aircraft and spurred the pilot to action. The helo lurched into the air and the sudden jolt rolled the corporal with the bad tooth over the edge of the tail ramp; he held on desperately for a few seconds but finally let go and fell about 20 feet to the ground. Cursing to himself, the young man limped back to his trench and waited for another chance.

Later that day, a UH-34 swooped in to pick up another casualty and the prospective dental patient quickly scrambled aboard. This trip also covered about 20 feet—10 feet up and 10 feet down—because the tail rotor of the UH-34 was literally sawed off by a burst from an enemy machine gun just after the bird became airborne. After the swirling craft came to rest, the passengers and the three-man crew quickly clamored out the hatch and dived into a nearby trench. A heavy mortar barrage ensued during which several more men were hit.

By the time another CH-46 arrived on the scene, the passenger list had grown to 14, including 10 casualties, the crew of the downed helo, and the original dental case. Because of the heavy concentration of enemy fire in the original zone, the Marines had blasted out another landing site on the opposite side of the hill. The chopper touched down and 13 of the 14 Marines boarded before the crew chief stated emphatically that the aircraft was full. As luck would have it, the young Marine with the swollen jaw was the 14th man. Thoroughly indignant, the three-time loser returned to his position and mumbled that he would rather suffer from a toothache than try and get off the hill by helicopter.

It was the consensus of both the ground commanders and pilots alike that the problem of getting helicopters to and from the hills was becoming critical. The technique then employed was resulting in casualties among both the air crews and the infantry units, as well as a rapid rise in the attrition of MAG-36 helicopters. The Huey gunships, though putting forth a valiant effort, did not possess the heavy volume of fire required to keep the approach lanes open. As a result, the 1st MAW adopted another system which provided more muscle.

The solution was basically a page out of the Fleet Marine Force Manual for Helicopter Support Operations. All helicopter flights to the hill outposts were to be escorted by strike aircraft which would provide suppressive fire. The A-4 Skyhawks of Chu Lai–based MAG-12 were selected as the fixed-wing escorts and the little jet was perfect for the job. Affectionately referred to as "Scooters" by their pilots, the A-4 was a highly maneuverable attack aircraft; its accuracy, dependability, and varied ordnance load had made it the workhorse of Marine close air support for many years.

The operation went into effect on 24 February. Because of the large number of aircraft utilized in each mission—12 A-4s, 1 TA-4, 12

CH-46s, and 4 UH-1E gunships—the overall effort was nicknamed the Super Gaggle by its planners. The difficulty in execution was primarily one of coordination and control because of the various agencies involved. Additional factors that had to be considered were departure weather, destination weather, and coordination of friendly artillery and air strikes around Khe Sanh. Lieutenant Colonel Carey, the 1st MAW Operations Officer and one of the planners, later described the mechanics of the Super Gaggle:

Success of the effort was predicated on timing, coordination, and often times luck. Luck, as used, refers to the ability to guess whether the weather would hold long enough to complete an effort once it got underway. The effort began with the TA-4 on station determining if sufficient ceiling existed for the "Scooters" of MAG-12 to provide sufficient suppressive fires to assure success. . . . Once the TA-4 called all conditions go, an "H" hour was set and the Super Gaggle began. Twelve A-4s would launch from Chu Lai while simultaneously 100 miles to the north 12–16 helos would launch from the Quang Tri helo base and proceed to the Dong Ha LSA (Logistics Support Area) for supply pickup. The object was for all aircraft to arrive in the objective area on a precise schedule. So the operation generally consisted as follows: (1) Softening up known enemy positions by four A-4s, generally armed with napalm and bombs; (2) Two A-4s armed with CS (tear gas) tanks saturate enemy antiaircraft and automatic weapons positions; (3) 30–40 seconds prior to final run in by the helos two A-4s lay a smoke screen along selected avenues of approach . . . (4) While helos make final run into the target, four A-4s with bombs, rockets, and 20mm guns provide close-in fire suppression. . . . Once the helos commenced their descent the factors of weather, their 4,000-pound externally carried load, and the terrain would not permit a second chance. If an enemy gun was not suppressed there was no alternative for the helos but to continue. They (the transport pilots) were strengthened with the knowledge that following close on their heels were their gunships ready to pick them up if they survived being shot down. Fortunately, these tactics were so successful that during the entire period of the Super Gaggle only two CH-46s were downed enroute to the hill positions. The crews were rescued immediately by escorting Huey gunships.

These missions, however, looked much more orderly on paper than they did in the air and the operation lived up to its name. Only those who have experienced the hazards of monsoon flying can fully appreciate the veritable madhouse that often exists when large numbers of aircraft are confined to the restricted space beneath a low-hanging overcast. Coupled with this was the fact that the fluffy looking clouds around Khe Sanh housed mountains which ran up to 3,000 feet. No doubt, the aircrews involved in the Gaggle were mindful of the standard warning issued to fledgling aviators: "Keep your eyes out of the cockpit; a mid-air collision could ruin your whole day."

Even though the missions were well-coordinated and executed with a high degree of professionalism, it often appeared that confusion reigned because planes were everywhere. A-4s bore in on the flanks of the approach lanes blasting enemy gun positions and spewing protective smoke; CH-46s groped through the haze trying to find the landing zones; the hornet-like UH-1E gunships darted in from the rear in case someone was shot down; and the lone 87TA-4 circled overhead trying to keep his flock from running amuck. During the missions to 881S, the men of India and Mike, 3/26, added to the hullabaloo with a little twist of their own. When the CH-46s settled over the hill, the Marines on the ground tossed out a few dozen smoke grenades for added cover and then every man in the perimeter fired a full magazine at anything on the surrounding slopes which appeared hostile. With some 350 men hosing down the countryside at the same time, the din was terrific.

Neither the deluge of lead from 881S nor the suppressive fire of the jets and gunships kept the NVA completely quiet. The 120mm mortar crews in the Horseshoe were especially active during the resupply runs to 881S and always lobbed some rounds onto the hill in hopes of knocking down a helicopter. These tubes had been previously registered on the LZs and the smoke screens had little effect on their fire; as a result, the Marines frequently shifted landing zones. The smoke did block the view of the North Vietnamese machine gunners and they were forced to fire blindly through the haze—if they dared fire at all. The choppers still took hits but nowhere near as many as before the Gaggle was initiated. The CH-46 pilots, poised precariously above the LZs during the few agonizing seconds it took to unload their cargo, often heard the sickening smack which meant that a bullet had torn into the fuselage of their thin-skinned helos.

The members of the two-man Helicopter Support Teams (HST), 3d Shore Party Battalion who were attached to the rifle companies were also prime targets. These men had to stand up while they guided the choppers into the LZs and, every few days, they had to attach bundles of cargo nets, which accumulated from previous missions, for the return trip to Dong Ha. This was dangerous for the aircrews as well as the HST men because, during the hook-up, the pilots had to hold their aircraft in a vulnerable position a few feet above the ground with the nose cocked up and the belly exposed to fire from the front. While they attached the bundles, the ground support personnel could hear the machine gun rounds zing a few inches over their heads and slap into the soft underside of the suspended helicopter. Not all the bullets and shell fragments passed overhead; on 881S, the defenders were operating with their fourth HST when the siege ended.

In spite of the seriousness of the situation, the Gaggle was not without its lighter episodes. In one instance, an HST man attached to I/3/26 hooked up an outgoing load and gave the pilot the "thumbs up" when he discovered that he had become entangled in the pile of nets. The CH-46 surged into the air with the startled Marine dangling helplessly from the bottom of the net by one foot. But for the quick reaction of his comrade on the ground who informed the pilot by radio that the chopper had taken on more than the prescribed load, the young cargo handler would have had a rather interesting trip to Dong Ha.

The CH-46 crews also provided a human touch during these missions. When the Sea Knights swept over the hills, it was not uncommon to see a machine gunner on board quit his weapon for a second, nonchalantly pitch a case of soda pop out the hatch, and then quickly return to blaze away at the enemy positions.

At 1st MAW Headquarters, Lieutenant Colonel Carey, who had been an infantryman in Korea before he went to flight school and who sympathized with the men on the outposts, felt that a small gesture acknowledging their continued outstanding performance was in order. Special efforts were made to obtain quantities of dry ice for packing and one day, without notice, hundreds of Dixie-cups of ice cream were delivered to the men on the hills as part of the regular resupply. This effort was dubbed Operation COOL IT. The only hitch developed on 881S where the Marines, unaware of the contents, allowed the cargo to remain in the LZ until after dark when it was safe to venture out of the trenchline. The ice cream was a little sloppy but edible and greatly appreciated.

The introduction of the Super Gaggle was a turning point in the resupply effort. Prior to its conception, the Marines on the outposts dreaded the thought of leaving their positions to retrieve cargo—even when it included mail—because of the heavy shelling. With a dozen Skyhawks pasting the surrounding hills during each mission, this threat was alleviated to a large degree and casualties tapered off. The Company I, 3/26, commander later stated: "If it weren't for the Gaggle, most of us probably wouldn't be here today."

The helicopter pilots, knowing that their jet jockey compatriots were close at hand, were also able to do their job more effectively. In the past, the transport crew chiefs occasionally had to jettison their external load prematurely when the pilot took evasive action to avoid ground fire. When this occurred, the cargo nets usually slammed into the perimeter and splattered containers all over the hilltop. With the Super Gaggle, the pilots had less enemy fire to contend with and did not bomb the hills with the cargo pallets as much; as a result more supplies arrived intact. In addition, the system greatly facilitated the picking up of wounded personnel.

The Marine helicopters continued their flights to and from Khe Sanh throughout the siege. In spite of the obstacles, the chopper pilots crammed enough sorties into those days with flyable weather to haul 465 tons of supplies to the base during February. When the weather later cleared, this amount was increased to approximately 40 tons a day. While supporting Operation SCOTLAND, MAG-36 and MAG-16 flew 9,109 sorties, transported 14,562 passengers, and delivered 4,661 tons of cargo.

Colonel Lownds was more than satisfied with the airborne pipeline which kept his cupboard full and he had quite a cupboard. The daily requirement for the 26th Marines to maintain normal operations had jumped from 60 tons in mid-January to roughly 185 tons when all five battalions were in place. While the defenders didn't live high off the hog on this amount, at no time were they desperately lacking the essentials for combat. There were periods on the hills when the Marines either stretched their rations and water or went without, but they never ran short of ammunition.

Understandably, ammunition had the highest priority—even higher than food and water. A man might not be able to eat a hand grenade but neither could he defend himself very effectively with a can of fruit cocktail. This did not mean that the men of the 26th Marines went hungry. On the average, the troops at the base received two C-Ration meals a day and this fare was occasionally supplemented with juice, pastry, hot soup, or fresh fruit. The men on the hills subsisted almost entirely on C-Rations and the time between meals varied, depending on the weather.

Within the compound, water was rationed only when the pump was out of commission and that was a rare occurrence. Lieutenant Colonel Heath's position on Hill 558 was flanked by two streams so 2/26 was well supplied but the Marines on the other four outposts depended on helilifts for water; it was used sparingly for drinking and cooking.

Besides the essentials, the 26th Marines also required tons of other supplies such as fortification material, fuel, tires, barbed wire, and spare parts—to name a few. PX items were on the bottom of the bottom of the priority totem pole because, as Colonel Lownds remarked: "If you have to, you can live without those." On the other hand, mail had a priority second only to ammunition and rations. The men at Khe Sanh received over 43 tons of mail during the worst month of the siege.

One portion of the airlift which affected morale as much as the arrival of mail was the swift departure of casualties. A man's efficiency was greatly improved by the knowledge that, if he were hit, he could expect immediate medical attention and when necessary, a speedy evacuation. Those with minor wounds were usually treated at the various battalion aid stations and returned to duty; the more seriously injured were taken to Company C, 3d Medical Battalion. Charley Med, as this detachment was called, was located just south of and adjacent to the aircraft loading ramp. There, U.S. Navy doctors and corpsmen treated the walking wounded, performed surgery, and prepared the litter cases for medevac. From Charley Med, it was a short, but often nerve-racking trip to a waiting aircraft and a hospital at Phu Bai. During the siege, the courageous men of Charley Med, often working under heavy enemy fire, treated and evacuated 852 wounded personnel.

Thus the Marine and U.S. Air Force transport pilots, helicopter crews, loadmasters, and ground personnel kept open the giant umbilical cord which meant life for the combat base. Without their efforts, the story of Khe Sanh would undoubtedly have been an abbreviated edition with a not-too-happy ending. On the other hand, accounts of the heroism, ingenuity, and skill demonstrated by these men would fill a book. But there were other things besides manna falling from the heavens at Khe Sanh and the vital role of the transports was frequently eclipsed by the efforts of air crews, who carried a much deadlier cargo.

SOURCES

"Paul Revere" from *Sons of Liberty*. Walter A. Dyer. New York: Henry Holt & Company, 1920.

"Bunker Hill" from *The Decisive Battles of America*. Benson J. Lossing, et al. New York and London: Harper and Brothers Publisher, 1909.

"Benedict Arnold's Navy" from *The Major Operations of the Navies*. Alfred Thayer Mahan. London: Sampson Low, Marston & Company Limited, 1912.

"Grant in Mexico" from *Personal Memories of U. S. Grant*. Ulysses S. Grant. New York: Charles Webster and Company, 1885.

"Stone River" from *Stone River: Personal Recollections and Experiences Concerning the Battle of Stone River*. Milo S. Hascall. Goshen, IN: Times Publishing Company, 1889.

"Vicksburg During the Trouble" from *Life on the Mississippi*. Mark Twain. 1883.

"Stealing the General" from *Capturing a Locomotive: A History of Secret Service in the Late War*. William Pittenger. Washington, DC: The National Tribune, 1885.

"Custer's Last Battle" from *A History of the Sioux War*. Frances Fuller Victor. 1881.

"The Battle of Las Guasimas with the Rough Riders" from *The Rough Riders*. Theodore Roosevelt. New York: Charles Scribner's Sons, 1899.

"Taking Mount Suribachi" from *Closing In: Marines in the Seizure of Iwo Jima*. Joseph H. Alexander. Marines in World War II Commemorative Series. Washington, DC: US Marine Corps Historical Center, 1994.

"The Loss of the *Indianapolis*" from *The Tragic Fate of the U.S.S. Indianapolis*. Raymond B. Lech. New York: Cooper Square Press, a division of the Rowman & Littlefield Publishing Group, 1982.

"Supplying the Embattled Marines at Khe Sanh" from *The Battle for Khe Sanh*. Captain Moyers S. Shore II. Washington, DC: History and Museums Division Headquarters, U.S. Marine Corps, 1969.